The
Come-Alive
Classroom

ABOUT THE AUTHORS

MYRA B. COOK has her Masters Degree in Education from Cornell University. She has taught multiple and single grades in Florida and overseas, and was associated with the Homebound Teaching Program of Lawton, Oklahoma and the Army Education Center of Fort Sill, Oklahoma. In addition, she has conducted reading improvement courses for military personnel.

JOSEPH H. CALDWELL received the Master of Science degree from Florida State University, was selected for further graduate study at the University of Florida by the National Science Foundation, and will complete work on the Specialist in Education degree this year. He has wide experience in teaching grades 4 through 8, has served as an elementary school principal, and as guidance counselor for the Florida Junior College at Jacksonville. His fields are science, mathematics and guidance.

LINA J. CHRISTIANSEN has taught high school, elementary school and Elementary Art to over 500 students in grades 1 through 6. She has given art seminars for graduate students at Cornell University, and art workshops for Ithaca, New York school teachers. In addition, the Liverpool, New York school system invited her to conduct a television seminar for classroom teachers; she was also selected to teach a summer workshop of art ideas and techniques in Santa Monica, California.

The
Come-Alive
Practical
for

Compiled and

Parker Publishing Company, Inc.

Classroom: Projects Elementary Teachers

Edited by Myra B. Cook
        Joseph H. Caldwell
        Lina J. Christiansen

Drawings by Myra B. Cook

The Come-Alive Classroom: Practical Projects
for Elementary Teachers
Compiled and Edited by
Myra B. Cook
Joseph H. Caldwell
Lina J. Christiansen

© 1967, by
PARKER PUBLISHING COMPANY, INC.
WEST NYACK, N.Y.

LIBRARY OF CONGRESS
CATALOG CARD NUMBER: 67-24797

PRINTED IN THE UNITED STATES OF AMERICA

B & P

DEDICATION

FOREWORD

by

Dr. Helen L. Merrill
Jacksonville University

The authors of this book are all talented teachers. This has been confirmed by the procedures they have used and their knowledge of their students. They did not, however, enter the classroom as master teachers, but have developed through study and effort in cosmopolitan atmospheres.

Most master teachers employ, to a large extent, a basic method of teaching, even though their techniques may vary greatly. With this in mind, the book has taken form. It has been written for experienced teachers who have not stopped for orientation and for beginning teachers who need assistance in quickly acquiring what all teachers need to know, so that both these groups are not overwhelmed and do not become discouraged.

The superior or master teachers who have authored this book have learned as others have learned; but they have made the additional step and interpreted this knowledge for others. It is to all dedicated teachers that this book is addressed.

INTRODUCTION

It has been my own experience that students frequently have been so conditioned as mere recipients of information that they disparage attempts to involve them creatively in the learning process. They want information handed to them literally, predigested, complete and unalterable. This attitude makes the creative teacher's job much harder, of course, but at the same time it offers a wonderful challenge: he must strive to prepare his students for a new kind of learning.

—*Edward Steichen*

Every chapter in this book has been written with one purpose—to give you, the creative teacher, a cross section of practical classroom projects.

The material has been gathered from twenty different classrooms: the best ideas, projects and philosophies of twenty teachers from kindergarten through college.

We have filled our book with drawings, photographs, charts, diagrams, clippings, worksheets and schedules to give you a starting point for your own projects and ideas.

These activities have already proven themselves in the classroom. They are creative, fun, demanding, exciting and rewarding. They are practical projects for a creative classroom. Put them to work and watch your classroom "come-alive!"

—THE AUTHORS

ACKNOWLEDGMENTS

> *Nobody ever writes a book all by him-self; behind every work stretches a long list of the people who made it possible.*
> —Glenn Doman

THE AUTHORS WISH TO GRATEFULLY ACKNOWLEDGE:

Dean Kimball Wiles of the University of Florida for his kind advice.

Dr. Joseph Crescimbeni of Jacksonville University, Dr. Rebekah Liebman of Forest Park High School, Baltimore, Maryland, Dr. William Carse of the University of Kentucky, and Professor Robbye Kinkade of Jacksonville University for their valuable comments, direction and guidance.

Mrs. Elizabeth Hobbs, former principal of the John N. C. Stockton School, for her encouragement and assistance.

Donald Cook who stood by patiently for five years while his home was cluttered with papers, documents, reference books, folders and files as this book was being written.

Mr. and Mrs. J. R. Brown, who supported the work, financially and inspirationally.

Mrs. Blanche Long who managed the children during the last few months of editing and typing the manuscript.

Mrs. Bernice Johnson who kept the household in order while the book was underway.

The authors wish to thank the following students for allowing the use of their school work: Jack Beckford, David Braddock, Janet Brooker, Jean Brooker, Donald Colson, Dick Draper, Bill Goelz, Kathy Jones, Alex Juhan, Catherine Logan, Danny Logan, David Logan, Marcia McCready, Linda Medders, Jerry Neuland, Stephanie Peterson, Margrete Saunders, Sandy Stout, and David Thames.

Mr. Ralph Parkinson for his assistance in the preparation of photographic material.

ABOUT THE AUTHORS

_____MYRA B. COOK

Myra Cook attended Rollins College, the University of Florida and Cornell University. She graduated from Florida with a BA in English and from Cornell with the MEd. She has taught multiple and single grades in Florida and Germany, was associated with the Homebound Teaching Program of Lawton, Oklahoma and the Army Education Center of Fort Sill, Oklahoma. She conducted Reading Improvement courses for military personnel at both Fort Sill and Fort Chaffee, Arkansas.

_____JOSEPH H. CALDWELL

Joe Caldwell received his BS and MS degrees from Florida State University. He was selected for the 1964-65 Academic Year Institute at the University of Florida, a year of graduate study sponsored by the National Science Foundation. He has taught the 4th through the 8th grades with experience in departmentalized and self-contained classroom organizations and was principal of Mill Creek School, St. Johns County, Florida. He is presently in higher education. His fields are science, math, and guidance.

_____LINA J. CHRISTIANSEN

Lina Christiansen received her BA from Atlantic Union College. She has taught high school, elementary school, multiple grades, single grades, and Elementary Art to over 500 students in grades 1 through 6. She gave art seminars for graduate students at Cornell University and art workshops for Ithaca, New York school teachers. The Liverpool, New York school system invited her to conduct a television seminar for classroom teachers. In Santa Monica, California she was selected to teach in workshops of art ideas and techniques.

_____RUTH H. GROSS

Ruth Gross held degrees from West Texas Junior College, the University of Missouri and the University of Florida. She taught in the states of Oklahoma, Texas, Nebraska, Mississippi, Florida, and with the Dependent Education Group in Japan. Her students were 3rd through 6th graders in the elementary school. She also taught English and physical education in high school. Her classroom projects were recognized by the publication TRENDS. In 1960 she won a regional award in the John Gunther's HIGH ROAD Teacher Awards Program. She was frequently recognized in the Florida Times-Union for her field trips and classroom projects. Mrs. Gross was a classroom teacher for 17 years.

_____JAMES ATKINSON

Jim Atkinson received his BME from Florida State University. He was a member of the University Singers and participated in numerous musicals, operas and Little Theatre productions. He teaches music to 250 students, grades 1 through 6, and science to 6th, 7th and 8th graders. His annual student productions of Gilbert and Sullivan operettas have received county-wide praise.

——————————————————————————————————GRETCHEN BLACK
Gretchen Black received her BA from Douglass College and MEd from Cornell University. She has taught 2nd and 5th grades in Lexington, Kentucky.

——————————————————————————————————JANE BROWN
Jane Brown graduated from the University of Florida with a BS in Business Education. She teaches high school classes in Business Education and junior high classes in mathematics.

——————————————————————————————————HARRIET COOK
Harriet Cook received her BA degree from Northwestern State College in Louisiana. She has taught single and multiple grades in the elementary school for 34 years.

——————————————————————————————————DALE DEVINE
Dale Devine received her BA in English from Carleton College and the MEd from Cornell University. She has taught 2nd and 3rd graders in the Irondequoit Schools of Rochester, New York, in Kaiserslautern, Germany with the U. S. Army Dependent Schools, and in the Hinsdale, Illinois school system.

——————————————————————————————————NENA GRIFFIS
Nena Griffis received the BA degree from Millsaps College. She continued with graduate work at Duke University. Her elementary classroom teaching has been in Mississippi and North Carolina. She also taught courses in English, math, science, history and Perceptual Reading to military personnel at Fort Chaffee, Arkansas. An accomplished organist, her work in the field of music has been extensive.

——————————————————————————————————SUSAN MABRY
Susan Mabry graduated from the University of Kentucky with a BA degree. She has taught in Kentucky, Oklahoma, and with the Dependents Education Group in Germany. She has tutored during the summer months and has been a full-time substitute for several years.

——————————————————————————————————SHIRLEY McGURRAN
Shirley McGurran received her BS degree from Davis and Elkins College and the MA degree from West Virginia University. She was selected for Extended Math Study courses at Denver University. Her first two years in the classroom were spent in a one-room school as the only teacher for six grades. She has taught multiple and single grades in West Virginia, in the Denver, Colorado sshool system, and with the Dependents Education Group in Germany.

——————————————————————————————————KATHERINE PRATER
Katherine Prater graduated from Ohio Wesleyan with the BA degree. She has taught in Florida, Georgia, Virginia and Texas. Her students have ranged from the 6th through the 12th grade level. Mrs. Prater has been a full-time substitute for several years.

_____MERKIN PURCELL

Merkin Purcell received the BS and MEd degrees from the University of Florida. She was a classroom teacher for 19 years and has been a principal for 9. Her school was featured in the Florida Times-Union for its work with the Ungraded Primary Classroom, the first of its kind in St. Johns County.

_____KAREN RUSH

Karen Rush received the BA degree from Carleton College and the MEd from Cornell University. She has done post-graduate work at the University of Rochester and Brockport Teachers College. She was a soloist with the Carleton College Choir and sang with the Cornell University Choir, the Rochester Ontario Society and the Ansbach Chorus in Germany. She has taught elementary and high school subjects in New York, New Jersey, Virginia and Germany. Her student projects in the field of music have received countywide praise.

_____GLENN SCHROEDER

Glenn Schroeder received a BS degree from Oregon College of Education and the MEd from the University of Oregon. He began work on his doctorate at the University of New Mexico in the fall of 1966. He has taught single and multiple grades at the junior high school level in Oregon and in Germany. Since 1961 he has been principal of an elementary and junior high school with the Dependents Education Group in Germany.

_____MORRELL SEXTON

Morrell Sexton graduated from the University of North Dakota with a BS degree in Commerce. He taught for three years at Niagara University. A Lieutenant Colonel in the U. S. Army, he has taught many classes to military personnel. The father of five children, he has been active in school affairs at all grade levels.

_____GENEVIEVE SKILES

Genevieve Skiles received her BA from the University of Redlands. She has taught Kindergarten, 2nd, 3rd, 4th and 6th grade classes in the state of California.

_____BETH STREET

Beth Street graduated from Louisiana Polytechnic Institute with a BA degree. She has taught high school classes in Oklahoma and Louisiana and was an assistant librarian at Fort Sill, Oklahoma.

_____JEAN WATSON

Jean Watson received her BA degree from Los Angeles State College. She has also studied at Jepson County Art Institute and the Los Angeles Art Center School. She has taught single and multiple grades in California and Germany. She was selected to conduct an art workshop for Los Angeles teachers during the summer of 1964.

CONTENTS

1. **Planning Ahead** 1

The Year at a Glance (1), The Weekly Plan Book (2), Planning Day by Day (3), Student Assignment Sheets (3), Challenging Assignments (4), Make Plans for Yourself (8)

2. **Classrooms as Workshops** 17

Put It On Paper (18), Creating Work Stations (18), Creating Storage Space (19), Creating Display Space (21), The Interest Center (21), Spruce Up the Room (23)

3. **Time Savers: Records, Files and Forms** 24

Make an Inventory (25), Label Everything (25), Keep an "Executive's Diary" (25), Keep a File on Each Student (26), Prepare an Easy-Check Class List (27), Keep Financial Records (27), Keep Track of Successful Lessons (27), Keep Handy Reference Files: Cards, Folders, Envelopes (28), Keep a Folder for the Substitute (29), Keep a File for the Visiting Specialist (29), On Your Desk Top (30)

4. **First Day Fevers** 31

The Classroom (31), Introducing Yourself (32), Getting to Work (34), Setting Standards (36)

5. **Setting Standards** 37

Setting Behavior Standards (37), Setting Standards of Appearance (40), Organizing Their Work (41), Setting Scholastic Standards (41)

6. **Classroom Testing and Evaluation** 42

What Are We Evaluating? (43), Why Give Tests? (44), Test Construction (44), Essay vs. Objective Tests (45), Evaluating Tests (46), A Fun Test to Take (47), Oral Tests (50), Marking Made Easy (51), Evaluating Behavior and Attitude (52), The Conference (52)

7. **Teaching Them to Study** 54

Teaching Motivation (55), General Guidelines (56), A Study Plan (56), Attacking an Assignment (57)

8. **Competition, Recognition, and Rewards** 73

Accentuate the Positive (75), On the Honor Roll (75), Posting Papers (76), Picturing Progress (77), Charting Progress (77), Keeping Them Reading (78), Telling Tales (79), Learning From Each Other (79), In the News (80), Tournaments and Contests (80), Get Some Gimmicks (84), Whiz Kids, Quiz Kids (84), Certificates of Achievement (84), Trophies (84), Plaques (84), Ribbons (85), Banners, Pennants, Flags (85), Emblems, Letters (85), Special Awards (85), Surprise! Surprise! (86)

9. Classroom Publicity and Public Relations 87

The Local Newspaper (88), The Classroom Newspaper (88), A Classroom Bulletin (90), Classroom Correspondence (90), Send Get Well, We Miss You, Congratulations, Happy Birthday and Holiday Cards (93), Send Papers Home for Signatures (94), Classroom Programs—Invite a Crowd! (94), Give Awards (96), Put Their Projects on Display (96), Bring the Community to Class (96), Gifts Which Reflect School Skills (97)

10. Drilling without Drudgery 102

From the School Supply Store (103), Flashcards With Flair (103), Manipulative Charts (105), Egg Carton Contests (107), Beat the Clock (107), Gold Star Papers (108), Alphabet Charts (108), Puzzles and Worksheets (108), Put It in Order (109), Magic Slates (109), A Creative Writing Corner (109), From the Playing Fields (110), Extemporaneous "Speeches" (111), Guess the Sketch (111), Textbook Relay (112), Role Playing (113), Twenty Questions (113), Teach a Class (114), Make a Movie (114), Give a Slide Show (114), Postage Stamp Detectives (115), The Listening Corner (116), Slides on Display (116), A Viewmaster Corner (116), Supplementary Reading Material (116), Reading Skill-Builders (119), Hand Puppets (119), Interesting Things To Do Sheets (120), Culture Corner Quest (121), Make a Grammar Kit (122), Punctuating Conversation (123), Perk Up Your Penmanship Program (123), Arithmetic With the Cuisenaire Rods (124)

11. Projects, Displays, Exhibition Techniques 125

Project Work (126), What Sort of Projects? (126), Setting Up a Project Period (127), Acetate Cover Sheets (128), Bulletin Boards (129), Charts (137), Dioramas (138), Dwellings (138), Exhibits and Displays (140), Flannel Boards (143), Graphs and Pictographs (143), Magnetic Charts and Boards (146), Maps (146), Murals (149), Posters (156), Sandtable Displays (157), Prepare a Project Kit (1958)

12. Teaching Them to Draw and to Letter 159

The Proper Tools (161), The Basic Strokes (161), Teach Shape (162), Teach Form (162), Teach Simple Perspective (164), Teach the Human Figure (166), Teach the Head and Face (166), Teach Expression (168), Teach the Hand and Foot (168), Teach Familiar Animals (168), Teach Standard Symbols (169), Teach Them to Cartoon (169), Teach Composition (170), Sketch Sessions (170), Teach Them to Letter (172)

13. Far-Reaching Field Trips **175**

What Can You Expect From a Field Trip? (175), Where Should You Go on a Field Trip? (176), What Advance Preparations Must Be Made? (177), How Many Trips Should the Class Take Each Year? (177), What Do You Do for Transportation? (177), How Much Do the Trips Cost? (177), Are Most of These All Day Excursions? (177), How Do You Keep Track of All the Children? (177), How Many Chaperones Go on the Trips? (178), What Safety Factors Have to Be Considered? (178), What Behavior Standards Are Set? (178), What Do You Do About Meals? (178), What About Bathroom Facilities? (178), Do the Students Have a Specific Assignment on the Trip? (178), Do You Have Standards for Dress? (179), Do You Refer to a Check List as You Plan the Trips? (179), What Do the Students Do While They Are Traveling? (180), Are the Follow-up Activities Planned Before the Trip? (181), What Do You Feel Are the Most Important Ingredients of a Successful Trip? (181), How Did You Handle Publicity? (181)

14. Teaching Through "Make Believe" Trips **184**

Making Plans (185), Student Committees (187), A Brief Case for Documents (188), The Passport (188), Shot Records (188), Planning the Itinerary (189), Planning Transportation (189), Financing the Trip (190), Packing for the Trip (192), Set Up a Ticket Counter in the Classroom (192), Sightseeing (192), Food on the Trip (195), A Taste of the Language (197), Have a Good Time on the Trip (199), How Can You Tell if They're Learning? (200)

15. The Activity Day **203**

The Oklahoma Land Rush: An Activity Day in Detail (206), Schedule of a Pioneer Activity Day (208), Schedule of Olympic Games Activity Day (209), Schedule of Middle Ages Activity Day (210), Schedule of a Revolutionary War Activity Day (211), Schedule of a House-Rasing—Sewing Bee (211), Early Days Antique Show (212), A Yurt on the Khirghiz Steppe (212), Baffin Island Afternoon (213), Covered Wagon Journey (213), Knighting a Squire (214), Safari (214), An Afternoon in Paris (214), Afternoon Tea in England (215), Along the Amazon (215), What Can You Do? (216)

16. Putting on a Program **217**

Writing an Original Play (219), Adapting a Play From a Story (221), Adapting a Play From the Classics (222), Adapting a Play From an Article (223), Plan and Produce a Classroom Musical (225), A Panorama of History Through Song (229), A Concert and Community Sing (230), Produce Your Own "Telecast" (231), A Poetry Assembly (231), Produce a Movie (233), Sound Effects and Slides (234), Open House (235), The Science Fair (235), The Book Fair (241), Open an "Art Gallery" (243), Creating Costumes (244), Scenery and Props (245)

17. Ten Units to Try 248

Bells Are to Ring (249), Water Is To Draw From (252), A Gem Is To Cherish (255), The Goodness of Grapes (260), Sugar, Spice and Everything Nice (262), Bridges Are To Cross—A Regional Winner (265), Early Days in America (267), Multiple Grades Look at the Middle Ages (272), A Portable Unit for Dental Health Week (274), The Wonderful Miracle Machine (275), A Unit . . . or More Than a Unit (278)

18. The Culture Corner 280

Featuring (281), Keep a Record (281), Choosing the Selections (282), "Story Hour" (282), Listen to Literature (283), Dramatize Literature (283), Work With Literature (284), Look at Literaure (286), Concerts in the Classroom (287), Early in the Morning (287), Work With Music (288), Take a Good Look at Art (289), Take Part in Art (292), Culture Corner Classwork (293)

19. Something to Live By 295

What Can You Do? (296), Where Can You Find Material? (297), To Get You Started (297)

20. Sources and Resources 307

Be A Catalog Collector! (320), Professional Help From the Magazine Rack (323), They Handle Films (326), They Make Slides (327), Helpful Addresses (328), Travel Posters (333), Parting Thoughts (334)

Bibliography 335

Index 341

The
Come-Alive
Classroom

CHAPTER 1

Planning
Ahead

*The man who can make hard things easy is
the educator.*

—*Emerson*

Good teaching is vivid, memorable, relevant—sharpened by
interesting detail. Such teaching requires careful planning; it
does not happen otherwise.

1. The Year at a Glance

At the beginning of each school year, it is important to take
a good long look at the year ahead. Pinpoint what *must* be covered in each subject you teach. Write it down!

An efficient planning sheet is a roll of shelf paper. Divide it
into the months of the school year. Along the side make divisions
for every subject you will be teaching. Rule off a section for

textbook pages, the major concepts involved, and the activities and special resources that will enrich your lessons.

Make your notations in pencil. Check your projected plans at least once a grading period. How nearly "on schedule" are you? Is the essential material being covered, or have you gotten side-tracked along the way?

■ Be practical when planning. Consider—

🖊 Holiday periods = excitement
🖊 Hot weather = apathy
🖊 Grading periods = tension

Keep these in mind as you schedule your introductory lessons.

■ Vary your lessons and assignments. There are many ways to explore and solve the same problem:

- Reading
- Written Work
- Oral Reports
- Experiments
- Demonstrations
- Drills
- Worksheets

- Research
- Visual Aids
- Physical Activity
- Projects, Exhibits, Displays
- Field trips
- Interviews
- Games

Don't attempt too many things. Unlimited activity is bankruptcy.
—Emerson

2. The Weekly Plan Book

Weekly plan books are required by most school systems. They provide a flexible framework for daily lessons and assignments.

A simple color code in your plan book greatly increases its value. One glance at what was accomplished *this* week makes it easy to plan for next week.

2

(Blue) → ✓ —a completed lesson
(Red) → ✓ —material planned for but not covered
(Green → ✓ —the class needs more drill
(Yellow) → ✓ —highly successful lesson; use this again!

THURSDAY	FRIDAY
PAGES 71-78	NEW LESSON 76
Essay on Thoreau	Verbs in action pg. 25-26

Indian signals

3. Planning Day by Day

A daily plan sheet will give you room for detail. Draw up
your own form on a ditto stencil:

Make spaces for

- The schedule, lessons and assignments
- Materials you will need
- Equipment you will need
- Things to remember
- Things to collect
- "Remind the class" items

SCHEDULE FOR _Sept. 12_

ABSENT: Robin Mark

LESSONS	ASSIGNMENTS
8:30 Rdg I	42-44
9:00 Music	(Auditorium)
9:30 Arith	Pg 41 # 8-15
10:00 Recess	
10:15 Rdg II	40-44
10:45 Science	Reports
11:15 Drill	
11:30 Lunch	
12:00 Soc. St	37-✓
1:00 P.E.	Play-off
1:30	
2:00 Film Strip	
2:30 Dismissal	

MATERIALS
Clay for Projects in S.S.

EQUIPMENT
Film strip –
2:00

REMIND THE CLASS:
Field Trip Friday

COLLECT: Permission Slips

BRING TO CLASS: Catalog

DON'T FORGET---

Punch the sheets for a loose-leaf notebook.

Use dividers and separate the plan sheets by grading periods,
months or weeks.

4. Student Assignment Sheets

At every grade level "assignment sheets" will help students
organize themselves to approach their assignments with efficiency
and purpose. These plan sheets can be set up on ditto stencils
with very little trouble.

*A problem well-stated is a problem
half solved.*

—John Dewey

5. Challenging Assignments

Ask your students to solve problems in new and interesting forms:

a. *Involve them in the assignment.*

1. *Be an author.* Write a three-paragraph description of yourself (your mother, your father, your early childhood.)
2. *Be a reporter.* Cover an historical event (a current event, a well-known event from a work of fiction). Include a headline, by-line, dateline, lead paragraph and five sub-paragraphs in your story.
3. *Be a political cartoonist.* Editorialize an event, situation, or idea.
4. *Be an architect.* Design a dwelling for a citizen of the past (of another country, of another area).

b. *Ask interesting questions.*

1. What do the names "Tallahassee," "Withlacoochee," "Ponte Vedra" and "Ribault" tell us of Florida's background and history?
2. Why did New Englanders settle in small towns and Virginians scatter over large plantations?
3. What happens when a cut gets infected?
4. If blood is red, why do people talk about "blue blood"?
5. What causes a person's face to break out?
6. What happens inside of you when you take a shot?
7. If you were visiting in Norway, what might you have for supper tonight?

c. *Prepare interesting work sheets.*

Type excerpts from their written or oral reports on ditto stencils and distribute copies as worksheets. Trace their original drawings. Make up questions and problems for the rest of the class to answer.

Top Left — Spelling Puzzle

Spelling Puzzle

Lady Margrete   March 15, 1907

I am "being thoughtful"
I am "being kind"
I am being <u>courteous</u>.

I am a written message
I inform.
I am <u>correspondence</u>.

THE CRUSADES SYMBOL

I am a jorney
I am people traveling
for a definate pupose
I am an <u>expedition</u>.

Food to sell!

I was a pilgrimage
I began in 1096
I was the first <u>Crusade</u>.

I live in town
I buy and sell
I am a <u>merchant</u>.

I am a union
My people are masters.
I am a <u>guilds</u>.

Top Right

NAME: —————————————— DATE: ——————————————

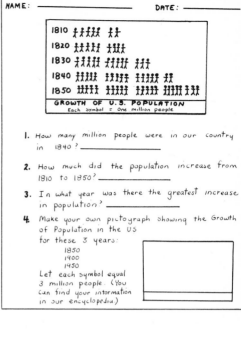

1810	𝍠𝍠𝍠𝍠𝍠 𝍠𝍠
1820	𝍠𝍠𝍠𝍠𝍠 𝍠𝍠𝍠
1830	𝍠𝍠𝍠𝍠𝍠 𝍠𝍠𝍠𝍠𝍠 𝍠𝍠𝍠
1840	𝍠𝍠𝍠𝍠𝍠 𝍠𝍠𝍠𝍠𝍠 𝍠𝍠𝍠𝍠𝍠 𝍠𝍠
1850	𝍠𝍠𝍠𝍠𝍠 𝍠𝍠𝍠𝍠𝍠 𝍠𝍠𝍠𝍠𝍠 𝍠𝍠𝍠𝍠𝍠 𝍠𝍠𝍠

GROWTH OF U.S. POPULATION
Each Symbol = One million people

1. How many million people were in our country in 1840? _____

2. How much did the population increase from 1810 to 1850? _____

3. In what year was there the greatest increase in population? _____

4. Make your own pictograph showing the Growth of Population in the US
   for these 3 years:
       1850
       1900
       1950
   Let each symbol equal 3 million people. (You can find your information in our encyclopedia)

Bottom Left — Special Spelling Flight To Hawaii!

Special Spelling Flight To Hawaii!

The Kuppinger plane, "Wiki-wiki", decided to take all the fourth grade keikis (children) on a Hawaiian spelling trip! It was Jonathan's idea that we learn to spell our Hawaiian words, so the two kumukulas (teachers) decided to help make-up the list. Your spelling list for the week are the underlined words in the sentence and paragraph stories below.

<u>Aloha</u> is a funny word because it means such opposite things. Aloha says hello if we come, and good-bye if we go!

To say thank-you in Hawaiian is <u>mahalo</u>.

The <u>Hawaiian Islands</u> has several other names. The other names are Hawaii, the <u>Territory of Hawaii</u>, the Sandwich Islands, the Paradise of the Pacific, and the Crossroads of the <u>Pacific</u>.

Every person who visits in Hawaii is given a <u>lei</u>, a pretty garland of flowers. Visitors to the Islands are called <u>tourists</u>.

Tourists are kept very busy. They visit the <u>sugar plantations</u>. They visit the <u>pineapple</u> canneries. They go swimming. They wear leis. They go to an old-fashioned Hawaiian fishing party called a <u>hukilau</u>. They look at <u>lava</u> rock from <u>volcanoes</u>. They eat Hawaiian <u>kau-kau</u> at a <u>luau</u>.

The most modern city in the Territory of Hawaii is <u>Honolulu</u>. Honolulu is the city most tourists first visit. Later they go to <u>Hawaii</u>, <u>Kauai</u>, and <u>Maui</u>.

Bottom Right

NAME: —————————————— DATE: ——————————————

1. { ◌ 🧂 } =
   □ { ◌ } ∪ { 🧂 }
   □ { ◌ } ∪ { }
   □ { ◌ } ∪ { ◌ }
      Which one?

2. Danny and David are jumping along a number line. Danny jumps 6 units each time. David jumps 4 units each time.
   0 1 2 3 4 5 6 7 8 9 10 11 12
   a) Danny starts at 0 and makes 2 jumps. He lands at _____.
   b) David starts at 0 and makes 2 jumps. He lands at _____.

3. { ♥ 🐟 } =
   □ { } ∪ { ♥ 🐟 }
   □ { ♥ 🐟 } ∪ { ◌ }
   □ { ♥ } ∪ { ◌ 🐟 }
      Figure it out!

4. Frankie ate 7 sandwiches and David ate three less.
   a) Write the equation. _____
   b) Solve the equation. _____

5. In our story of MOBY DICK, Queequiq harpooned 6 whales and Ishmael harpooned 4 less.
   a) Write the equation. _____
   b) Solve for N. _____

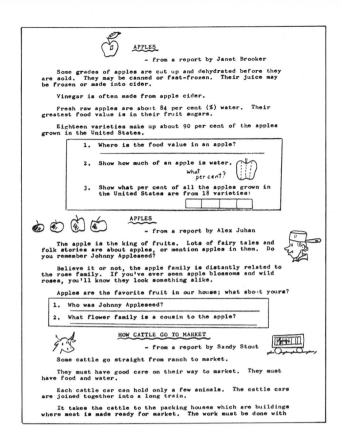

d. Present interesting problems.

1. Clip one column of news from the front page of today's paper. Underline all of the adjectives (nouns, verbs, pronouns, etc.) that you can find.
2. Alphabetize this stack of 10 books. Write your list in your best penmanship.
3. Write a 5-sentence report on Corn (any topic). Choose your facts from either set of encyclopedias.
4. Give the geographical history of a rubber tire.
5. Prepare a picture dictionary from our unit in science (social studies, math, reading, etc.).
6. Prepare a 2-minute oral report on Pioneer Schools (any topic).
7. Draw a pictograph to compare the amount of cotton produced in Georgia, Alabama, Louisiana and Florida (any comparison).
8. Using your new vocabulary from this chapter, prepare a puzzle for someone else to answer.

6

e. *Let your textbooks become "workbooks".*

1. Change all singular nouns to plural on page 6.
2. Write abbreviations for as many words as possible on page 18.
3. List all 2-syllable words on pages 101-102.
4. Find 10 words in Chapter Two with long a. List them.
5. Find 20 words in Chapter Four with silent letters. List the words and draw a line through the silent letters.
6. Find 15 words in Unit One that end in -er (-ing, -ed, -ful, -le, etc.). List them. Alphabetize them.
7. Choose one paragraph from page 10. List all its words in alphabetical order.
8. List all the words in paragraph 2 on page 10. Beside each word write another that rhymes with it.
9. Outline paragraph four on page 101.
10. Make up six word problems using the people and the situation on page 101.
11. Find and list 15 words from Chapter 3 that have prefixes.
12. Write all the words you can find in Chapter 6 with the phonogram "ight" ("ough," "ite," "ing," etc.).

MEMO

Be a catalog collector!

Ask your office supply dealer, druggist, grocer, and display materials dealer for copies of their suppliers' catalogs—or for a chance to look at them. They're chock full of ideas and inexpensive tools and materials that can give a real boost to your lessons and projects—

Pages 320-321 list many catalogs of interest to teachers.

6. Make Plans for Yourself

Perhaps you don't feel "fully qualified" in some of the subjects you teach. Or perhaps you feel more could be accomplished if you had a little help. Make plans for yourself!

a. *Subscribe* to a professional journal in the field. Every month you will be exposed to articles, ideas, projects and advertisements that will stimulate your own thinking.

b. *Read* anything and everything you can find on the subject. Comb the library shelves for both specific and related works. Prepare a reading list.

c. *Audio-visual aids* will help *you* as much as your students. Study the catalogs of films, slides and recordings which are available to you. Request any and all that bear on your subject.

d. *Take a course* that will further your understanding of the subject—a workshop, a summer program, an extension course.

e. *Get involved* right away with a classroom project centered in this subject—something new and different and stimulating that you've never tried before.

GUIDELINES FOR PLANNING

1. The human mind works best upon those things in which it is interested. Interest is the channel for energy and enthusiasm.
2. The central truth of every lesson usually has many applications. Help your students apply it.
3. Students must start from their own experience if they are to find meaning in what they study.
4. Better to cover only a portion of the text and do it well, than to hurry through all of it and have none of it clear.
5. New steps and new material should be developed in class.
6. Unless you are thoroughly familiar with a subject, you should work out each exercise and problem in the text before presenting it to or assigning it to the class.
7. Excessive writing deadens interest.
8. Rivalry should be between the student and his previous record. Help your students measure their progress through diagnostic tests, charts, and graphs.
9. Good work should be praised more than poor work should be criticized.

10. Variety is the spice of life . . . and learning. Present your
    lessons in many forms:

- films
- charts

- lectures
- trips

- experiments
- visitors

IT'S TRUE!

You can take a child of average ability
and make him a prodigy with the right
approach.

—Caleb Gattegno

> *Method and procedure are the only*
> *sound basis of teaching, for without*
> *them creative ability has no chance.*
> —*Andrew Loomis*

Any adult who does not understand
the power of the pleasure principle in
dealing with young children is very
much deluded.

—Nancy McCormick Rambusch

> *You cannot elevate people by going*
> *down to their level. If they succeed in*
> *getting you there, there they will keep*
> *you, for it is easier to get you to stay*
> *down than for them to move up.*
> —*Mortimer Adler*

The child's mind in order to rise into
the abstract needs first to move in contact with the solid and the concrete.

—Maria Montessori

> *Nothing in education is more vital to*
> *the future of America than that* all *its*
> *children shall learn to read and write*
> *easily, rapidly, accurately and enjoy-*
> *ably.*
> —*Romalda Bishop Spalding*

When the Chinese wrote that "one picture is worth a thousand words" this statement was based on hundreds of years of experience. They knew that a message placed before the observer in picture enabled his mind to grasp the idea much more rapidly than from the printed word alone.

—John de Lemos

Much teaching consists in explaining. We explain the unknown by the known, the vague by the vivid. The students usually know so little that they are delighted to hear you explain what you know and tie it up with what they are trying to understand.

—Gilbert Highet

No idea is going to be clearly conveyed unless it is clear in the mind that conceives it. Let not this be passed over as an idle statement of the obvious. At least half the failures in the propagation of ideas are due to lack of definition. The idea being muddy at its source continues muddy along its course.

—John M. Shaw

One of the most common criticisms from college teachers is that students cannot express themselves in writing. They can't form sentences and paragraphs, or make clear written statements to say what they want to say. In my opinion, too much ready-made material handed out to children in elementary and secondary school is largely responsible for this situation.

—Lila Sheppard

The most important personal element
in making a class interesting is your
own enthusiasm for your subject.
—Henry W. Simon

*Abstraction is an inner illumination
and if the light does not come from
within, it does not come at all. All we
can do is to help the children by giving
them the best possible conditions which
includes presenting them with external
concrete materials.*
—Maria Montessori

The pupils must continually be enjoying some fruition and starting afresh.
—Alfred North Whitehead

*If it is the job of the teacher to put the
children in direct contact with what
they are learning, then it is further her
job to free them and let them alone
once they begin to learn, and not to in-
trude herself constantly upon what
they are doing.*
—Nancy McCormick Rambusch

My eyes were opened to the difference
between the learning that occurs when
pupils do assignments and when they
work on some project or problem they
have deemed important enough to
tackle. Never again could I be com-
placent about making an assignment.
—Kimball Wiles

*How does one learn to identify prob-
lems, to observe with discrimination,
to hypothesize, to distinguish good
from questionable evidence, to sort fact
from assumption, to make reasonable
interpretations from evidence, and to
generalize? Only by continuous practice in actual situations.*
—Ellsworth S. Obourn

We don't waste enough in school. We
hoard our old ideas on charts to be
used again and again like stale bread.
Ideas are never the same again, even
those of the masters; even if the only
change is in our own mood of reap-
proach.

—Sylvia Ashton-Warner

*Throw away your notes at least every
other year and make new ones, new
ones based on what you have found out
about your subject meantime.*
—Henry W. Simon

We help by continually expecting more
from pupils than they are able to deliver, rather than by protecting them
from making major decisions simply
because we believe that they are not
ready.

—Kimball Wiles

*Part of teaching proficiency comes from
the memory of the way we were taught,
part comes by learning from the experience of others, and part is based upon
our own willingness to work at tasks
that we feel must be accomplished.*
—Paul S. Anderson

The process of learning should be fun
of the highest order, for it is indeed the
greatest game in life.

—Glenn Doman

PLANNING FOR MULTIPLE GRADES

*. . . the methods . . . must be simple
and direct and such as will take the least
time possible to carry out effectively.*
—W. W. Charters

1. Combine, Combine, Combine

First, accept the fact that you cannot teach every subject to every grade! Before the school year begins, go through your curriculum guides and textbook material for each of the grade levels.

Decide—
    a. What must be taught separately
    b. What can be taught to the entire class
    c. What can be eliminated

Then list on separate sheets of paper those subjects you will try to—
    a. Teach every day
    b. Teach every other day
    c. Teach once a week
    d. Assign for individual study; no group work
    e. Teach during one semester or grading period only

The third step is to take a roll of shelf paper and block off the hours in your school day—

    a. Put the hours across the top.
    b. List the number of grade levels down the side.
    c. Show what each class will be studying or working on for each period in the day.
    d. Color in the block that shows what you will be teaching each period.

Now, check your schedule to make sure that—

    ✔ All subjects are being covered
    ✔ Group work and individual work are balanced
    ✔ Every grade level has a share of your time

Keep working with and adjusting your schedule after the year begins. When you find the arrangement that seems most productive, stick with it!

2. General Guidelines

    a. *Use the Buddy System.* Let your stronger students help children in a lower grade level or weaker students at their own level. Schedule specific "study halls" for children to pair off and work.

> *All of this, of course, takes time and involves noise and movement and personal relations and actual reading, and above all communication, one with another: the vital thing so often cut off in a schoolroom.*
>
> —*Sylvia Ashton-Warner*

b. Prepare "Learn From Each Other" work sheets so that students may benefit from the variety of activity in the different grade levels.

LEARN FROM EACH OTHER

1. Study Nan's project on Metamorphosis. What illustrations does she use?
2. Read Chris' story in the folder on the library table. Draw a picture to illustrate it.
3. What fact impressed you the most on the 5th Grade's bulletin board?

c. Teach as many subjects by the unit method as possible. Lectures and visual aids can be prepared for whole class presentation and followed by graded assignments.
d. Develop interest centers with games, drills, books and experiments that can be handled independently.

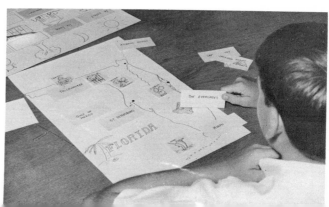

e. Build a strong room library.
f. Build a collection of enrichment activities.
g. Encourage students to work independently. Let them check their daily work by keys.
h. Write to SRA for their catalog of multi-level instructional labs in reading, science, social studies and math.

These laboratories permit the average, above-average and superior student—or students of different grade levels—to work side by side in the same classroom.

The teacher enters no scores, corrects no papers, keeps no records. The student corrects his own mistakes, records his daily work and plots his own progress. The teacher sets the program into operation, makes sure each student knows what to do and consults with each individual every few days to check his progress.

Write for informational brochures:

Science Research Associates, Inc.
259 E. Erie Street
Chicago, Illinois 60611

i. For class, group or individual work, the workbook series READING TO SOME PURPOSE, answers many needs.

Books 1-4 are graded to provide work for half a year each; books 5-7 for one year each. Prices range from 50¢ to 80¢ each.

The workbooks include stories, descriptions, expositions, dialogue, verse, indexes, dictionaries, diagrams, graphs, tables and maps. Answers are *not* written in the books themselves, so they may be used with group after group.

A minimum amount of guidance is required of the teacher. The work is prepared in such a way that children cannot help but write correct answers.

An excellent reference for preparing your own practice worksheets and exercises, an excellent skillbuilder for individuals or groups—

READING TO SOME PURPOSE, Books 1-7
by
Phyllis Flowerdew and Ronald Ridout

For information on ordering single or multiple copies, write:

Clarke, Irwin & Co., Ltd.
Clarwin House
791 St. Clair Avenue W.
Toronto 10, Canada

j. Contact Scholastic Book Services for a free kit of materials to start a classroom book club for your students:

The Lucky Book Club for Grades 2-3,
The Arrow Book Club for Grades 4-6.

Outstanding children's titles in paperback editions are available for 25¢ and 35¢ each. Illustrated newsletters describe the current choices. Dividend copies for your classroom library!

For further information write:

Scholastic Book Services
904 Sylvan Avenue
Englewood Cliffs, N. J.

k. Write the Cuisenaire Company for their catalog of Cuisenaire arithmetic materials—an activity-centered math program:

The Cuisenaire Co. of America
9 Elm Ave.
Mt. Vernon
N. Y.

l. Let students assist you whenever possible—calling out spelling, checking work with keys, taking up money, preparing bulletin boards, handling supplies and equipment, and the like.

CHAPTER 2

Classrooms
as Workshops

Youth resists the dull, the dingy, and the dusty. They are attracted to light, to brightness, to color. The appearance of the school should give the impression that the school is a place where it would be fun to live and work.

—Kimball Wiles

Classrooms are important workshops! See them as a series of work centers—the best possible arrangement of furniture, tools, equipment, storage, and display areas. Do everything you can to create a feeling of order and purpose in your room. Can you improve your present setup? How well planned and efficient is your room's—

     floor space?   display space?

     storage space?   work space?

            general atmosphere?

*This is not a museum where materials
are kept, but a workroom where materials are used and where there is always space for a new project.*
        —*Prudence Bostwick*

1. Put It On Paper

Sketch your present room arrangement on graph paper using
a ½ inch scale. Show windows, door, furniture, and storage areas.
Don't forget to indicate electrical outlets!

Take a red pencil and trace the traffic flow through the room.
Where are the congested areas? Do present traffic routes pass
through your work centers or discussion groups?

Now place sheets of onion skin over the graph paper and
sketch new possibilities. Make a list of pros and cons. Can you—

   a. Rearrange desks for more floor space?
   b. Widen the aisles?
   c. Turn work areas away from windows?
   d. Put the pencil sharpener and waste basket out of the main
      traffic routes?
   e. Put materials near work centers?
   f. Plan for group work areas and individual work areas?
   g. Plan for interest centers, display areas?
   h. Use rugs, curtains, plants, dividers?

Sketch a dozen plans on paper before you shove the first piece
of furniture!

2. Creating Work Stations

Try placing desks and tables next to each other instead of in
rows. This almost doubles the unoccupied floor space and creates
a feeling of quiet and order in the room.

Try several arrangements:

L Shapes   M Shapes   U Shapes

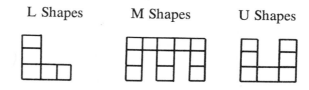

Create specific work stations with your desks or with conference tables. Let student committees set up their materials for discussion groups, committee meetings, art work, project work, and the like.

3. Creating Storage Space

If your room is short on storage space, consider building or buying your own:

a. *Cement blocks and planks*

Paint and decorate!

b. *Wooden grocery crates*

Paint and decorate!

c. *Flip top, removable top and pull drawer storage cartons*

Sturdy, specially constructed office storage cartons are excellent organizers. Buy the kind that store flat and can be assembled quickly without tape, staples or tools.

- For file folders, manuals, magazines—the Letter Size or Legal Size boxes are best.
- For charts and rolled illustrations, the Check Size boxes are best.

Most of these cartons have index panels on both ends with hand holes front and back. They are built to carry a 200 pound or better load and can be stacked from the floor to the ceiling or stored on inexpensive shelving.

MEMO

Most office supply stores can order R-Kive File Boxes for you. They have a removable top.

Atlantic Advertising, Inc. carries the Flip Top and Pull Drawer style boxes. Write for their illustrated brochures and catalog:

Atlantic Advertising, Inc.
Atlantic City, N. J. 08404

Their cartons must be purchased in quantities of 6 and 12 or more, but cartons disappear quickly when several teachers combine their orders.

Sears, Roebuck & Company carries inexpensive steel shelving. Your local industrial supplier could also direct you to some.

d. *Subject matter kits*

Get rid of the realia and equipment that so often clutters a classroom. These same cardboard storage cartons are ideal Subject Matter Kits.

Partition your cartons. Label and index both ends.

e. *Pegboard panels*

Pegboard panels are ideal for your housekeeping, gardening and athletic tools and equipment. Paint silhouettes of the objects onto the panels.

f. *For primary classrooms*

A simple storage sack can be stitched together to hang at the side of each student's desk to hold crayons, scissors, paste, pencils, and the like, leaving the desk free for books and paper. Your room mothers will be glad to help!

g. *Office letter baskets*

Letter baskets of wire, wood or plastic can be stacked on top of each other to provide neat collection spots for papers, worksheets, and supplies.

4. Creating Display Space

a. *Bulletin boards*

Consolidate small display areas by covering them with one large bulletin board. Three-quarters of an inch of chipboard covered with monks cloth and bordered by a 2″ wooden frame is inexpensive to install. You will find a 4′ x 16′ board a highly motivating teaching tool.

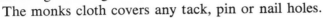

The monks cloth covers any tack, pin or nail holes.

b. *Portable panels*

Pegboard and corkboard panels can be hinged for desk or floor display pieces, or mounted on the wall.

c. *Pegboard strips*

Mount a strip of pegboard along a wall or chalkboard area. Display papers, illustrations, articles, charts in acetate jackets. Notes can be written directly onto the acetate surface without harming the paper. Clipboards, charts and corkboard panels can be hung along the strips.

d. *Concrete blocks and planks*

Concrete blocks and inexpensive pine planks can create additional permanent or temporary shelving for displays.

e. *Wooden crates*

Stack and nail together wooden grocery crates for display cubbyholes and dioramas.

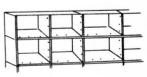

5. The Interest Center

The Interest Center is an important teaching tool for every elementary classroom. Here are some Guidelines to help you plan yours:

GUIDELINES

a. *Accuracy is the keyword!* Better not to have something displayed than to have it improperly labeled. If there is any question, use a "?" and give suggestions for clearing up the doubt.

b. *Use a variety of display areas:* tables, shelves, sandtable, wall space, desk tops, bulletin boards, chalkboards.

c. *Display a variety of materials:*

student projects	pictures, paintings
realia	magazines
record jackets	book jackets
bulletins	posters
simple experiments	earphones and phonographs
games	worksheets, drills
Viewmaster reels	filmstrips
binoculars	slides
models	radio

d. *Do not clutter the Center.* Keep the arrangements, background, lettering and labels quite simple.

e. *Place the most important objects*—charts, experiments, models—*in strategic positions.*

f. *Set up an experiment or activity* whenever possible.

g. *Encourage students* to handle the material, read the pamphlets, solve the problems.

h. *Use sound, color and motion whenever possible.* Earphone jacks can be added to record players or tape recorders. Color and texture can be achieved with light, paint, paper and material. Revolving turntable display units can be purchased for under $10.

MEMO

See the discussion of General Electric's
SHOW 'N TELL units
on page 281.

6. Spruce Up the Room!

Bright and interesting classrooms evoke a definite response. How does your room rate with regard to—

- ☑ Freshness
- ☑ Neatness and order
- ☑ Brightness and color
- ☑ "Atmosphere"

See what you can do to create a pleasant atmosphere for learning!

A quart of water-base paint will brighten cartons, shelves and display areas with a minimum of mess. Students can assist in these projects since cleaning up spilled paint involves only water and elbow grease.

Ask your students, room mothers and friends to help collect special furnishings for your room—

- Drapes
- Lamps
- Magazine Racks
- Bookshelves
- Paintings
- Paint
- Tables
- Flowers
- Rugs
- Easy Chairs
- Plants
- Dividers
- Pottery

Some classrooms appeal to a visitor as soon as he sees them. It is apparent that someone cares about them. Steps have been made to make them attractive . . . The room is inviting—the type of place the visitor would like to spend the day.

—Kimball Wiles

Make even the simplest tasks easier through improving the physical arrangement of your room. Better working conditions will have an immediate effect on you *and* your students. A cheerful, well-organized and attractive classroom workshop is your goal!

CHAPTER 3

Time Savers:

Records, Files

and Forms

The intelligent use of good records will help us decide what to do as well as what not to do. If we fail to keep a record, how can we learn from experience?

—Gail Plummer

The classroom can be run as efficiently and smoothly as the busiest downtown office. It has to be if you are to meet all your housekeeping, clerical and teaching responsibilities!

Chapter 3 is concerned with saving time. Does it suggest something you could be doing, could stop doing, or could do differently? Look for short cuts you can use, ways you can simplify, or steps you can eliminate. You'll see a big difference in your daily schedule!

24

1. Make an Inventory

Everything in your classroom should have a particular place and its place should be recorded in an indexed inventory—
                    Paper clips,
                    Permanent records,
                    Pictures,
                    Scraps—everything! Sound impossible?
Far from it, and once you work out your storage arrangements you'll find your inventory is a great time saver. Let your students help you organize. Keep track of where things are *and* how much you have on hand. Pencil in the quantities—keep your records up to date. Use 3 x 5 cards or loose-leaf notebook sheets to file your information. Each category should have its own card or page and be filed alphabetically. You'll never regret the time you spend on this inventory.

2. Label Everything

Simplify the search for materials. Use self-stick labels freely—on shelves, cartons, drawers, cabinet doors. They make it much easier for you, the students or a substitute to find materials and return them to their proper places.

3. Keep an "Executive's Diary"

An Executive's Diary on your desk top will simplify many problems. A ¼-inch ring binder with dividers is all you need.
Include a section for:

☐ Frequently used phone numbers
☐ Frequently used addresses
☐ A check list of reports due
☐ A Year-At-A-Glance calendar showing important dates, holidays and themes
☐ A student list
☐ Special information—school policies, substitute policies, and the like.

4. Keep a File on Each Student

Prepare a separate manila file folder for each of your students. Insert material to use in conferences and to evaluate their progress at the end of grading periods.

- Progress sheets
- Notes
- Significant daily papers
- Important test papers

Prepare forms which can be duplicated and checked quickly and easily.

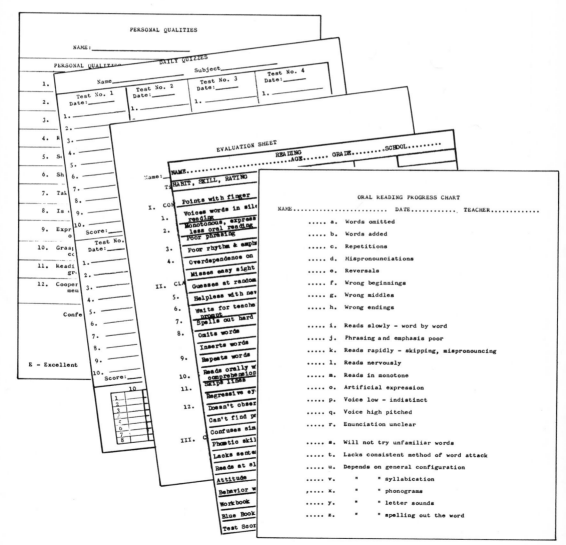

5. Prepare an Easy-Check Class List

Many many times during the year you will be asked for a list of your pupils! Prepare an easy-check form at the beginning of the year. Run off a generous supply of copies.

 ✔ Take the information from your register.
 ✔ Leave a few spaces for new pupils.
 ✔ Use the lists for any occasion that requires names, addresses or information on your students:

- attendance
- collections
- organizing grades
- checking in work
- permissions
- long-term assignments

Time is capital. Invest it wisely.

6. Keep Financial Records

Keep track of what it costs to run your classroom. Staple bills and receipts into a manila folder so they can be referred to easily. Income tax deductible!

Improvements, refinements and changes come easier when one has a pattern to follow.

—Gail Plummer

7. Keep Track of Successful Lessons

Keep notes on your successful lessons—preparation and presentation. It's a simple matter to adapt a lesson; it is not so simple to start from scratch and replan. You think you won't forget but the time-consuming details may escape you.

Glancing through a Successful Lesson File brings an activity into sharp focus and makes it easy to present it again. Ditto a form and punch it for notebook filing—

Everything . . . can be classified . . .
This is the principle used in office sys-
tems—a separate folder for each sub-
ject.

Apply this principle to everything
you have and you will soon bring order
out of chaos.

—*Lillian M. Gilbreth*

8. Keep Handy Reference Files: Cards, Folders, Envelopes

Keep a separate manila folder, brown envelope or 3 x 5 card file on each of your reference materials—

>Special units
>Class programs
>Bulletin board themes
>Articles, pamphlets, bulletins

Each folder, envelope or card should deal with one topic, subject or period and be tabbed for quick reference:

>Artists and their works
>Continents
>Countries
>Holidays
>Mythology
>Physical Features of the Earth

- Note the contents on the front of the folder or envelope.
- Give every folder and envelope an identification number and mark each item you insert with that same number.
- In warmer climates, spray your envelopes and storage boxes to keep bugs away.
- Collect a variety of materials—

clippings	pictures	quotations
recipes	articles	puzzles
pictographs	jokes	cartoons
anecdotes	worksheets	essays
reading lists	project ideas	observations
visual aids	realia	

- Encourage your students to be alert for material and to contribute to the files.
- Store your envelopes and folders in file cartons.

(See page 19 for a discussion of low cost, sturdy containers.)

9. Keep a Folder for the Substitute

How efficiently the substitute could function in your absence if you kept a special folder just for her. She will need—

- An up-to-date seating chart (unless you keep your students' names taped on their desks)
- The daily schedule
- The location of the tools she will need to carry on your work—

> Grade book
> Plan books
> Register
> Chalk, pencils, erasers
> Manuals
> Texts
> Maps
> Equipment and supplies

- A list of Lunchroom—Playground—Restroom standards
- Bus duty responsibilities
- Lunch duty responsibilities
- Favorite playground games of your class
- Suggestions for recess activities on rainy days
- A list of special routines and responsibilities of your students

Tab each section for easy reference. A ¼-inch ring binder with dividers makes a nice folder.

10. Keep a File for the Visiting Specialist

Prepare a special file for the visiting specialist. Bring it up to date and leave it in the office on the day of his visit so he can acquaint himself with the current activities in your classroom. Include—

- An up-to-date seating chart (unless you keep your students' names taped to their desks)

- Your daily schedule
- Current class interests or projects
- Current work in his field of art, music, physical education, etc.
- Special work by individuals in the class
- Ways you would like him to help

Use a ¼-inch ring binder and dividers.

11. On Your Desk Top

3 x 5 card files are handy reference sources for your desk top. Keep several boxes with your notes on—

- Independent activities—games, puzzles, projects, papers
- Physical Education activities—indoors and outdoors
- Games and drills—athletic, academic, recess
- Reference materials—books, films, records, articles, pictures, clippings, tapes
- Ideas to follow up—your own personal brain-storming

They're easy to add to, easy to use!

Whenever possible, simplify; eliminate; trim down every routine task. Be constantly alert for short cuts—better, quicker, more efficient ways of keeping your records, files and forms. You'll soon find yourself with more time—and energy—to *teach!*

CHAPTER 4

First Day
Fevers

The first hour in the morning is the rudder of the day.

—Henry Ward Beecher

Just as the first hour in the morning sets the pattern for the day, so the first few days in the classroom are important to the pattern of your year.

The first day—the first few minutes—are perhaps the hardest of the whole year. Careful planning is the most effective medicine for those "first day fevers."

1. The Classroom

What should the students find when they come through your door to begin their year?

a. Brightness!

Even in rooms where students and teachers rotate from hour to hour, there should be something displayed which indicates the material the class will be studying and which proves your enthusiasm for what you are teaching!

The most important personal element in making a class interesting is your own enthusiasm for your subject.
        —Henry W. Simon

- A bulletin board display
- Pictures
- Interest centers
- Books on the library table
- Maps
- Flowers or potted plants
- Splashes of color through curtains, cupboards, furniture

Any of these will give your students the feeling that in *this* classroom learning will not be humdrum and routine. Beginning enthusiasm is contagious!

b. The desks and chairs

Arrange the desks and chairs before your students arrive. Have name cards on the desks, or let the children sit where they please, but avoid the confusion of assigning seats and moving students on the first day.

c. You!

Be at the door to welcome each of your students. Have your name written on the board. Know exactly what you are going to do the entire day. Impress the class with your firmness, friendliness and self-confidence.

2. Introducing Yourself

The most important thing about your introduction is simply— Be Yourself! In some way you will want to get across these four points:

1. You are happy to be teaching this class.
2. You have definite standards of behavior.
3. The responsibility for learning is on your students' shoulders.
4. You have many special and interesting activities planned for the coming year.

There are any number of ways you could introduce yourself. Try a "chalk talk":

a. Put the following circles and shapes on the board.

b. Then introduce yourself—

"Good morning! I'm Mr. Smith and I'm delighted to have you in my class this year. Right now I'm probably as much of a blank to you as these circles I've drawn on the board. You're wondering what I'll be like. Will I be grouchy and grumpy?

Will I fuss all the time?

Or will I be pleasant to work with?

Well, I'll tell you a secret—it's not up to me! It's entirely up to—-

YOU!

Think of the kind of class you'd like to be in—one that takes field trips, that has projects and activities, contests, exciting ways of learning. Surely you would prefer that to a class that can't have the extras because there's no time left for fun.

I'm not a baby sitter and I'm not here to nag you every minute. You're here to work for yourself, for the knowledge and skills *you* can gain. If you finish an assignment ahead of the others, there will be many things in our room to help you keep learning—

> good books to read,
> experiments to try,
> drills and games to practice with.

I expect you to take advantage of every minute we have together.

Now there's another picture on the board. It may remind you of me today because while we learn about each other and distribute our books and materials, I may seem to be as slow as a

turtle; But I shall expect you to be courteous and patient, and take the extra minutes to get acquainted with your text books or with a library book from the table.

3. Getting to Work

You have already warned them that the first day may move slowly but that's no excuse for poor planning. Perhaps no other day in your year should be more carefully planned than this first one—

Plan to:

a. Distribute and examine the new textbooks together. Point out particularly interesting units. Hint at special activities the class will undertake.

b. Discuss a general outline of the daily schedule.

c. Introduce them to the interest centers and enrichment materials in the room.

d. Be sure and have some actual work planned for them to do. There should be papers to carry home the first day! For instance,

> 1. *A Vital Statistics Sheet*
>   Ask them to fill out an information sheet. Ditto a

form or write the questions on the board and let
them answer in sentences.

*If we want to teach boys
and girls in terms of their
individual capacities, interests, and needs, we
must be willing to listen
to them.*

—*Kimball Wiles*

> 1. My name is ____
> 2. I have ____ brothers and ____ sisters.
> 3. My father's job is ____
> 4. My mother's job is ____
> 5. My pet is ____
> 6. I spent the summer ____
> 7. My favorite TV program is ____
> 8. My favorite movie star is ____
> 9. The subject I like best is ____
> 10. The subject I like least is ____
> 11. My birthday is ____
> 12. My home address is ____

2. Give diagnostic tests in different subjects.
3. Distribute paper and ask for an illustrated essay or
   composition on:
   > My Goals For This Year
   > How I Spent This Summer
   > All About My Family
   > If I Had Three Wishes
4. Ask them to list from memory the facts, rules, or
   special vocabulary they remember from a specific
   subject.
5. Get a sample of their penmanship:

   *This is a sample of my penmanship
   on the first day of school, September 8, 1966.
   George McLatchey*

6. Ditto a puzzle to be completed with their first week's
   spelling words or with a special set of vocabulary
   words.
7. Distribute a map to be labeled and colored.

e. For minutes that lag, have
   —An exciting story on hand
   —Flash cards for a quick review
   —A special phonograph record

f. Be sure you have these in your classroom:

   ✔ A clock or watch

✔ Paper, pencils, crayons for forgetters
✔ Physical Education and Recess plans and equipment
✔ A flag for morning exercises

4. Setting Standards

From the very beginning you will want to let your students know what you expect. Chapter Five is devoted to setting standards on that first day and all through the year.

Before You Know it——
the first day will be over! You will have

✔ Introduced yourself
✔ Introduced the textbooks and materials
✔ Previewed the year's work
✔ Set behavior and academic standards
✔ Discussed the daily schedule
and
✔ Sent your students home with papers to prove that the first day of school was one of accomplishment!

CHAPTER 5

Setting
Standards

For the spirit to live its freest, the mind must acknowledge discipline.

—Sylvia Ashton-Warner

What are your standards for behavior, appearance, and scholastic achievement? What are the school's policies? Whatever you expect of your students, tell them at the very beginning.

1. Setting Behavior Standards

Don't be afraid to be firm! Let the class know you mean business—you do no idle talking. Speak with confidence and be specific about what you expect. Prepare charts to lead your discussion. Use magazine pictures or drawings for emphasis and humor. Ditto a similar chart to be filled in by the students.

37

All Year Long

1. We will do our best.
   - We will be industrious.

   GRADE A

   - We will use our time wisely.
   - We will take pride in our work.

2. We will think of others.
   - We will be courteous,
     kind,
     thoughtful,
     considerate.

3. We will take care of our room.
   - We will be neat,
     orderly,
     careful.

   THIS WILL BE THE BEST YEAR YOU'VE EVER SPENT!

ALL YEAR LONG

GRADE A

1. WE WILL DO OUR BEST.

_____

_____

_____

Tell some of the ways you can use your time wisely.

_____

2. WE WILL THINK OF OTHERS.

_____

_____

_____ and

_____

What can you do to be considerate?

3. WE WILL TAKE CARE OF OUR ROOM.

_____

_____ and

_____

What can you do to help take care of our room?

_____

The amount of noise or quiet in a room is no measure whatsoever of the discipline in it.

—*Henry W. Simon*

Allow time before activities to discuss courteous and proper behavior:

- On the Playground
- In the Hall
- In the Lunchroom
- When You Are Absent
- In the Restroom
- Waiting for the Bus
- Riding the Bus
- When There Are Guests

Establish a definite procedure for leaving and returning to the classroom.

Establish definite safety rules for playground and physical education periods. Use a whistle and demand prompt obedience. Wait until everyone is listening before you attempt to talk.

Mount pictures in potential trouble spots. They are effective silent reminders. Cover them with acetate.

38

She ate too fast
at lunch!
DON'T YOU !!

No Pushing
At The Sink,
Please !

Any teacher will attest to the fact that tight and efficient control in the classroom usually makes for a wholesome atmosphere. Only when rules are suspended does confusion set in.

—O'Donnell, Taylor, McElaney

She went to bed
late last night!
DID YOU ??

Let's Take Care Of
Our Equipment!

Please put things
back neatly
and
carefully!

QUIET,
PLEASE !

We're
reading!

Once the class knows exactly what you expect, snap up the first offense. Make the punishment sober, worthwhile.

Remember that you, not the students, must take the initiative if an unpleasant situation begins to develop. Nip it in the bud.

If a student needs correcting, it could be because he is trying to attract attention. Take him out of the room and talk to him personally. Do not try to match wits in the classroom.

You will be tested—just expect it. Interest your students, love them, help them, praise them and they will respond.

Consider it a compliment if you find at first that they are saying, "I don't know if I'm going to like my teacher or not. He's awfully strict." You can ease up after you know the children better and after they know positively that you have the upper hand.

You must prove that you like all of them—even the troublemakers. Give the problem child special jobs: line leader, note taker, errand boy.

When you find that their feeling of working for a teacher has changed to working with the teacher, then the real learning begins!

Be as courteous to students as you ex-
pect them to be to you.
                          —Kimball Wiles

2. Setting Standards of Appearance

If the school has policies on personal appearance, discuss them with your students the first day of school.

Establish your own standards for their written work. A specific format and the use of pen and ink or a soft pencil will greatly simplify the grading of papers and will encourage neat, carefully done work.

- Ask for a heading on all papers: Name
                                    Date
                                    Subject
                                    Assignment (page number)
- Insist on margins.
- Insist on the use of a straight edge when preparing material for unlined paper.
- Have lines skipped on the first and second drafts of essays, compositions and reports. This makes it easy to indicate errors and to make suggestions for rewriting.
- Block off math problems so they are not crowded and difficult to check.
- Have answers listed in a side column for quick checking.
- Insist on student proofing. Ditto a chart for them to check against before they turn in their papers:

> Heading?
> Paragraphs indented?
> Capitals?
> Spelling?
> Complete sentences?
> Punctuation?
> Legibility?
> Neatness?

And ask for the signed statement, "I have proofed my paper.
_____"

3. Organizing Their Work

You can help your students organize their work by deciding ahead of time whether or not you will want them to—
- File their notes or assignments in a particular way.
- Keep notebooks, composition books or assignment books.

Establish a policy on classwork and homework:
- Will there be specific homework assignments or will unfinished classwork ordinarily constitute homework?
- If there is no written work, do you expect students to use their homework time to:

> go over previous notes?
> pre-read assignments?
> drill on weak areas?
> read supplementary material?

Children learn by doing, but they learn
more surely by doing correctly.
—Reading To Some Purpose

What about long-term projects? Should your students begin gathering material for term papers, research units, charts, scrapbooks, science projects?

Whatever you expect, tell your class at the very beginning of the year!

4. Setting Scholastic Standards

In terms of Intelligence Quotient, Creativity Quotient and individual drive, there will be many levels of achievement represented by your students. To what standards will you hold the entire class? What allowance will you make for individuals?

There are established standards of achievement—diagnostic tests, penmanship scales, reading level charts—which give students specific goals. They should have no doubt as to what standards they are trying to meet.

Let the students chart their progress on graphs. Keep standards high at all times. We usually ask too little, rather than too much.

We aim above the mark to hit the mark.
—Ralph Waldo Emerson

CHAPTER 6

Classroom Testing
and Evaluation

Part of our job is to help students see evaluation as a way of getting more satisfaction out of school work.

—Kimball Wiles

. . . evaluation is not something that is done just before the report cards are given out. It is involved in each experience and provides evidence regarding the needs, interests and behavior of children, as well as information regarding the effectiveness of the program.

—John U. Michaelis

Happily, there is a gradual turning away from the old-fashioned marking and reporting method that tended to make grades, rather than knowledge the goal of education.

—Benjamin Fine

Evaluation is a never-ending responsibility of the teacher *and* the pupil. Tests serve a purpose—but so do conferences, drills, graphs, check sheets and projects. There should be many opportunities for self-examination, both with and without grading. The best teachers provide these!

1. What Are We Evaluating?

The student's achievement can be measured in several areas:

A. *Academic Skill*

> Mastery of subject
> Critical thinking
> Creative thinking
> Class participation

B. *Work Habits*

> Ability to work independently
> Follows directions
> Accurate
> Neat
> Works to fullest capacity

C. *Adjustment*

> Self-controlled
> Cooperative
> Responsible

Achievement can be measured by many devices and techniques.

☐ Anecdotal records	☐ Drills	☐ Profiles
☐ Autobiographies	☐ Essays	☐ Questionnaires
☐ Case studies	☐ Exhibits	☐ Rating scales
☐ Charts	☐ Graphs	☐ Recordings
☐ Checklists	☐ Interviews	☐ Samples of work
☐ Conferences	☐ Learning games	☐ Tests—oral
☐ Cumulative records	☐ Logs	written
☐ Discussions	☐ Observation	standardized

There is no one "best means;" the purpose of the evaluation will determine which approach the teacher takes. Generally, a combination of devices and techniques gives the most accurate appraisal of the student.

The teacher-constructed or classroom test is probably the most popular evaluative device.

2. Why Give Tests?

The well-constructed classroom test can serve four important purposes for the teacher and the students:

    a. It provides a definite incentive for learning.

    b. It serves as a teaching tool, helping to organize and emphasize the main points of the lessons.

    c. It provides a basis for evaluating achievement.

    d. It gives the teacher a basis for planning new work and reinforcement drills.

Generally, teachers who give frequent quizzes will find that their students are more alert, better organized, and gain more from the instruction.

Of the things we want, a frighteningly large and expanding number are dependent upon the showing we make in one kind of formal test or another.
        —Darrell Huff

3. Test Construction

The best tests have both an evaluative and a diagnostic function. They indicate how successfully the teacher has taught, how well the students have learned, and where more work needs to be done.

In developing a test it is only fair to the student to consider carefully

    ✔ the objectives in teaching the material,
              and
    ✔ which points were stressed in class as being significant.

For the student the test will reflect a philosophy of the course and will affect his future study methods and values.

Emphasis can be accomplished by weighting different sections of the test, and by adjusting the number and type of questions on particular topics.

A worksheet is helpful. List the main points and important details on which the students are to be tested. Lesson plans, assignments, lecture and class notes will provide the material. From this information develop your test outline showing the number, type and point value of each question.

Topic	No. of Questions	Type of Questions	Scoring
1. Army of Northern Va.	5 1	Completion Essay	2 ea. 10 pts.
2. Battle of Bull Run	4	Matching	2 ea.
3. Lee & Grant	4 1	Completion Essay	2 ea. 10 pts.

- Be consistent: don't emphasize memorization one time and expect understanding the next, unless you have plainly indicated this change in your subsequent teaching.
- Trivial details should not be part of a test.
- No trick or catch questions.

Remember—the test reflects your philosophy of the course.

4. Essay vs. Objective Tests

Much has been written with regard to the merits of essay and objective tests. In general, you will find that the essay test can be more quickly prepared. It is, for the most part, free from guessing and requires the student to organize and reproduce his own thoughts. It can be an excellent learning situation.

On the other hand, scoring of the essay is more difficult and more time consuming. It is also quite difficult to obtain reliability in scoring. The following techniques have been useful to experienced teachers:

   a. Have the student write his name on a cover sheet so you cannot tell whose paper you are reading.
   b. Prepare yourself for scoring by listing the information you expect on each question. You can easily determine how much of what you expected has been included in the student's answer.

c. Grade the corresponding questions on *all* papers before going to the next question. There can be a tendency to require more or less information as you grade through the papers—the total effect can be great. Scoring the same question at one time will minimize this effect.

Construction of the objective test is more time-consuming but it can be more easily and quickly scored; in fact, this can be accomplished by someone other than the teacher—even the students. The main drawback is no provision for organization of thoughts and expression of understanding.

Many teachers like to combine the advantages of the essay and objective test by giving sections of each in a single test.

Some teachers who cover similar material each year keep a file of both objective and essay questions on 3 x 5 cards. It is a simple matter to select and adapt questions which apply to current classroom teaching.

5. Evaluating Tests

Tests should be evaluated and an analysis made of the student responses. It is helpful to prepare a summary of errors made on each item.

- If most items relating to a teaching objective are missed, it may be due to inadequate instruction.
- If virtually everyone marked the question right or wrong, the question should be discarded as not discriminating.
- The test should provide questions with varying degrees of difficulty so there will be an adequate range of discrimination between the poorer and the better students.

Most test publishers have free bulletins on standardized tests, test construction and test interpretation. Write for catalogues.

■ Bureau of Educational Research and Service
University of Iowa
Iowa City, Iowa

■ Bureau of Publications
Teachers College
Columbia University
New York, New York

- California Test Bureau
5916 Hollywood Blvd.
Los Angeles, California

- Houghton-Mifflin Co.
2 Park Street
Boston, Mass. 02107

- Psychological Corporation
522 Fifth Avenue
New York, New York

- Science Research Associates
57 West Grand Avenue
Chicago, Illinois

- World Book Company
750 Third Avenue
New York 17, N. Y.

MEMO

For those who wish further details on the construction and evaluation of teacher-made tests, the book MEASUREMENT AND EVALUATION IN PSYCHOLOGY AND EDUCATION is an excellent source.

MEASUREMENT AND EVALUATION
IN PSYCHOLOGY AND EDUCATION
Robert L. Thorndike and Elizabeth Hagen
New York: John Wiley & Sons, Inc., 1955

For a handbook on test construction:

HOW TO IMPROVE CLASSROOM TESTING
C. W. Odell
Dubuque: W. C. Brown Co., 1953

6. A Fun Test to Take

The most interesting and challenging tests include a variety of question types. Frequently used are:

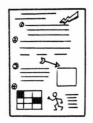

Multiple Choice	True-False	Listing
Completion	Recall	Essay
Matching	Identification	Situational

But there are other forms which make the same test more fun to take. Keep these in mind as you prepare your questions!

a. *Puzzles*

CROSSWORD   KRISS-CROSS   FILL-IN-THE-SQUARES

b. *Time lines*

VERTICAL   HORIZONTAL — GRAPHIC

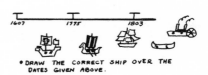

• DRAW THE CORRECT SHIP OVER THE DATES GIVEN ABOVE.

c. *Color the answers*

I. | THE | DOG | RAN | AWAY. |

• Color the nouns yellow
• Color the verb blue.
• Color the adjectives brown.
• Color the adverbs orange.

• Color the flag correctly.

Susquehana	Mississippi
El Paso	Miami
Baton Rouge	Los Angeles

• Color the names that show our:
▲ French heritage **BLUE**
▲ Indian heritage **YELLOW**
▲ Spanish heritage **Green**

Education isn't play—and it can't be made to look like play. It is hard, hard work. But it can be made interesting work.

—Thomas A. Edison

d. *Diagrams and graphs*

DRAW ONE.   LABEL ONE.   EXPLAIN ONE.

• Complete this pie graph.

• Label each step.

• Answer these questions:
1.
2.

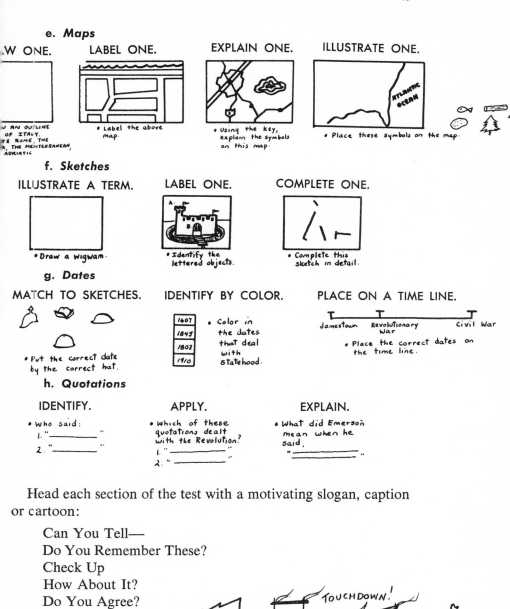

e. Maps

W ONE.

LABEL ONE.

EXPLAIN ONE.

ILLUSTRATE ONE.

J AN OUTLINE
OF ITALY.
E ROME, THE
, THE MEDITERRANEAN,
ADRIATIC

• Label the above
map.

• Using the key,
explain the symbols
on this map.

• Place these symbols on the map.

f. Sketches

ILLUSTRATE A TERM.

LABEL ONE.

COMPLETE ONE.

• Draw a wigwam.

• Identify the
lettered objects.

• Complete this
sketch in detail.

g. Dates

MATCH TO SKETCHES.

IDENTIFY BY COLOR.

PLACE ON A TIME LINE.

• Put the correct date
by the correct hat.

1607
1845
1803
1910

• Color in
the dates
that deal
with
Statehood.

Jamestown Revolutionary Civil War
War

• Place the correct dates on
the time line.

h. Quotations

IDENTIFY.

APPLY.

EXPLAIN.

• Who said:
1. "_____"
2. "_____"

• Which of these
quotations dealt
with the Revolution?
1. "_____"
2. "_____"

• What did Emerson
mean when he
said,
"_____"

Head each section of the test with a motivating slogan, caption
or cartoon:

Can You Tell—
Do You Remember These?
Check Up
How About It?
Do You Agree?
Be A Winner
Whodunit?
How About That?
Pick A Number
What Would You Do?

Signs of the Times
Who's Who?
Where In The World?
Win, Lose or Draw
Map A Course
In Your Opinion
Sez Who?

. . . for the test to simply measure factual knowledge is not enough; it must be so constructed that it will measure ability to apply and use the information and skills that have been taught.

—*Techniques of Military Instruction*

Use ditto stencils and emphasize with color—

   ✔ the test printed in purple,
   ✔ the highlights added with blue, green, black or red stencils!

7. Oral Tests

Get your students on their feet before a group as often as possible. Ask them to give:

Show and Tell talks
Prepared talks
Extemporaneous timed talks
Experiments
Demonstrations
Recitations of memory work
Round table discussions
        and
to participate in skits or plays.

Prepare special marking sheets for your evaluation.

ORAL TEST
Marking Sheet

NAME: _____ DATE: _____

SUBJECT OF SPEECH: _____
(REPORT, TALK, ETC.)

Item DESCRIPTION	Comments STRONG POINTS	Circle the SCORE	Comments WEAK POINTS
1. Knowledge of Subject		2 4 6 8 10	
2. Development of Subject		2 4 6 8 10	
3. Projection of Voice		2 4 6 8 10	
4. Use of Gestures		2 4 6 8 10	
5. Mannerisms		2 4 6 8 10	
6. Poise, Self-confidence		2 4 6 8 10	
7. Enthusiasm		2 4 6 8 10	
8. Props, Visual Aids		2 4 6 8 10	
9. Audience Response		2 4 6 8 10	
10. Question-Answer Period		2 4 6 8 10	

(100 Points Possible)

SCORE: ____

SUGGESTIONS FOR IMPROVEMENT:

8. Marking Made Easy

As you plan both tests and assignments, plan an efficient way
to check the answers.

a. Have the students use an answer sheet.

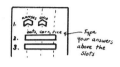 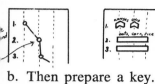

b. Then prepare a key.

c. Use a check sheet.

e. Use a standardized scale.

d. Use a score sheet.

The Ayres Handwriting Scale may be
purchased for 55¢ (35¢, plus handling and
postage) from

e Bureau of Educational Research and Service
iversity of Iowa
va City, Iowa

The Freeman Scientific Evaluation Scales for
Grades 1–9 may be purchased in sets of
nine for $3.35 or single copies for 45¢.

rder from:

The Zaner-Bloser Company
612 North Park Street
Columbus 15, Ohio

rite for their free informational brochure.

DAILY QUIZZES

Name_____   Subject_____

Test No. 1 Date:___	Test No. 2 Date:___	Test No. 3 Date:___	Test No. 4 Date:___
1.	1.	1.	1.
2.	2.	2.	2.
3.	3.	3.	3.
4.	4.	4.	4.
5.	5.	5.	5.
6.	6.	6.	6.
7.	7.	7.	7.
8.	8.	8.	8.
9.	9.	9.	9.
10.	10.	10.	10.
Score:___	Score:___	Score:___	Score:___

Test No. 5 Date:___	Test No. 6 Date:___	Test No. 7 Date:___	Test No. 8 Date:___
1.	1.	1.	1.
2.	2.	2.	2.
3.	3.	3.	3.
4.	4.	4.	4.
5.	5.	5.	5.
6.	6.	6.	6.
7.	7.	7.	7.
8.	8.	8.	8.
9.	9.	9.	9.
10.	10.	10.	10.
Score:___	Score:___	Score:___	Score:___

CHART
YOUR
PROGRESS!

How're You Doing?

90

Fourscore and seven
years ago our fa-
ther brought forth
upon this continent
a new nation, con-
ceived in liberty,
and dedicated to
the proposition that
all men are created
equal. Now we are
engaged in a great
civil war testing

f. Indicate the type of error in the paper and have the student locate and correct his mistake.

g. Stamp Your Comments.

Wise owls, stick men, sunshine, ghosts, and seasonal designs are among the clever marking stamps you can buy. Comments include—

Perfect Paper
Very Good
You Were Not Listening
Messy
Did Not Finish
You Can Do Better
See Me
Do Work Over
Careless

For information and prices, write to:

Gemini Industries
205 West Wacker Dr.
Chicago, Illinois

Summit Industries
Dept. 93, Box 415
Highland Park, Illinois

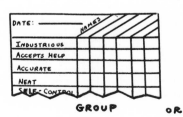

9. Evaluating Behavior and Attitude

Periodic checks on behavior, work habits, attitudes and adjustment are important to your comprehensive picture of each child.

Prepare a check sheet and keep the record for conference discussions. Let the students evaluate themselves. Can they recognize their weak areas, their strong points? Can they see progress?

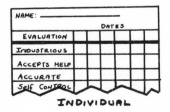

10. The Conference

Your conferences with the principal, guidance counselor, parents or children will be more effective if you can produce a file of pertinent material:

- Significant daily work
- Test papers
- Progress charts
- Check sheets for behavior and attitude
- Anecdotal records
- Student evaluations

. . . and added to the file should be your notes taken during the conference.

> *We believe intelligent, personal discussion is the only effective way to report on a child's progress and to keep that progress at a peak.*
> *—Dr. Benjamin Fine*
> *Sands Point Country Day School*

CHAPTER 7

Teaching Them to Study

When you give up facts, all you can teach is that citizens ought to work together happily, and attend a church of their choice at least once a week.

—*Harry Golden*

Scholastic success depends primarily on the efficiency with which a student applies himself to his studies.

—*O'Donnell, Taylor, McElaney*

There are specific techniques to help a student understand and remember what he is learning. At every grade level and with every subject, you can help students organize themselves for efficient studying. Teach them the skills of scholastic success!

54

1. Teaching Motivation

Give your students a motivating push. Inspire them! Use slogans and captions on their assignment sheets, across the chalkboard, in the margins of their test papers. Enthusiasm is contagious:

Achievement seldom exceeds effort.
—Mortimer Adler

Genius is 1% inspiration and 99% perspiration.
—Thomas Edison

What you don't know, you can always learn.
—Old Maxim

Every day gives you another chance.
—Old Maxim

The real essence of work is concentration.
—Old Maxim

Be ashamed to find yourself idle.
—Old Maxim

We aim above the mark to hit the mark.
—Emerson

Do well the duty that lies before you.
—Pittacus

Patience is bitter, but its fruit is sweet.
—Rousseau

Let me do the thing that ought to be done, when it ought to be done, as it ought to be done, whether I like to do it or not.
—Maxim

A problem well-stated is a problem
half solved.

—John Dewey

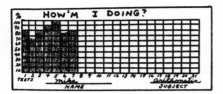

*We may provide learners with a mental
meal and persuade them to partake of
it, but we can neither digest it nor as-
similate it for them. Ultimately the
learner must do his own learning.*

—L. Wilkes

Let them chart their progress in daily work as well as on tests.
Individual graphs stimulate the most wholesome type of rivalry
and competition—that between the student and his previous
record.

2. General Guidelines

Each student should be aware of the efficient way to study.
Teach these guidelines in your classes and urge your students to
follow them as they plan out their study sessions.

    a. No distractions—quiet and order for work.
    b. Comfortable seating; good lighting; all materials
       and tools gathered and ready to use.
    c. Concentrate! Give the assignment your fullest at-
       tention.
    d. Survey! Get an overview of the material.
    e. State the problem to be solved.
    f. Plan your study time. Pace yourself. Don't bog
       down on any one aspect of the assignment.
    g. Study actively—use pencil and paper. Outline.
       Make notes. List points. Underline. Diagram.
       Sketch. Ask questions.
    h. Review. Recognize the need for drill. Prepare flash
       cards.
    i. Check and test yourself.
    j. Be careful! Always proofread written material.

3. A Study Plan

Until your students develop efficient study habits, you might help them by writing a study plan on the board or by dittoing a study sheet:

Assignment: The Battle of Bull Run
Due: Friday
Read: Pages 30–35, 38–41, 108
Skim: Pages 35–37
Omit: Pages 42–45
Review: Outline pages 30–35;
Make flashcards for page 34
Test: Write exercises 3 & 4 on page 42 as a self-test.

4. Attacking an Assignment

The six steps of covering an assignment should be taught to every student:

SURVEY: Get the general gist of the material. Note the author, copyright date, preface, titles, headings, illustrations.
NOTES: Jot down questions, comments, unfamiliar words as you survey.
READ: Read discriminately: read to answer the purpose of the assignment—some skimming, some scanning, some omissions, some intensive studying. Take notes. Underline.
ORGANIZE: Organize your notes and questions. Complete the written portion of the assignment.
REVIEW: Make flashcards. Answer questions. Outline. Drill.
TEST: Answer questions. Solve problems. Apply the material. Check yourself carefully.

Practice applying these steps in class; then ask students to follow them at home as they work with their assignments.

The six steps involve many important skills which should be taught in the classroom:

a. Surveying the assignment

Students will find a preliminary survey to be a great time-saver. Clues to the content of any assignment can be found in:

1) Introductions
2) Titles
3) Headings
4) First and last paragraphs
5) Illustrations
6) Tables and graphs

No one should plunge into intensive studying without first
getting an overview of the material. Ideas are more meaningful
and easier to relate after a survey. Be sure that your students
are familiar with the parts of a book. To fully illustrate the function of each part, put together a mock-up of a book as a class
project:

> Cover
> Title page
> Copyright page
> Preface, Introduction
> Table of Contents
> List of maps, illustrations, tables
> Chapter, sectional and topical headings
> Footnotes
> Index
> Bibliography
> Glossary
> Appendix

b. Locating and gathering information

You and the librarian can greatly increase student efficiency
by teaching what resource and reference materials are available
and how to use them.

- Take a field trip to the library! Give specific assignments
  to be completed during the visit—
    1) On a floor plan of the library have students indi-
       cate the location of important reference materials,
       card catalog, periodicals, and the like.
    2) Answer a list of questions by referring to the card
       catalog.
    3) Answer questions by referring to current material
       in the periodicals.
    4) Answer questions by referring to a special refer-
       ence work.
- Have students prepare author, title and subject cards for
  their textbook.
- Familiarize them with the library's classification system.
    1) Let each student prepare an illustrated chart of the
       10 classifications.

2) Give them a series of call numbers and ask for the classification.

3) Give a list of titles and subjects and ask for the classification number.

- Familiarize them with standard library abbreviations.
    1) Chart them.
    2) Drill with flash cards.
    3) Give matching tests.
- Plan FIND THE FACTS sheets.
    1) Ask students where they would look to find the answer to specific questions (i.e., in the

    dictionary
    atlas
    encyclopedia
    yearbook
    biography
    anthology
    periodical
    manual
    telephone book
    etc.)

    2) Ask them to answer specific questions by referring to a particular source.

NAME: _____ DATE: _____

ENCYCLOPEDIA
ENCYCLOPEDIA
ATLAS
WORLD ALMANAC
CURRENT BIOGRAPHY
DICTIONARY
TELEPHONE DIRECTORY

FIND THE FACTS!

The Problem	The Solution	The Source
1. In what time zone is Utah?		
2. How many synonyms can you find for the word "happy"?		
3. Where was Andrew Carnegie born?		
4. List 3 interesting facts about General Westmoreland.		
5. What day of the year is Thanksgiving?		
6. Show the location of the city of Atlanta.		
7. How much does it cost to mail a letter to Europe?		
8. Give 3 interesting facts about the grasshopper.		
9. Who won the World Series in 1953?		
10. Where is the city of Munich?		
11. Define and syllabicate the word "catastrophe".		
12. Who would you contact to ask the price of a flag wholesale?		

c. Reading improvement

You *can* teach your students to read faster and more efficiently because you can break down bad reading habits and replace them with efficient ones. Most adults could learn to read 75 to 100% faster than their present rate— with a little instruction and lots of practice.

Once a young person can read well, the door is open to other learning. If he can't read well, he'll find locked doors for the rest of his life.

—Dr. Calvin E. Gross

Vocalization, reading word by word, regression and a constant rate of speed are what cripple most adult readers. These bad habits are hold-overs from the elementary school classroom. Check your students carefully. If any one of these cripplers is part of their approach to reading, you cannot begin too soon to replace it.

MEMO

Two excellent books with practice materials which can be adapted for your classroom are

HOW TO READ BETTER AND FASTER
Norman Lewis
Thomas Y. Crowell Co. 1954

and

READING IMPROVEMENT FOR ADULTS
Paul D. Leedy
McGraw-Hill   1956

d. Building vocabulary

Students who do below-par work almost always have limited vocabularies. Some systematic study of words should be part of every classroom teacher's program. Develop a weekly vocabulary list with your students. Choose important words from their textbooks, from current events, and from their resource and reference materials.

1) Duplicate the word list. Include:

> *The Word*—(Its Phonetic Spelling)
> Part of speech
> Definition
> The word in a sentence

2) Prepare different drills, tests or puzzles which give students an opportunity to use the words.
3) Use charts, pictures, models, films, recordings—whatever you can find to build concrete images of the words on your lists.
4) Create special dictionaries from your lists.

MEMO

The Cat in the Hat Beginner Book
DICTIONARY
by
P. D. Eastman
Random House   1964
shows a fun way to approach vocabulary building!

*Increasing your vocabulary—
properly, intelligently, and
systematically—means treating
yourself to an all-round liberal
education.*
—Norman Lewis

All vocabulary textbooks and workbooks use a variety of tests
and drills to help the student determine how well he has mastered
a new word. Include at least 10 questions on each of your drill
sheets.

Multiple Choice
   1. naive   a / unfriendly   b / unsophisticated   c / warm

Matching
   1. naive   a / unfriendly
   2. hostile   b / unsophisticated

True–False, Yes–No
   1. Is a naive person unsophisticated?   Yes–No
   2. A hostile person is friendly.   True–False

Recall the word
   1. He is an unfriendly person. _____

Homonyms
   1. The (principal–principle) wrote the letter.

Correct spelling
   1. noo-ROL-o-jist   neurologist

Change the part of speech
   1. confirm   His testimony was a _____ of the report.

Describe the situation.
> The doctor is worried. You are on antibiotics. You are feverish. You are beginning to imagine things. You are (delirious).

Categorize a list
> color   health   food   puny   cuisine   robust
>   hue   shade   culinary

Completion
> When I think about high school days, I am overcome with (nostalgia).

Match or Illustrate

Match these with the correct picture.	island peninsula	Draw a picture to illustrate these words.

Identify a phrase
> 1. Queen Elizabeth II   (monarch)
> 2. Super Suds   (detergent)

■ Crossword puzzles as vocabulary drills are always fun. Duplicate a copy for each member of the class. A chart of winners will keep interest high.

■ Clip full-color magazine advertisements and cover or cut off the text. Ask students to list descriptive adjectives and phrases which would apply to the illustration.

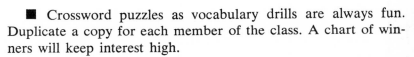

■ Assign a colorless or lifeless word and ask for as many synonyms as possible.

> SAY: shout, urge, demand, utter, whisper, shriek, etc.

■ Assign a general category and ask students to write as many specifics as possible within a certain time:

> RIVER: Nile, Amazon, Rhine, Mississippi, St. Johns, etc.
> COLOR: violet, crimson, chartreuse, dubonnet, red, etc.

■ Assign a general category and ask students to write as many descriptive adjectives as possible within a certain time:

> BOY: industrious, handsome, shrewd, courageous, happy-go-lucky, intelligent, sinewy, lithe, etc.

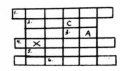

■ Prepare worksheets which deal with a special vocabulary—history, science, math, music, grammar, etc.

1. SETS: a—elements
              b—collections
              c—factors

2. EMPTY SET: a.
                    b.
                    c.

■ Collect, post and study homonyms. Use in puzzles, riddles, worksheets, games, contests.

e. Taking notes

The act of writing something down helps most people learn new material—but many students do not know what to write down.

> They write too much.
> They become distracted.
> They lose the main points.

Give your students some general guidelines for note-taking and plenty of opportunity to practice.

GUIDELINES

1. Listen carefully.
2. Take notes on 3 x 5 cards or on loose-leaf sheets.
3. Be alert for main points. Don't bog down in details.
4. Be brief. Write only enough so the meaning is clear to you.
5. Take notes in outline form.
6. Keep all your notes relating to one subject in one section.
7. Review your notes before they get "cold."
8. Use a red pencil to circle or underline main points as you shuffle and re-organize your notes.

As you present a new lesson, make notes on the board. Let your students copy these notations and use them to complete an assignment. Even primary students can acquire this skill.

Have your students practice taking notes from reference materials.

1. Take notes from a chapter in the textbook.
2. Use 3 x 5 cards and include:

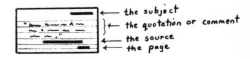

3. Quote some material: be sure it is copied exactly and enclosed in quotation marks.

3. Check to see that all notes are accurate and really reflect what the author says.

To facilitate their note taking, teach your students a dozen or so basic shorthand symbols—learn the Gregg or Speedwriting forms, or make up your own for the words they use most frequently:

and	go
is	will
was	would
were	be
to	have
the	with
it	are

Any sort of symbol will do so long as you agree on what it stands for! ∧ ⊓ ○ — ૪ ✓ ⏖

Practice taking notes during:

- Discussions
- Field trips
- Films
- Lectures
- Meetings
- Reports
- Radio and Television programs

f. Outlining

Outlining material is a major study skill. These four steps can be developed in your classroom:

I. *Write the outline of a paragraph with which the class is familiar.*
    A. They will easily recognize main points, and sub-points.
    B. Have them copy your outline.
    C. Use the outline to
        1. Write a paragraph, or
        2. Answer questions.
II. *Make an assignment in the textbook.*
    A. Write the main topics on the board.
        1. Indicate the sub-topics.
    B. Have students read the assignment.
    C. Students copy the main topics and
        1. Fill in the sub-topics.
III. *Make an assignment in the textbook.*
    A. Show a skeleton outline on the board.
    B. Have students read the assignment.

      C. Students fill in:
          1. Main topics
          2. Sub-topics
  IV. *Make an assignment in the textbook.*
      A. Ask students to prepare a complete outline.

g. Summarizing material

An important study skill is the ability to summarize. Students cannot say in a few words what they do not understand. Have your students test their comprehension by writing summaries of material they are studying:

1. Select a paragraph or poem.
2. Count the total number of words.
3. Have the students read, then rewrite the selection in ⅓ the total number of words.

> *It usually takes more than*
> *3 weeks to prepare a good*
> *impromptu speech.*
> *—Mark Twain*

h. Preparing a speech

Help your students learn to prepare and give a talk before the class.

There are several ways to give life and drama to a speech:

1. The first sentence should be dramatic, bold, arresting.
2. The material should be well-organized.
3. There should be animation and variety:

      ✔ anecdotes   ✔ charts
      ✔ conversation   ✔ demonstrations
      ✔ gestures   ✔ quotations
      ✔ personalized statistics

4. The body of the speech should be *spoken* language:

      ✔ simple words   ✔ familiar phrasing
      ✔ short sentences   ✔ positive statements
      ✔ few adjectives

5. The summary should be bold, easy to remember and spur the audience to action.

Borrow a collection of toastmaster jokes, anecdotes, quotations, etc. from the library.

If the speech is well-written, it should be easy for the student to deliver it effectively. He should remember to:

1. Stand easily and naturally before the audience.
2. Pick out one or two individuals to speak to.
3. Have the first and last sentence of the speech committed to memory.
4. Have the outline of the talk well in mind.
5. Have any gestures, demonstrations or presentation of charts rehearsed until they can be handled naturally.

As with any other skill, practice makes perfect!

> *More men have achieved success by*
> *their ability to speak than through any*
> *other skill.*
>
> *—Bruce Barton*

i. *Thinking on their feet*

To help students learn to think on their feet, plan one- or two-minute extemporaneous speeches. Give the class a subject, allow a few minutes to collect thoughts, then ask individuals to speak to the group.

j. *Oral reports*

Assign oral reports well in advance. Set up your schedule so that only a few are given each day. Help your students get organized:

1. Ask for an outline of the report at least a week before it is to be presented to the class.
2. Urge students to use a variety of reference materials, interviews and visual aids.
3. Ask that the report include an experiment, demonstration or presentation of some audio-visual aid.
4. Ask for a checklist of materials. Be sure the necessary materials are gathered a day or so before the report is to be given.
5. Have the student time his report. A dress rehearsal is a good precaution.
6. Provide for a question and answer period. The student should

be able to repeat any part of his report that may have been misunderstood.

7. Have the student prepare and post a list of follow-up activities to be carried out by other individuals in the class.
8. Before the report is given, make sure that every person in the room can see and hear.

k. Written compositions and reports

Literature is one of the fine arts; but everyday writing, as all of us are called upon to practice it, is a craft. Genius, which produces literature, is born in its possessor, and cannot be acquired; but the craft of writing can be learned by anyone, like carpentry or dancing.
—*James W. Linn*

Compositions, essays, reports and term papers can be required in connection with every school subject. Even very young students can be taught the step-by-step procedure of a well written paper. The importance of practice in writing is spelled out in HOOKED ON BOOKS by Daniel N. Fader, Ph.D., and Morton H. Shaevity, Ph.D. This 50¢ paperback is an appeal to teachers of *every* subject.

MEMO

Prentice-Hall has published a handbook for young writers with everyday requirements for correct and effective writing in elementary classes. The text is divided into two parts: "101 Rules for Correct Writing" and "Guidelines for Effective Writing."

A HANDBOOK FOR YOUNG WRITERS

Hansen • Johnson • Walker
Webb

Prentice-Hall, Inc.
1965

1. *Choose the topic carefully.*

Insist that your students explore their own backgrounds, feelings and experiences for topics which are important to them. What is vague and abstract to them will be dull if they put it on paper.

2. *Limit the topic.*

It is important to consider the "audience" factor when limiting the topic. The paper should be written with someone or some group in mind. The student must settle on one approach:

    a) What is my point of view?
    b) What aspect do I know best ?
    c) What will be most interesting?

3. *Organize the material.*

Notes can be made on 3 x 5 cards. From the shuffled and re-shuffled cards comes an outline with all points in logical order.

4. *Write a first draft.*

The first draft should be written hurriedly, spontaneously—dashed off in "the heat of the moment." It will lack polish and contain mechanical errors but it should carry the idea of the composition forward promptly and in logical order.

5. *Let it cool.*

One can be objective only when one comes back to a composition. It is foolish to try and revise immediately.

6. *The final draft comes later.*

There may be several drafts between the first and the last. But when the student is satisfied with the sharpness of his vocabulary, the quality of his expression, the orderliness of his organization and the correctness of his grammar, spelling and punctuation—then he should re-copy the final draft and turn it in.

You can take your students step-by-step through the writing of a sound composition. Choose one topic which could apply to every student—My Favorite Program, My Best Friend—and have everyone write on the same subject. Jot down examples, ideas, illustrative material and leave these on the board for reference. Outline a sample paper to help them get started.

MEMO

Show students Julian Cate's experiment with style: "A Style-ish Fable." He taught his classes to compare the styles of Shakespeare, TIME magazine, the King James Bible and the Uncle Remus stories. Then he assigned "The Three Bears" to be re-written in each of the four styles.

You'll find the stories on pages 423–425 of the high school literature text:

ADVENTURES IN APPRECIATION

by

Loban, Holmstrom, Cook

Harcourt, Brace & World

1958

Set a time limit—5, 10 or 15 minutes—and ask the class to follow the outline and write a composition. If they will double-space, corrections can be made easily.

While they begin another assignment, go over their papers. Return them to be revised for homework. Discuss different paragraphs in class.

After several such practice sessions, ask the students to write a composition on their own from start to finish.

Don't wait until the junior and senior years of high school to help students with formal papers. The basic steps can be taught in an elementary fashion in the elementary school.

MEMO

Warriner's handbook, ENGLISH GRAMMAR AND COMPOSITION, takes a student step-by-step through the writing of a research paper. A teacher at any grade level could profit from his ideas and suggestions.

ENGLISH GRAMMAR AND COMPOSITION
John E. Warriner

Harcourt, Brace and World
1957   Paperback

Kahn and Mulkerne's THE TERM PAPER, STEP BY STEP is also excellent. Key points are applied to a sample paper. You and your class could cover the manual step by step, writing a paper as a group.

THE TERM PAPER, STEP BY STEP
Gilbert Kahn & Donald Mulkerne

Doubleday and Company, Inc.
1964 $1.00 Paperback

One way to help a student write his paper is to show how it will be evaluated. Give each student a form when you make the assignment. It can be clipped to the completed paper for the score and comments:

Name_____ Title_____ Score_____

1. *Format*

_____ a. Correct Format (5 pts)

_____ b. Bibliography, annexes, illustrations (5 pts)

2. *Writing Ability*

    a. Mechanical Errors

_____ (1) Spelling (1 pt each to 5 pts)

_____ (2) Punctuation (1 pt each to 5 pts)

_____ (3) Capitalization (1 pt each to 5 pts)

_____ b. Grammar (1 pt each to 5)

_____ c. Style (1 pt each to 5)

3. *Organization*

_____ a. Logical Presentation (20 pts)

_____ b. Thorough Discussion (15 pts)

_____ c. Reliable Data (15 pts)

_____ d. Relevant Material (15 pts)

Any scoring arrangement can be developed. Spaces can be left between each item for written comments.

l. *Memorization*

The more often a person memorizes material, the easier it becomes. Building this skill is an important part of a study program. Practice with poems, paragraphs, plays, quotations, lists, formulas.

m. *Reviewing*

Teachers of little experience often underrate the value of practice work, and do not realize what a large proportion of the learner's time should be given to this type of work.

—L. Wilkes

Forgetting begins when learning stops! Frequent reviews are essential if learning is to be lasting. Hazy, fuzzy impressions are often more confusing than no impression at all.

There are several interesting and effective ways to review:

1. *Drills*

    ✔ Worksheets   ✔ Contests

    ✔ Games   ✔ Tournaments

    ✔ Boardwork   ✔ Practical application

2. *Transferring Information to Displays and Charts*

Organizing material for a display or a chart forces students to review, select, re-state, and present important ideas and facts.

3. *Manipulative Charts*

Alice Liechti and Jack Chappell have prepared an excellent manual of charts and games which you and your students can make.

MEMO

MAKING AND USING CHARTS
Alice Liechti & Jack Chappell

Fearon Publishers, Inc.
828 Valencia St.
San Francisco 10, Calif.

$1.50 paperback

4. *Flashcards*

One of the simplest but most effective study aids is the flashcard. Flashcards are easy to make, easy to carry and easy to use. They provide a pleasant way to practice.

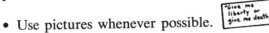

- Use pictures whenever possible.
- Use color codes.
- Pages 103-105 cover flashcards and manipulative charts in detail.

n. The art of taking tests

Test taking is an art and can be learned like any other.

—*Darrell Huff*

Like it or not, a great deal depends on whether or not youngsters do well on tests. There is an art to taking tests and you can help your students learn it. Give them lots of tests, quizzes and exams. Teach them to follow certain steps in taking any kind of test:

1. Read each problem carefully—be sure you understand what is wanted.
2. Go straight through the test and answer all the questions you know.
3. Look for clues in other questions which will help you answer the puzzlers.
4. Go back and attack the questions you skipped. Pace yourself and leave time for this.
5. Check back through the test for carelessness and omissions. Proofread!

Before an important exam give a "pre-test." By checking it together as classwork, the students receive an important review. The same test sheet can serve as a guide for their home study sessions.

MEMO

One of the best books we've seen on the subject is:

SCORE: THE STRATEGY OF TAKING TESTS

Darrell Huff

Appleton-Century-Crofts, Inc.

1961

Mr. Huff gives sample tests, guidelines, short cuts and solutions! Lots of help here for your students.

CHAPTER 8

Competition, Recognition, and Rewards

Like it or not, people have evidently been sorting themselves out into chiefs and Indians, nobles and peasants, executives and hourly workers from time immemorial, and they show no signs of stopping. . . . History gives no sign of any long-range leveling of prestige.

—Saul W. Gellerman

You must find someplace where they have some success and build them up all the time. They don't think too well of themselves and they won't do well until they say: "I'm a good person. I'm capable."

—Mona Dayton
1966 Teacher of the Year

Competition, recognition, awards, rewards: lots of pros and cons on this subject! Scouting, camping and athletic programs, the Armed Forces, social groups and most business establishments strive to generate a competitive spirit among their membership and to reward this energy monetarily or through public recognition.

Competition is a natural instinct and, properly used, a valuable one. Yes, it can become obsessive, destructive—even brutal. But also true, it can be channeled into constructive, creative activity. What it *does* become is the teacher's responsibility.

73

We do not want to falsely motivate our students. *Whether or not one is best or worst, it is a good thing to learn.* But who among us does not relish a bit of public praise? Some tangible proof, some positive recognition of achievement can be a keen stimulus to learning.

> *Outside school, competition develops many good qualities as well as some bad ones: courage, determination, industry; conceit, selfishness, envy. Inside school, therefore, it should be used —and controlled. It should be used with moderation and a very careful sense of fitness, so that it brings out good qualities and encourages keen learning—and is braked, if possible, before it becomes bitter.*
> *—Gilbert Highet*

A word of praise pays dividends out of all proportion to the effort involved.
—Kimball Wiles

> *The pupils must be continually enjoying some fruition and starting afresh.*
> *—Alfred North Whitehead*

Any adult who does not understand the power of the pleasure principle in dealing with young children is very much deluded.
—Nancy McCormick Rambusch

> *There lies a certain danger in inculcating in the individual the ambition to win prizes and scholarships, and holding up to him as success the securing of pay, position and power, unless there is a corresponding instruction in service for others.*
> *—Lord Baden-Powell*

> People seek prestige throughout their
> lives in countless ways, some of them
> subtle and others blatant.
> —Saul W. Gellerman

1. Accentuate the Positive

There are general guidelines which can be followed in every classroom:

1. Praise honest effort.
2. Find something to commend in the work of every student.
3. Encourage those who are discouraged.
4. Keep high standards at all times.
5. Remember that "Nothing succeeds like success."

2. On the Honor Roll

At the beginning of the year take a roll of 35mm film and make a close-up shot of each student. Keep a set of prints and a packet of photo corners handy. With magic marker and bright construction paper, you can quickly give recognition for achievement.

The child who does not excel scholastically can find himself recognized for Good Citizenship, Courtesy, Perfect Attendance, a contest winner, and the like.

☆ ON THE HONOR ROLL ☆

CITIZEN OF THE WEEK

OUR CHAMPION SPELLER FOR OCTOBER

100 BOOKS READ AND ENJOYED!

WINNER OF THE 50 YARD DASH

Ditto an Honor Roll list periodically. Include students who deserve recognition for:

- Scholastic Achievement
- Special Reports and Projects
- Cultural Contributions
- Athletic Achievement

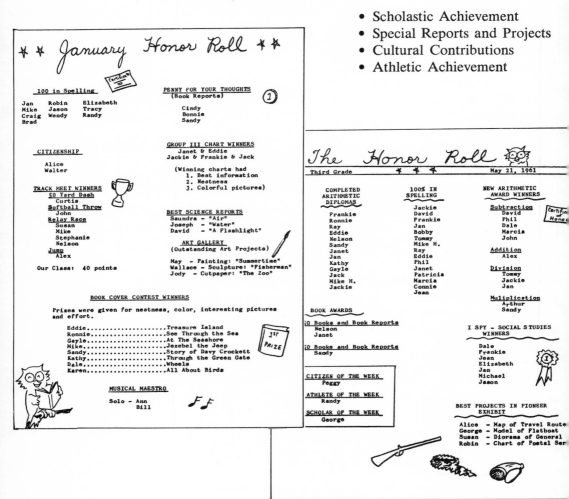

These are welcome sights to parents and find special places in scrapbooks.

3. Posting Papers

Exhibit outstanding papers in industrial jackets. Use a marking pencil on the acetate to point up highlights of the papers.

4. Picturing Progress

Liven up your comments while grading papers. Order a set of marking stamps for papers or for honor rolls.

5. Charting Progress

Prepare and post Progress and Achievement Charts. Change them frequently. Keep interest high.

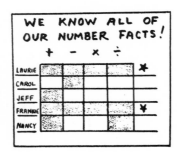

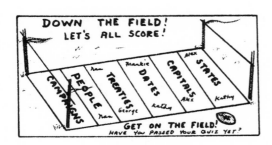

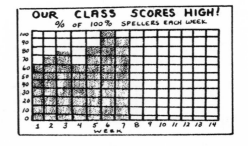

6. Keeping Them Reading

Plan different individual or wall charts to keep track of how many and what kind of books your students are reading.

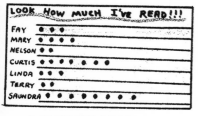

A TACK PER BOOK

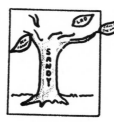

A LEAF PER BOOK

A FEATHER PER BOOK

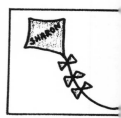

A BOW PER BOOK

A PETAL PER BOOK

A PAPER DOLL PER BOOK

A FLOWER PER BOOK

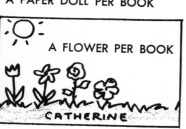

MY READING BOOKCASE

A STAR PER BOOK

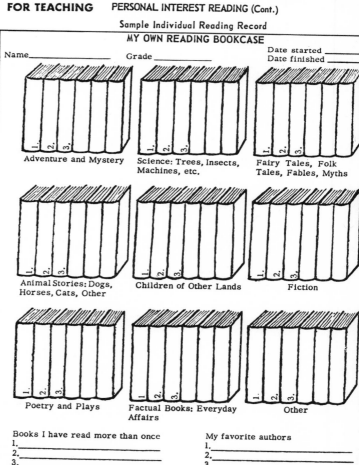

SUGGESTIONS FOR TEACHING   PERSONAL INTEREST READING (Cont.)   READING, GRADE 3

Sample Individual Reading Record

MY OWN READING BOOKCASE

Name_____   Grade _____   Date started _____
Date finished _____

Adventure and Mystery

Science: Trees, Insects, Machines, etc.

Fairy Tales, Folk Tales, Fables, Myths

Animal Stories: Dogs, Horses, Cats, Other

Children of Other Lands

Fiction

Poetry and Plays

Factual Books: Everyday Affairs

Other

Books I have read more than once
1._____
2._____
3._____

My favorite authors
1._____
2._____
3._____

Note to the teacher: This is one type of reading record. Enlarge for pupil use.

7. Telling Tales

After playground activities, lunchroom or restroom trips, or for general classroom behavior, schedule a Compliment Time:

> Who came in quietly?
> Who set a good example?
> Who showed good sportsmanship?
> Who has been industrious?
> Who observed good manners?

Compliments instead of tattle-tales!

8. Learning From Each Other

Give recognition through "Learn From Each Other" sheets. Prepare questions on the various exhibits, projects, reports and assignments in the room. Duplicate worksheets and have every student complete one. The efforts of each student will then be studied and appreciated by the entire class.

A Report On The Pelican
- by Jack Beckford

A clever bird is the pelican.
His bill holds more than his bellican.

All of them are birds of large size. They take their prey by hovering over the water and plunging upon it when it appears. They store up their prey in their pouch from which they can bring it out at their leisure either for their own eating or to feed their young.

Pictures of Birds by David Braddock

A Report On The Seagull
- by Kathy Jones

Seagulls are usually found around the ocean or rivers that flow down to the ocean.

Seagulls keep the beaches clean. They eat fish and clams that are washed in by the tides.

They follow the fishing boats.

WHO AM I?

1. I sleep all day and hunt at night. Jimmy told you about me. I am _____.

2. I live near David's house. I live in a covey. I am _____.

3. Jack wrote a 7 page report about me. You will find me at the beach. I am _____.

4. Sharon brought my picture. I have a ruby throat. I am _____.

5. I am a copy cat. I am your state bird. I am _____.

6. I am a plasterer. Jan told you about me. I make my nest of mud and straw. I am _____.

9. In the News

Create opportunities for students to write up their school activities for the newspaper—a classroom bulletin or the local journal.

Many newspapers welcome contributions from the schools. Clear it with your principal and set up a flow of student articles describing their outstanding classroom projects.

PONTE VEDRA PALM VALLEY

By Kathy Jones, Janet Brooker and Jean Brooker.

The Fourth Grade at the Ponte Vedra-Palm Valley Elementary School have built a cabin in their room.

The outside walls have skins, Indians and the name of the town.

On the inside we have a fireplace, two rocking chairs, a loft and ladder, a bed and spinning wheel. There are also skins, quilts, a cradle and samplers.

When we had our house-raising it took three days. We had the cabin because we wanted to see what it was like in the olden days and to get the real feeling of really being three families in those days. We learned how hard a pioneer family had to work for a living.

Our teacher split the room into three families: the Beckfords, the Mc-Latcheys and the Thames. Each family has 5 children.

The town that we have is called McLatcheyville after George H. McLatchey. We voted on the name for our town.

We got all of our ideas about our cabin and room from the book we are reading named "Singing Wheels".

We have made up 3 plays about McLatcheyville and also 3 songs. We keep a diary of what we read. We are planning a Box Supper with a Spelling Bee.

We have many different projects of "Singing Wheels" and they are all around the room.

THIS MAKING OF A PIONEER town was a project of students at the Ponte Vedra-Palm Valley School. Taking part in the program were George McLatchey and Janet Brooker. Incidently the students selected George's name for the primitive village calling it McCatcheyville.

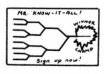

10. Tournaments and Contests

Sponsor classroom tournaments in scholastic fields:

- Our Champion Speller
- Genius At Work
- Mr. Modern Math

Plan classroom contests:

My favorite symphony is (in 25 words or less)

My favorite artist is (in 25 words or less)

> Moby Dick, the whale,
> Turned all who saw him pale—
> He rode the seas,
> Did as he pleased,
>   (Write the last line)

• Encourage participation in local, state and nationally approved contests:

> essays
> posters
> speeches
> debates
> projects

MEMO

Freedoms Foundation
sponsors
an annual
SCHOOL AWARDS PROGRAM
—

The award recipients may win *cash, medals, plaques, trips* and *certificates.*
Write for the current announcement:

Freedoms Foundation
Valley Forge, Pa.

Solve This Puzzle!

WHO'S WHO and What Did He Do?
(TIME covers)

WHAT DO YOU KNOW?
(A list of
questions)

SAYS WHO?
(Questions to
be identified)

The Parker Pen Company
219 East Court Street
Janesville, Wisconsin
U.S.A. 53545

AFFIX 5¢ STAMP HERE

An opportunity to form an International friendship... A 1570

As a member of the Parker International Penfriend Program, you will join over a million other Penfriends personally benefiting from international correspondence while contributing to world peace through understanding...through writing.

People from many nations of the world apply for Penfriends and these names, gathered by a world-wide network of Parker distributors, are fed into our electronic computer. One of these people will be selected as your Penfriend. It may take several weeks to find someone who shares your interests, but we will try to locate your Pen friend as soon as possible.

Before you detach and mail your Penfriend registration form, be sure you:
1 Print your complete NAME and ADDRESS
2 Circle the LANGUAGE number in which you will correspond
3 Circle the number of your AGE GROUP
4 Circle the number of your SEX
5 Circle the number of the preferred SEX OF YOUR PENFRIEND
6 Print names and code letters of your SPECIAL INTEREST PREFERENCES

Save this part of your registration form. If you have not been successfully matched within 120 days, send us the serial number appearing on this card along with a letter explaining your situation. We will re-process your request.

SPECIAL INTERESTS

Choose up to three special interests. Print names and code letters in the space provided on the other half of this form.

GENERAL INTERESTS	A
ANIMALS AND PETS	B
ART, DRAWING AND PAINTING	C
AUTOMOBILES	D
BUSINESS AND INVESTMENTS	E
COLLECTING (Stamps and others)	F
COOKING, SEWING AND GARDENING	G
CRAFTS AND MODEL BUILDING	H
DANCE	I
GAMES (Chess and others)	J
GOVERNMENT AND POLITICS	K
HISTORIES	L
LANGUAGES, STUDY OF	M
LITERATURE	N
MEDICINE AND NURSING	O
MOVIES, RADIO AND TV	P
MUSIC	Q
PHOTOGRAPHY	R
RELIGIONS	S
SCIENCES AND STUDIES	T
SCOUTING	U
SPORTS	V
TEACHING	W
THEATER AND ACTING	X
TRAVEL	Y
WRITING	Z

What Your Students Should Know About Advertising

by Howard L. Hurwitz, Ph.D.

Jamaica High School (New York)
Co-author of ECONOMICS IN A FREE SOCIETY
Teacher-Editor, SENIOR SCHOLASTIC (1948-62)

11. Get Some Gimmicks

School journals and magazines carry advertisements of kits and programs designed to motivate and interest students in better work, study and health habits. Write for some for your class.

12. Whiz Kids, Quiz Kids

Sponsor a "Classroom Bowl" or "Password" bout patterned after the television shows. Organize committees to research and write the questions. Divide your class into groups. If interest runs high, challenge other classes in your school.

13. Certificates of Achievement

Printed certificates can be obtained through school supply stores. Prices range from 25 to 75 cents a dozen. There are Certificates of Honor, Attendance, Merit, Promotion and Special Awards. If there is no school supply store in your area, write to Newton School Equipment Company, 2221 Pearl Street, Jacksonville, Florida for information and prices.

F. A. Owen Publishing Company, Dansville, N. Y. carries packages of 10 certificates, envelopes and seals for $1.50. Write for their catalog.

You can make your own certificates with correspondence cards and India ink. A legal seal makes it special.

14. Trophies

Plastic loving cup trophies cost less than a dollar in dime-stores, sporting goods stores or school supply stores. Paste on your own award title.

15. Plaques

Plywood or beaverboard plaques can be cut from a pattern by a lumber company. Novelty stores sell printed plaques which you could cover with your own award.

16. Ribbons

Staple a cardboard square to a strip of ribbon.
Crepe paper, a heavy cardboard circle and a safety pin can create effective merit ribbons.

17. Banners, Pennants, Flags

Banners, pennants and flags can be cut from felt. Stitch a symbol onto the material or paint the letters on with enamel. Johnson Smith & Company, 6615 E. Jefferson Avenue, Detroit 7, Michigan sells colorful felt emblems, numbers and pennants for 25¢ to $1.00.

18. Emblems, Letters

Felt emblems and letters can be used to identify teams or given as awards. You can order from:

Johnson Smith and Company,
6615 E. Jefferson Avenue
Detroit 7, Michigan.

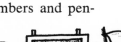

19. Special Awards

Plan special awards for your activities:

An olive wreath for the Olympic team captain.

A sword for the champion of the Knight's tournament.

A sewing kit for the winner of the Quilting Bee.

An autograph book for outstanding penmanship.

A box of stationery for excellence in Language Arts.

A dictionary for the winner of the Spelling Bee.

A record for the winner of a Culture Corner contest.

A Quizmo game for a math expert.

A puzzle map for a social studies whiz.

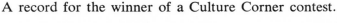
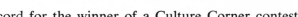

20. Surprise! Surprise!

The world is so full of a number of things—and so is the classroom! Prepare a list of activities you know the students enjoy. Write each activity on a 3 x 5 card and drop it in a Surprise Box. On days when everyone has been especially cooperative, industrious and diligent, plan a treat by letting someone draw out a Surprise Activity for the following day—

- A special story
- A favorite recording
- A neighborhood walk
- A Koolaid and Cookie treat
- A movie
- A slide show
- A trip to the library
- A project period
- Games and contests

CHAPTER 9

Classroom Publicity
and Public Relations

*With public sentiment nothing can fail; with-
out it, nothing can succeed.*

—Lincoln

*Publicity can be a constructive, reconstructive
or destructive force.*

—Joseph W. Hicks

*Publicity is publicity, whether we sing it, say
it, picture it, or act it. Advertising is any way
in the world to get people to look or listen.*

—Andrew Loomis

It pays to advertise your classroom! It pays in good will, in
understanding, in appreciation and parental support. And there
are so many, many ways to publicize your youngsters' achievements.

1. The Local Newspaper

Names sell newspapers. Most news staffs are very happy to receive potential news stories. Clear yours through your principal and then let the editors decide whether or not the material will do. But give them an opportunity to relate the achievements and the activities of your students:

- Scholastic honors
- Contest winners
- Special projects
- Sports events
- Guest speakers
- Field trips

2. The Classroom Newspaper

Plan a weekly, bi-monthly or monthly news sheet covering major events in your classroom.

A typewriter, ditto stencil or two, a pack of newsprint, 20 minutes of pounding the keys and your students' journalistic efforts can become a published fact! Include—

Articles and reports
Drawings
Special achievements
Special projects
Honor rolls
Coming events

First Grade News

MARCH 12	FRIDAY	ROOM 3

The Policeman

Today Marks's daddy came to our class. He gave us 3 posters. He told us to watch the traffic. He showed us his gun and bullets and handcuffs. He showed us his car. He said NEVER walk alone.

– Nancy, Donald

Kathy's Birthday

Kathy had her party at school! We all got cake. We got ice cream too. Kathy is 7. We had fun. Thank you, Kathy.

– Pat, Alexander

Our Grocery Store

We made a grocery store in our room. We have shelves and a counter. Mary brought her cash register. We have steak for 89¢ a pound. We have milk for 62¢. We need more groceries.

– Kathy, Steve

Brush Your Teeth

We wrote reports on teeth. We know about cavities. It is important to brush our teeth. Anna's daddy is a dentist.

– Sara, Billy

A bird
– by Tommy

☆ The Star-Journal ☆

Grade 2		October 5

A New Flag

We got a new American flag. It has the same stripes and 50 stars. We used it this morning.

– Marcia

Our Fish

Mrs. Williams fixed our aquarium. We have 8 fish and 2 snails. We have seaweed and clean sand. We are drawing pictures and writing reports.

– Mark

PTA TONIGHT

PTA is at 8:00 tonight. We are on the program. We will sing 2 songs. Robert will read a report. If all our parents come we win a prize.

– Carl

Trip To The Museum

Our class is going to the museum Monday. A special exhibit on Eskimo life is there. We will see a movie. We are going on the school bus. We will be back for lunch.

– Becky

TO THE JUNGLES ON A SAFARI

We went to the zoo on a safari Wednesday. We saw alot of animals. We saw bears and monkeys, camels, lions, snakes, baby goats, and others. Mrs. Burdges, Mrs. DeLoach and Mrs. Harris went with us. We enjoyed them. Mary drove the bus for us. We were hot and thirsty and tired. It was a good safari.

– Betty Sue, Connie

PLANE TRIP FROM NORWAY

We went on a plane to Africa from Norway this week. The plane we went on had 27 seats and 16 beds, 1 bathroom, 1 kitchen and 2 baby beds. That is just a few things from the Air France plane; it's the World's Largest Airliner. It's just like your home. You should go on it.

– Bobby, Eddie

TRAVEL POSTERS

We have travel posters. We are making them from the book, IF I WERE GOING. We are in Africa in it. Mr. Sanders gets in trouble in Africa. We have posters on Lapland and Africa.

A man in town gave us some travel posters. They are from a real steamship company. They are from Britain, France, South Africa and the Pyranees.

– Phil, David

NICE MANNERS

Mrs. Brown, Miss Brown's mother, helped at the track meet Friday. She said our boys had the nicest manners of any she knew. And she said they were all good sports. We are proud of our class and how it behaves.

JACK AND HIS COLLAR BONE

May 1, 1958 we were practicing up for a track meet. We were practicing jumping a high rope. All of a sudden it was Jack Beckford's turn. He jumped over the rope. He made it but for one thing---he broke his bone.

He landed on his shoulder. His whole weight was on his shoulder. He came in the building. His mother came and took him home. She took him to the doctor.

The next day, Friday, Miss Brown told us that he had his shoulder in a cast and that if he felt better he might come to school.

Thursday Miss Brown had thought he might have just disconnected it.

We know it hurt Jack. We are very very sorry for that to happen. Jack was supposed to be in the Track Meet down at the other school but now he can't. He was one of the best ones to be entered.

– Connie, Dale, Janet, Ronnie

MAP OF AFRICA

This week in the class we have had a map of Africa. It is very big and it is good. And there are trees, camels, men and tents. And the Equator. That is where the part of Central Africa is where the jungles are.

– Mike D., Mike H.

THE TRACK MEET

We are having a track meet at the other school. Half of it was yesterday and the other half is today.

You have to do the high jump, the 25 yard dash, the 40 yard dash, the 3-legged race and the relay.

The winner will be given a prize. We have entered.

– Patricia, Kathy

Ocean Park Reporter

Miss Brown's Room	Issue # 2	November 4, 1963

ENGLISH VISITORS

Today 2 girls came to school. They are 2 of my best friends. They came from London, England.

It was the first American school they had been to.

Their names were Josy and Barbara. They had a tent that was pumped up and had no sticks.

And they got to be in the Jacksonville Journal, and so was I.

We saw pictures of Josy's brothers and dogs. One of them was named Sandy and they had 10 of them.

– Sandy Stout

ST. AUGUSTINE TRIP

One day we went to St. Augustine. We went to the Old Fort and for a train ride, too. It was fun and scary, too.

My mother was there, too.

Peggy, Linda and I and Darlene made a flag, too.

We made the Old Fort and a ship in school, too.

– Fay Rawson

CONQUISTADORE GENERALS' LETTERS

A few weeks ago we got letters from General Burdges and General Brooker. They were our generals on a trip. They went with us to St. Augustine.

The generals wrote very long, wonderful and interesting letters. They answered all the questions that we asked them.

– Kathy Jones

HALLOWEEN PARTY

On Friday the 31st we had a Halloween party in which we had a costume parade. We also dunked for apples and bowled for points and had pumpkin pie. It was my birthday.

We had lots of fun. Well, I think it was fun. I don't know about them but I think it was fun.

– Stephanie Peterson

AMERICAN HISTORY

In school we have been learning about great people. But now we are starting to learn about American History.

Today we wrote a report on Vikings. Miss Brown is drawing a picture of a Viking's ship. She also borrowed the 5th grade history book and read to us about the Vikings.

– Jean Brooker

THE VIKINGS

We are beginning to learn United States History and we are starting by the Vikings and their travels and we have a poster called "The New World".

And Dan made a report on them and I am making one on them also.

– Jack Beckford

SANTA MARIA MODEL

Today we got through with the Santa Maria. It took us about 2 or 3 weeks to get through with it. The hardest part about the ship was the crow's nest. We could not bore a hole through the crow's nest and finally we just stuck it on. It kept on falling down and then it broke off, so we had to glue it on again and finally it stayed up. The people that helped me do it were Peggy, David T., Janet and myself, George.

– George McLatchey

ELECTRIC EXPLORER'S MAP

We made an electric map. It showed the voyages of Columbus, De Luna, Narvaez and De Soto. It has Christmas lights.

– Frankie Burdges

3. A Classroom Bulletin

A weekly one-page bulletin written by the teacher or the pupils will publicize classroom activities. Announcements, honors, projects and achievements, quotations, notations—something different every week.

Ask your principal to consider preparing bulletins and newsletters for other teachers, other schools. Share the best from every classroom. Include—

> Successful projects
> Ideas for lessons
> Coming cultural events
> Helpful books, records, periodicals
> Creative writing topics
> Pertinent reprints and quotations

Post them on the bulletin board, or circulate individual copies.

4. Classroom Correspondence

There are few things more important than teaching your students to write letters—to enjoy corresponding. Never miss a chance, no matter how small, to have your whole class write. Create make-believe situations if no real ones exist.

Teach them how simple but how important it is to write a letter:

> a. Post charts showing correct letter and note forms.
> b. Plan a bulletin board showing all types of correspondence.
> c. Let them write for information
> > place an order
> > cancel a subscription
> > say thank you
> > RSVP an invitation
> > send an expression of sympathy
> > write a note of congratulations
> > make an inquiry
> > extend an invitation
> > ask for a job
> > send family news

MUSIC and the ARTS NEWSLETTER

SANTA MARIA ELEMENTARY SCHOOL DISTRICT

September - October, 1965

GETTING TOGETHER -- FOR AN EXCITING YEAR!

A brand new year, and a fresh opportunity is offered us all in the Santa Maria School District to not only share our faith in each other, but also, to renew our highest professional ideals in order that this year becomes the best ever!

Let us join together and build a bridge of fine education across our community!

We can do this as we dedicate ourselves:

To use the power of positive action in all aspects of our work. Petty misunderstandings, the false and ineffective thinking that stands between us and our potential as artist teacher fade beneath a solid spirit of professional comeraderie. An enthusiastic attitude can work wonders to inspire those around us.

To really work together in ways that bring about change-for-the-better in each of us. An innovation-oriented school system sets the climate for the very essence of true education to be lived by adults as well as by students.

To expand,and to keep flexible our classrooms and schools so that youngsters can learn in many ways. A school built on the concept of "family" offers a vitality that cannot happen where each classroom is an "island" of learning.

To stress emerging values -- the giving of self, and self-selection rather than to impose standards -- with all of it's implied inflexibility.

Finally to build our classroom environment around aesthetics that re-create children and ourselves each day we are together.

As Kahlil Gibran has said:

We live in beauty - - -

All else is a form of waiting.

We recommend you explore having these works in your room--to brighten a display, or for motivation of your next art lesson.

SCULPTURE ART PIECES IN THE LIBRARY

Auguste Rodin (1840-1917)	Nat Werner
The Thinker	Spirit of 1776
The Cathedral	Ellen Lord
Edgar Degas (1834-1917)	Spring
Dancer	Rima
Albrecht Durer	Llama
Praying Hands	Musician
Edward Schillaci	Banjo Player
Town Crier	Family
Owl	Oriental Art
Nathaniel Kaz	Tang Horse
Sonata	Middle Eastern Art
Pablo Picasso	Assyrian Goat
Owl (13")	Egyptian Art
Cat	Cat
Bob Schindler	Falcon
String Quintet	African Art
Bull	Tji Wara
Lincoln Memorial	Elephant Tusk
Ernst Barlach (1870-1938)	Greek and Roman Art
The Singer	Greek Horse
Michelangelo	Boy With Thorn
Moses	Terracotta Horse
The Discus Thrower	Cycladic Horse

RECORD CLUB IS PROVING SUCCESSFUL!

"Let's raise the flag and see who salutes", seems an apt description of feelings that often accompany new techniques tried within our schools. Teacher response to the sending of records from the district collection directly-to-teachers for their evaluation has been most gratifying--and educational. Many teachers are listening to an average of two records per week.

The reviews of records will be summarized and added to the jacket of each recording for future guidance in where, and when, to play the music. Numerous recordings are being judged "Extremely valuable--to be added to the school's record collection". Other recommendations include statements such as "Probably better in upper grades", "Too heavy", and "This was great", "Children enjoyed some of these songs...".

Mrs. Wilson, 6th grade teacher at Alvin had each of her youngsters write an evaluation of the recording they heard in November. Their penetrating comments made for fascinating reading.

SPEAKING OF RECORD CLUBS

Many of us consider the "Record Club of America" to offer the best advantages to any collector of recorded music. Under its plan you may purchase any record on the market at savings from 1/3 to 3/4 off list price.

The enclosed order form at the back of the newsletter gives specifics.

. . . .

The mediocre teacher tells. The good teacher explains. The superior teacher demonstrates. The great teacher inspires.-------William Arthur Ward

---

popular song, or a song of solace and comfort may be just the thing needed in order to help a boy or girl over some particularly difficult emotional block. The classroom teacher, not the music specialist, can best accomplish this because she understands the emotional needs of the children, and because the music specialist is not always present when needed.

NEW COURSE OF STUDY

Music goals to "shoot for" have been added to this year's Course of Study for Santa Maria teachers. Specific skills and understandings are described which, when taught children, will offer them opportunities for continual aesthetic growth.

Art goals per grade level are recommended in terms of minimum number of art experiences for children.

We believe that through music and art experiences such as these, our students are provided a trellis of understandings and likings upon which can grow a lifelong pleasure of active aesthetic enjoyment.

Follow the Course of Study in order to add breadth as well as depth to your teaching.

THE PERFORMING ARTS IN SANTA MARIA

It seems that Santa Maria is well on its way to being a model community in terms of its rich aesthetic climate.

Performance dates to jot on your calendar are:

THE ALLAN HANCOCK INTEREM THEATRE lists--

"The Fantasticks", November 4-20
"The Empoeror's New Clothes", from January 15 on to tour Elementary schools.
"The Mad Woman of Chaillot", February 10-19
"Romeo and Juliet", May 19-June 4.

A special performance of the "The Trojan Women", direct from New York will be presented October 10, 8:30 p.m. at the Ethel Pope Auditorium.

THE SANTA MARIA CIVIC THEATRE presentations--

"Mary, Mary", for three weekends starting October 28
"The Rainmaker", January 13 through January 22
"The Boyfriend", March 17 through March 26
"A Shot in the Dark", May 12 through the following three weekends.

THE SANTA MARIA CONCERT ASSOCIATION schedule--

"Jose Echaniz, pianist", October 21
"Orchestra San Peitro of Naples", November 17
"Pacific Ballet Company", February 14
"Madam Butterfly" opera, March 17

It is hoped that through this record distribution   , teachers will become better acquainted with the wealth of music contained in the district record collection and at the same time that they will offer guidance to the Music Supervisor for future purchase of recordings.

You can expect the first record to be sent to you around the end of October.

'Hope you enjoy the idea.

IT'S A FACT!

Major topics in art within World Book Encyclopedias in our libraries include: Understanding Painting, How the Painter Works, The History of Painting, Collections of Paints, Famous Painters and Pictures of Famous Paintings.

Major topics in music are: Learning to Enjoy Music, Elements of Music, Musical Forms, Vocal Music, Instrumental Music, Sacred Music, History of Music, Music Around the World, Famous Musicians and Careers in Music.

SONGBOOKS FOR SANTA MARIA

"Songs We Like In Santa Maria" is the title of the new songbook compiled for use at assemblies and multi-room songfests within our schools.

The 143 songs in the booklet represent favorite tunes gathered from all parts of the world.

Intermediate grades should find the book a valuable aid in learning songs which can be sung whenever two or more youngsters get together in our community.

As a start, 100 copies are being sent to each school.

"QUICKIE" ITEMS OF INTEREST --- MAYBE!

- If your records sound poorly, one major cause is a worn needle on your phonograph. Your principal can supply you with a new needle.
- A piano bench is needed for the Alvin School Auditorium piano. 'Know where we can buy one?
- A squirt of liquid soap added to tempora paints (liquid or powder) will make the removal of paints from clothing a much easier task.
- The first Santa Maria Symphony Orchestra Concert will feature "The Moldau", by Smetana. Borrow a recording of this fine selection from the District Library to "set the stage" for having your children and their family attend the concert.
- The September issue of Instructor magazine has a number of excellent suggestions to liven-up your art and music program.
- The October 20th, 4 P.M. meeting of A.C.E. to be held in an Orcutt School,will feature Nat Fast demonstrating the making of Tissue Paper Collages. 'Sounds like fun.

Paris, France
April 16, 1961

Dear Mother and Daddy,

We landed at Cherbourg and took the boat train to Paris.

Our hotel is right off the Champs-Elysees so we are in the center of things.

We visited the Louvre today. We saw the Mona Lisa. It is not a very big painting. I saw others I liked better.

We walked along the Seine and crossed over to the Left Bank. We looked at paintings and books in the stalls.

Here is my picture by the Eiffel Tower. We climbed to the second landing. You can see all over Paris from there.

Tomorrow we will still be in Paris. Then we will drive through the Chateaux country on our way to Germany.

I will write again tomorrow.

Love, Chrissy

d. Using situations in social studies, history or reading texts, write make-believe letters to parents.

Don't let them tell you they have nothing to say!

Everybody has something to say, a something colored by his background —the place where he lives, the way he spends his leisure time, the manner in which he earns his living, the people who inhabit his daily existence. The more complete the person is, with respect to his capacity to understand and to feel, the greater will be the variety of his experiences and the depth of his responses.

—Jacob Deschin

You might encourage students to correspond with a pen-pal in an overseas dependent school or schools in another part of the United States. Pen-pals living in areas you plan to study can sometimes provide up-to-date information on a first-hand basis.

5. Send Get Well, We Miss You, Congratulations, Happy Birthday and Holiday Cards

Greeting cards involve the students in language arts projects and draw on their creative talents. Have each person design and make his own verse, greeting and card for all possible occasions.

AND THE BEST OF GOOD WISHES

FOR A HAPPY NEW YEAR

JOSEPH H. CALDWELL

SEASONS

GREETINGS

6. Send Papers Home for Signatures

One way to publicize classroom work is to send significant papers home for the parents' signatures. Some daily papers and all test papers should go home. Then report cards will reflect what you, the parents and the students have noted throughout the entire grading period. File the papers for use in conferences. At the end of the year they can be placed in an inexpensive binder to serve as a record of the students' work and progress from September to June.

7. Classroom Programs—Invite a Crowd!

It's not as difficult or as time-consuming as you might think! And classroom programs give parents and friends a wonderful opportunity to see what's going on at the school. Publicize the events, issue invitations, urge people to attend.

Seeing is believing, and the family and friends of employees are always interested in seeing the inside of the plant, how it operates, what is necessary to produce the finished commodity, and —most important of all—the conditions under which the employees work.
—James W. Irwin
Your Public Relations

- Plan open houses
    plays   song fests   speeches
    antique shows   sports events   debates
    science fairs   art exhibits   demonstrations.
    library fairs

Ditto programs or catalogs for souvenirs, bulletin boards and family discussions.

"H. M. S. Pinafore"
OR
THE LASS THAT LOVED A SAILOR

"H. M. S. PINAFORE"

W. S. Gilbert   Arthur Sullivan

presented

by

The Seventh & Eighth Grades of

PONTE VEDRA-PALM VALLEY SCHOOL

8:00 P. M.   25 April, 1963

Cast in Order of Appearance

Boatswain	Ramsey Huston
Little Buttercup	Stephanie Peterson
Dick Deadeye	David Thames
Ralph Rackstraw	Tom Ellis
Captain Corcoran	Rod Henson
Josephine, the Captain's Daughter	Patti Reed

The Rt. Hon. Sir Joseph Porter, K. C. B. - Ivan Browning

Hebe, Sir Joseph's first cousin - Charlotte Haymans

SIR JOSEPH'S SISTERS, COUSINS & AUNTS

Patsy Beckford, Nimi Bradford, Mimi Brewer, Joyce Cason, Edna Haworth, Robin Hicks, Brenda Mickler, Kathi Sheridan, Judy Tribble, Merry Trumble, Janet Brooker, Jean Brooker, Nancy Brown, Peggy Cason, Mary Haworth, Darlene Hunter, Linda Medders, Faye Rawson.

SAILORS

Tommee Carr, Ricky Devereux, Dick Draper, Bill Harrison, Robbie Hruska, Gus Kroner, Dave Parrish, Jack Beckford, Bobby Bridges, Kent Buckley, Ronnie Hawks, Ken Hutchison, Alex Juhan, George McLatchey, Nelson Sayford, Eric Searcy, Sandy Stout, Jim Tinsley Joe Jerner, Todd Harris, Dell Richardson.

SCENE

Deck of H. M. S. Pinafore off Portsmouth

ACT I Noon   ACT II Night

SYNOPSIS OF MUSIC

ACT I

We Sail The Ocean Blue	Sailors
Little Buttercup	Buttercup
The Captain of the Pinafore	Captain
Over the Bright Blue Sea	Girls
Sir Joseph's Barge is Seen	Sailors
I Am the Monarch of the Sea	Sir Joseph
When I Was a Lad	Sir Joseph
Finale	Ensemble

ACT II

Things are Seldom What They See -	Buttercup & Captain
Bell Trio	Josephine, Captain & Sir Joseph
The Merry Maiden and the Tar	Captain & Dick Deadeye
Carefully on Tiptoe Stealing	Chorus
HE is an Englishman	Chorus
Farewell, My Own	Ralph Rackstraw
A Many Years Ago	Buttercup
Finale	Ensemble

END OF THE YEAR PROGRAM

McLatcheyville, Florida • Fourth Grade • June 1, 1957-1959

Announcer: Jack Beckford   Music: Janet Brooker
      Lights: Frankie Burdges

America the Beautiful

Our Welcome Song

A Program of Slides and Songs............Fourth Grade

    THIRD GRADE
    The Church
    The Fire Truck
    Halloween
    The Garden
    "If I Were Going"
    FOURTH GRADE
    The Church
    Florida History
    The New School
    Kickball
    "Singing Wheels"
    McLatcheyville

Awards Earned During the Fourth Grade

    Play Day Award
    Look-It-Up Certificates
    64 Point Questions
    Honor Roll
    Gold Cards
    Scholarship
    Blue Cards
    Spelling
    Arithmetic
    Reading
    Comprehensive Exam Announcement
    E-S Honor Roll Medals
    Attendance
    First Six Weeks Citizenship
    Fox Fire Award
    Freckles Contest
    Best Pioneer Family
    Citizenship
    Honor Point Awards

America

Parents will please file outside; the children will follow.

Songs Written by the Fourth Grade: "We're the People from McLatcheyville", "In 1857 The Finest Town of All", "Mother's Song", "Father's Song", "A Hard Life", "Great Fun", "This Is Our Town"

OPEN HOUSE of the SPRING WORK
BEFORE THE PROGRAM

The Ditch The Menehune Built

Second Grade   10:30 AM
Belle Sherman School   February 15, 1957

CAST

King Umi.........Davo Br.   Jim B.

King of the Menehune..........Gary

Wise Man..............Jim Lattin

King's Men..... Tom   Bobby
     Larry   Robert

Dwarfs....Cindy Sandy   Bob   Faith
    Billy David   Nancy S.   Danny

Fishermen... Pat   Deb   Dave

Women... Margie   Robin   Pam
   Katya   Penny Lee Rachel Penny P.

Children... Susan Alt Sharon   Susie A.
    Valoie   Nancy Jean   Anne Lynne

PIRATES OF PENZANCE

or
The Slave of Duty

by
W. S. GILBERT
and
ARTHUR SULLIVAN

Ponte Vedra-
Palm Valley
School
FRIDAY—MAY 14—8:00 PM
1965

Cast of Characters

Richard, a Pirate King	Rand Sharp
Samuel, his Lieutenant	Ivan Stout
Frederic, a Pirate Apprentice	Nelson Sayford
Major-General Stanley, of the British Army	Ed Merritt
Edward, a Sergeant of Police	Sam Veal
Mabel, the General's youngest daughter	Ellison Hite
Kate,	Susan Peacock
Edith } Three of the General's many	Sharon Cason
Isabel, } Daughters	Suzanne Sapier
Ruth, a Piratical Maid of all work	Sherrie Fills

Chorus of Daughters, Pirates and Policemen:

Julia Brooks		Lewis Booker
Robin Brooks		George Bridges
Lori Goetz		Spencer Cason
Cayetha Hancock		Tommy Ellis
Marion Herzman	7th Grade	Jim Gray
Pegi Hewitt		George Harney
Susie Hunter		Steve Hughes
Barbara Justice		David McCall
Beverly McCall		Ed Oesterreicher
Donna Reitz		Glenn Peacock
Helen Searcy		Leo Sheridan
Janie Utter		Kurt Sizmon
Dena Villa		Glen Spoares
Cynthia Young		Bink Kinsley
Kathy Barboskie		Mike Olson
Joanly Cason		Bill Oppont
Penelane Jasquier		Jeff Carroll
Jan Davis	8th Grade	Gus Cobb
Diane Felcer		Mike Denly
Wesley Fielder		Bill Goetz
Robin Hicks		Bill Henderson
Linda Harris		Joe Jgata
Betty Scarborough		Bink Knight
Shelley Snoser		

Director   Joanne H. Atkinson

"The Pirates of Penzance" was first performed in New York City on December 31, 1879. Sir Arthur Sullivan conducted.

8. Give Awards

Recognition, prizes and awards are appreciated by all ages—note Pop's bowling trophies, Mother's bridge club prize, brother's letter sweater, sister's scout badge.

Award prizes, emblems, ribbons, certificates, trophies to your students for their achievements.

9. Put Their Projects on Display

Students will strive diligently if they feel that their work is of importance. They are vitally interested in what others are doing —and in others knowing what they are doing. Put your student projects on display.

Type excerpts from their written or oral reports on ditto stencils and distribute copies as worksheets. Trace their original drawings. Make up questions and problems for the rest of the class to answer.

10. Bring the Community to Class

All of the people who share in the life of the community have something to teach your class. Most adults are more than willing to talk with children if they are given a definite idea of what they should cover and how long they should plan to speak to your class.

    a. Be specific about subject matter. Prepare a list of questions developed through class discussion. Ask your visitor to plan his talk around these points.

    b. Set a time limit so your visitor can plan his talk and his day.

    c. Suggest visual aids or realia which are available.

    d. Give him a brief outline of the students' background in that area.

Prepare your class for the visit!

    a. Discuss audience manners.

    b. Discuss welcoming and thanking the guest.

    c. Discuss the question-and-answer period.

    d. Designate a host and hostess for the visit.

File an information sheet on each speaker.

Name _____ Occupation _____
Address _____ Phone _____
Date of Talk _____ Length _____
Theme _____
Visual Aids _____
Questions class submitted (attach)
Thank you notes written (date) _____

11. Gifts Which Reflect School Skills

The holiday gift-giving times of Christmas, Valentine's, Easter and Mother's Day all fall within the school year. Let your students prepare gifts which reflect the skills they are developing in the classroom:

a. Anthologies

Save your students' best creative writing. Type excerpts or entire selections on stencils and assemble a class anthology.

Art Linkletter capitalized on the fact that kids *do* say the darndest things—especially when you have assigned provocative themes:

> The Most Wonderful Person I Know
> Good and Bad Points About Teachers
> Improvements I Should Like To See
> My Life Thus Far
> The Autobiography of a Pair of My Shoes

MEMO

Excellent help for your creative writing program can be found in
WRITING CREATIVELY
J. N. Hook

D. C. Heath & Co.
1963

It is filled with ideas, topics, and approaches to creative writing—adaptable to whatever grade level you are teaching.

Don't let your students shy away from poetry. Read it, post it, collect it, dramatize it, illustrate it—then ask them to create it.

Ruth Gross was enthusiastic about the Japanese poetry form HAIKU. Her sixth-graders became interested in the verse form during a social studies unit on Japan. Their verses caught the attention of the *Florida Times-Union* which ran a feature article on the young poets in its Sunday edition.

Haiku is a verse of three unrhymed, unmetered lines. The first line must contain only five syllables; the second, seven syllables; and the third, five. This total of seventeen syllables centers on one moment of insight, appreciation or experience.

The meter is not always perfect in these sixth-grade efforts, but the thought is certainly in the oriental vein.

Young trees sing;
In the glen soft wind stirs.
Storm approaches.

Wild thunder crashes.
Mighty winds rush madly.
Storm hurls itself.

Old bell rings mournfully,
Senses death in stillness.
The tolling weeps.

It is morning.
Dawn stealthily approaches.
Hour of the tiger.

The sly fox pauses.
Snow drifts in dark ravine.
Goose hangs limp.

The falcon sweeps
Like swift wind from nowhere
On unwarned prey.

b. Out of my life and thought

From the beginning of the school year, assign essay topics which reflect the thinking of your individual students. Have these compositions copied into special notebooks to be given as gifts.

- My Mother
- When I Grow Up
- I Want To Be

- My Father
- Responsibility
- Friendship

- My Brothers and Sisters
- My Home

c. Something to live by

Collect poems, prose passages, quotations and apothegms from the beginning of the year. Use them for Penmanship exercises which are copied into a special notebook. These become gifts which can be added to by the recipient.

d. Calendars

Small paste-on calendars can be ordered through stationery shops or a calendar form can be dittoed and filled in for each month.

Follow a theme with your twelve illustrations and the cover:

> Arithmetic Around the Year
> Great Art
> Historical Events
> Highlights of the Season
> School Days

Illustrate with drawings, magazine cutouts, sketches, cloth, art reproductions, postcards, and the like.

e. Songbooks

Purchase music composition books from your school supply store. Have the students copy the music of the songs the class has enjoyed throughout the year. Illustrate each page. Include a sentence or two about the song and its composer.

f. Potted plants

Purchase small flower pots and let each student grow his own plant. Wrap the pots with tinfoil and tie with a ribbon.

g. Paintings

Mount and frame each student's best painting. Cover the cardboard with a cellophane or clear plastic.

h. *Maps*

Mount decorative or realistic maps prepared in Social Studies or Language Arts programs. Wrap in cellophane or plastic:

> Historical maps
> Storyland
> Travel
> Current events

i. *Personalized stationery*

Pen a sketch, design, cartoon or initial in the left hand corner of unruled paper. If you add color, use India ink or drawing pencil so it won't smear. Buy envelopes that match the paper. Back each packet of paper with a sheet of shirt cardboard. Wrap the package in Saran Wrap or put it in a thin plastic bag. Tie with a bright ribbon.

If the stationery is for "little folks," draw in the lines.

j. *Recipe books*

When studying measurement in arithmetic, ask each student to bring in his mother's favorite recipe. Add to the collection any dishes, menus and meals connected with social studies. Have them copied and illustrated in small notebooks or on looseleaf sheets to be put into binders.

There are, indeed, so many ways to advertise and publicize your classroom:

> ☐ Bulletins
> ☐ Bulletin Boards
> ☐ Celebrations
> ☐ Ceremonies
> ☐ Charts
> ☐ Clippings
> ☐ Conferences
> ☐ Displays
> ☐ Dramatizations
> ☐ Exhibits
> ☐ Fairs

- ☐ Films
- ☐ Gifts
- ☐ Interviews
- ☐ Letters
- ☐ Meetings
- ☐ Posters
- ☐ Reports
- ☐ Significant Papers
- ☐ Slides
- ☐ Special Occasions
- ☐ Special Class Projects

. . . . What Have You Tried?

MEMO

Investigate the monthly newsletter of classroom public relations ideas—

IT STARTS IN THE CLASSROOM
published by
The National School Public Relations Association
1201 Sixteenth Street, NW
Washington, D.C. 20036
$3 per year

Public relations is concerned with public opinion and attitudes. And as long as we live in a society where freedom of speech prevails and public opinion is the ultimate power, public relations will be an essential and important force.

—John W. Hill

CHAPTER 10

Drilling
without Drudgery

Teachers of little experience often underrate the value of practice work, and do not realize what a large proportion of the learners' time should be given to this type of work.

—L. Wilkes

Our experience has proved that concentration comes when children are occupied with the material, always with the material. So then it is a material we must have, not a person.
—Maria Montessori

Self-learning is the key to that inner discipline so necessary for anyone who will educate himself to the hour of his death.
—Nancy McCormick Rambusch

Drills, games, skill-builders, independent and group activities are a vital part of your classroom program. Choose your materials wisely—for specific learning value, for clear purpose and for challenge.

The same facts that seem so terribly dull and dry take on new life and color when they become the key to winning or losing a game, solving a puzzle or completing an activity. There are so many interesting things to do—so many exciting ways to approach the necessity of practice and drill.

1. From the School Supply Store

Even if your budget prohibits many purchases, pore over school supply catalogs or visit the store and you will find many ideas for making your own materials.

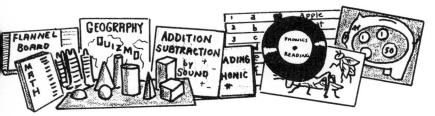

2. Flashcards With Flair

Almost anything that has to be learned thoroughly can be printed, pasted or drawn onto flashcards. They can be wonderfully interesting when they are prepared with imagination and flair.

Use illustrations on your cards whenever you can.

Perry Pictures is an excellent source of illustrative material for your flash cards

Use color codes. For instance,

History—

All cards dealing with the Colonial Period in white,
Westward Expansion in green,
the Civil War in blue and grey,
Spanish explorers in orange.

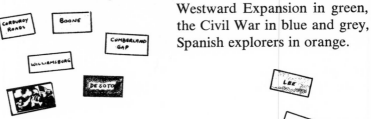

States and capitals—

All cards dealing with the New England States in grey,
the Southern states in orange,
the Far Western states in yellow.

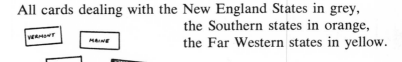

For English grammar—

Prepare cards showing the parts of speech at work (each part of speech a different color)—

Nouns on yellow cards,
Pronouns on pink,
Verbs on blue,
Adjectives on brown,
Adverbs on orange,
Prepositions on red,
Conjunctions on purple,
Interjections on green.

Example:

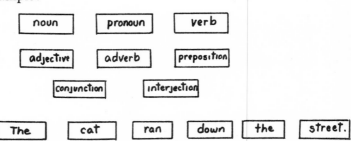

(See page 122 for a detailed discussion of flashcards and
English grammar.)

And for foreign languages—

• Choose three different shades of yellow to differentiate be-
tween masculine, feminine and neuter nouns.
  • Put idioms on white.
  • Follow the above color coding for all other parts of speech.

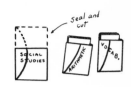

You can buy your sheets of paper from a printing company
and have them cut into cards of any size you like.

Students can carry their cards in special packets made by
trimming the top of a standard 3⅝" x 6½" letter envelope.

Urge students to carry a set of flashcards at all times. Waiting
for the bus, standing in line, between classes or at home, they
can whip out their cards for a quick review. Use them alone or
with manipulative charts. Practice individually or in groups.
Flashcard drills can cut many hours off "homework."

3. Manipulative Charts

Manipulative charts can be about anything your students are
studying. They are highly effective study aids and very easily
prepared. You are limited only by your imagination!

Oaktag sheets are best for desk work. Larger wall charts can
be prepared on posterboard, oak tag, flannelboard or magnetic
boards.

Store the cards and an answer key in a plainly marked envelope
which can be clipped to the chart.

Students place the flashcards in the correct positions on the
charts and check themselves with the answer key.

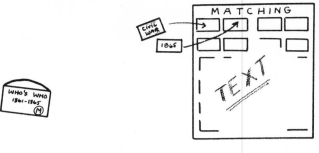

MATCHING charts can be used with any number of card sets: Vocabulary, Who's Who, Quotations, Dates, Documents, Battles, Formulas. Put the questions on one color card and the answers on another. Mark these envelopes with an M to show that they are used on the MATCHING charts.

If you don't have enough room right on your picture, letter the points you wish identified and leave spaces *around* your chart to place the cards.

106

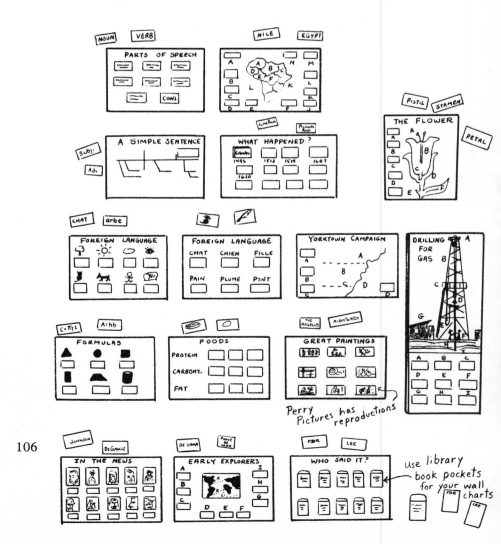

4. Egg Carton Contests

Turn egg cartons into a means for drill.

    a. Put the rules in the top of the box.
    b. Put the carton on a shelf or table. Players step back a specific distance.
    c. Toss in buttons, pennies or markers—one point for each correct response.

      Number facts
      Music symbols
      Abbreviations
      Phonics

Keep a paper and pencil handy for scoring. Let fast students work with slow ones.

5. Beat the Clock

Place several drill sheets and sign-up sheets on a table with two or three egg timers. Put your answer key on the back of the sheets. Change the drills frequently. Keep them in loose-leaf notebooks.

MEMO

For a wonderful collection of Arithmetic enrichment activities for elementary school classrooms, get a copy of

ARITHMETIC ENRICHMENT ACTIVITIES
FOR ELEMENTARY SCHOOL CHILDREN
by
Joseph Crescimbeni

Parker Publishing Co., Inc.
West Nyack, New York
1965

Puzzles, games, group activities, teaching materials, bulletin board ideas—hundreds of activities.

6. Gold Star Papers

On an Independent Activities table place 5 or 6 Gold Star projects to choose from. Folders are made from oak tag. The project is explained on the left side and materials for completing it are on the right side of the folder. A chart can be posted to indicate participation. Any sort of drill, project or creative assignment can be part of the Gold Star Papers. Completed papers are placed in a designated box to be corrected by the teacher.

7. Alphabet Charts

Let your students attempt an Alphabet for any subject. Some of the letters will be easy to illustrate. How cleverly can they picture the others? P. D. Eastman's approach to dictionary definitions is exceptional. Show your students a copy of his:

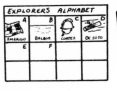

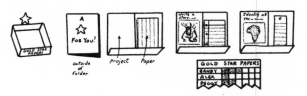

The Cat in the Hat
Beginner Book
DICTIONARY
Random House, Inc.
1964

8. Puzzles and Worksheets

Whenever you prepare a special puzzle or worksheet for your class assignments, run off extra copies and keep them available for extra drill and review.

9. Put It in Order

Print a poem, quotation, description, situation or experiment onto tagboard sentence strips. Have students place the strips in proper order on a Sentence Pocket Chart. (School supply stores can furnish 3″ x 24″ strips for approximately $1.25 per hundred.)

10. Magic Slates

Magic Slates with penmanship practice alphabets and arithmetic number facts are nice for extra practice. AERO Products, Department 224, St. Charles, Illinois 60174 handles several kinds. Write for information.

11. A Creative Writing Corner

Arrange an exhibit or display pictures which illustrate a situation: realia, stuffed animals, a painting, a model or picture folders.

The folders hold up better if they are constructed from manila file folders. Mount an illustration on the left side. On the right-hand side list the words the students might need in their story, poem or paragraph.

Children may work independently or you can read the vocabulary list and discuss the illustration with a group before they begin writing.

When the written portion is completed, encourage the students to illustrate their writing through cutpaper work, drawings, stick puppets or dioramas.

MEMO

To give your students an appreciation and awareness of style, read them the very clever experiment of Julian Cate and his students: "A Style-ish Fable". (After studying the styles of Shakespeare, TIME magazine, the King James Bible and the Uncle Remus stories, Cate's students wrote the story of "The Three Bears" in each of the four styles.)

You'll find these stories on pages 423-425 of the literature text book—

Adventures in Appreciation

by

Loban, Holmstrom, Cook

Harcourt, Brace & World

1958

12. From the Playing Fields

Whatever the season, capitalize on student interest in sports. Draw footballs or fields, softballs or diamonds, basketball courts, track fields, golf courses, swimming lanes and scoreboards for your drill sessions.

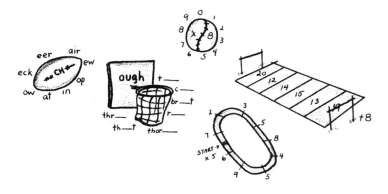

☐ Let the team "come to bat" or "kick off" in Spelling Bee fashion. Let them move down or around the field, court or lane as they answer questions correctly.

☐ Prepare a set of flashcards for a given subject. Put a word or problem on one side and a given value (home run, touchdown, base hit, 10 yard gain) on the other side. An incorrect answer gives the other team a turn.

☐ Chalkboard Golf is exciting. A score sheet indicating 9 or 18 holes is drawn on the board.

Team A is given a problem, question or word. If it misses, Team B gets a chance. Each attempt counts as one stroke for that hole. Lowest score wins.

13. Extemporaneous "Speeches"

Divide the class into teams or simply call on individuals. Ask a student to stand and give as much information as he can about any word or any subject. He receives one point for each fact. If another student thinks he can give more, he must repeat what has already been given before he adds to it. For example, in Spelling—

> Steven, tell us about the word *catastrophe*.
>
> The word catastrophe is a noun.
> It has four syllables.
> It means a disaster.
> An antonym is "windfall".
> The accent is on the 2nd syllable.
> It is spelled c-a-t-a-s-t-r-o-p-h-e.
> It has 4 vowels.
> It has 7 consonants.
> It has one silent vowel.
>
> Score: 9 points

14. Guess the Sketch

Divide the class into teams or call on individuals. Choose a subject area: spelling, literature, social studies, art. A student chooses a word to illustrate. He makes one line which suggests the meaning. A member of the class or the other team makes a guess. If the guess is incorrect, the artist makes an additional line and calls on a second person. Lines are added until the sketch is guessed. Each guess counts as a point. Lowest score wins.

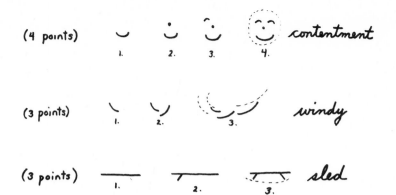

(4 points)   1.   2.   3.   4.   *contentment*

(3 points)   1.   2.   3.   *windy*

(3 points)   1.   2.   3.   *sled*

15. Textbook Relay

Place a dictionary or textbook on the first desk in each row. (Make sure the rows are even in number.) On the board write a word or problem for each person in the row. Start on a signal. Each student looks up a word or problem, writes the answer, passes the book to the student behind him. First row finished wins.

With the dictionary: Copy the phonetic spelling for each of these words.	With the math book: Work the 6th problem on each of these pages:	With any text: Answer the 1st question on these pages:
career	19	41
honest	47	65
stingy	82	83
weary	97	95
total	108	114

16. Bingo, Lotto, Quizmo

Have each student fold a sheet of notebook paper into 16 squares. In each square he writes a letter or word, phonetic symbol or figure—depending on the subject of the game.

Since each student makes up his own sheet, they are all different. Call out a problem, ask a question, give a word or sound. Let them cross out or circle the answers that appear on their sheets. First to complete a row or first to complete all 16 squares is the winner.

112

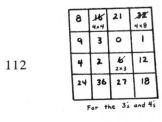

For the 3's and 4's

For Spelling

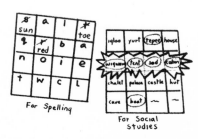

For Social Studies

17. Role Playing

A fine way to review is to assign a person being studied to each member of the class. Have the individual researched as to his or her personality, role in history, appropriate costume, importance to us today. Let the student present himself as that person. Excerpts from speeches and writings, presentation of charts and maps, costumes and realia make the role playing even more convincing.

18. Twenty Questions

One student or team chooses a date, person, place, period or event which the class has studied. He (or they) may be asked 20 questions to which he may answer only YES or NO.

> Is it a place? No.
> Is it a person? Yes.
> Is it a man? Yes.
> Is he still living? No.
> Is he from American History? Yes.
> Is he from the Industrial Revolution? No.
> Is he from the Colonial Period? Yes.
> Was he a statesman? Yes.
> Was he a president? Yes.
> The first president? No.
> The third president? Yes.
> Thomas Jefferson? Yes.

19. Teach a Class

Assign committees to present a flannelboard lesson, a chalk talk, or to set up an experiment or a lesson. They can't teach what they don't know! And they'll exercise the skills of planning, organizing and speaking as they set up their class.

20. Make a Movie

If you own or can borrow an 8mm movie camera, an exciting class project and review can be developed. Let student committees plan the script and scenes around some area the class has studied.

A 200 foot film will run for 15 minutes. Tape narration, sound effects and music to accompany the film.

Plan to edit each 50′ reel before splicing together your movie. Cut out the bad spots!

MEMO

An excellent reference for planning, shooting, editing and projecting your movie is:

THE AMATEUR'S 8mm MOVIE GUIDE
Sid Norinsky
Universal Photo Books
1957

21. Give a Slide Show

Any snapshot, drawing, or negative of your students and their work can be turned into a 2 x 2 projection slide for a classroom program.

A program of commercial slides *and* your own, with narration and sound effects can be an excellent review and an exciting project.

MEMO

Projection Slides, Inc. will make 2 x 2 black and white slides from prints for 35¢ each and from negatives for 15¢ each.

Projection Slides, Inc.
P. O. Box 26072
Indianapolis, Indiana

22. Postage Stamp Detectives

Purchase several packets of postage stamps from the dime store. Let each student choose a different stamp and do a research paper on its subject. Paste the stamp to the completed paper.

23. The Listening Corner

For approximately $5.00 an earphone jack can be installed in your record player. Inexpensive ear phones can be purchased from your record dealer. Feature a *Record of the Week* or *Composer of the Week* in your Listening Corner. Encourage students to spend a few minutes every day listening to something special in music.

24. Slides on Display

Purchase a 2 x 2 slide sorter from your local camera shop. Prepare a display of 36 slides and an information sheet or question sheet to accompany it.

Cover the front with a sheet of acetate to keep slides from falling and to insure that no fingerprints get to the transparencies.

25. A Viewmaster Corner

Begin a collection of Viewmaster reels. Set up a Viewmaster Corner with the viewer, reels and information or question sheets. Change the reels frequently.

When motivated, pupils engage in exploratory and completing activities; and as they explore, as their curiosity causes them to probe, they become educated.

—James S. Kinder

26. Supplementary Reading Material

Build a library of supplementary reading materials for your classroom. Start with:

✔ *Single or duplicate copies* of other readers at many different levels. (Sometimes your School Book Depository will let you have readers which have been discontinued for regular classroom use.)

 *Magazine stories and articles,* mounted and placed in acetate jackets.

 *Pamphlets, booklets, brochures.*

 *Your own or your students' creations*—Type or print the stories. Illustrate them with drawings, magazine cutouts or snapshots. Store them in acetate jackets and loose-leaf notebooks.

MEMO

Contact Scholastic Book Services for a free kit of materials to start a classroom book club:

The Lucky Book Club
(Grades 2–3)

The Arrow Book Club
(Grades 4–6)

Outstanding children's titles are available for 25¢ and 35¢ each. The paperbacks are described in illustrated newsletters. Dividend copies for your classroom library!

For further information write:

Scholastic Book Services
904 Sylvan Avenue
Englewood Cliffs, N. J.

An Artist

Elizabeth is an artist.

She is painting a picture. She uses four colors in her picture: red, blue, green and yellow.

What do you think she painted?

What happened to her hands? What should she do now?

Would you like to paint a picture? You can be an artist too.

A NEW BABY

Alex has a new baby sister. She is a lovely little baby.

Alex says she cries alot. Most new babies do. He says she sleeps alot. New babies get tired in a hurry.

Alex helps take care of his sister. He feeds her. He rocks her to sleep. He takes her to walk. He plays with her.

Do you know her name? Ask Alex! He will tell you all about her.

Our German Friends

Hello from Hans and Erika! They live in Germany. They live near some very high mountains.

Do you like their clothes? Hans has on leather shorts. He wears them in summer and winter.

Do you see the pins on Hans' and Erika's hats? They add a new pin every time they climb a mountain. They have been on top of the highest mountain in Germany. It is called the Zugspitz.

Would you like to climb a mountain?

Buried Treasure

Buried treasure! The pirates plan to search for a chest of gold. They study their map carefully. It shows the lonely island where the gold is buried.

Danger ahead! Adventure!

Read all about it in "Treasure Island". The book is in our library.

✔ *Poems*—Type or print them; illustrate; store in acetate jackets and loose-leaf notebooks.

118

27. Reading Skill-Builders

Cut a story out of a magazine or discarded reader. Mount it on cardboard and then cut it into six or eight sections. Store the pieces in a manila envelope with the title on the front. Ask your students to first skim the material, put it in order, read and answer a set of questions.

Purchase a set of bulletin board display letters. Paint all the consonants one color and all the vowels another. Mount pictures of their vocabulary words on 3 x 5 cards. Let students build words to match the pictures.

> *. . . it is always better if the child can teach himself—that is, learn by his own active experience. In this way he genuinely apprehends or grasps knowledge by an active assimilation, instead of a passive receiving.*
>
> —*E. M. Standing*

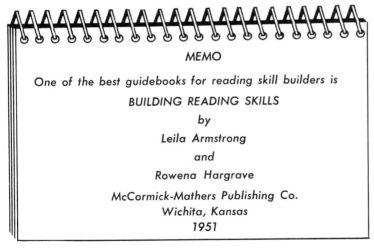

MEMO

One of the best guidebooks for reading skill builders is

BUILDING READING SKILLS

by

Leila Armstrong

and

Rowena Hargrave

McCormick-Mathers Publishing Co.
Wichita, Kansas
1951

28. Hand Puppets

Hand puppets can be related to all areas of the curriculum: historical figures, story book characters, and the like. With careful costuming and an information card, they are wonderful research projects.

A. Mix two cups of fine sawdust with one cup of wall-paper paste. Add enough water to give a good modeling consistency.

B. Tape a ball of newspaper over a toilet paper roll. Shape the puppet's face around the newspaper with the sawdust paste.

C. Stand the puppet on a soda pop bottle or plastic detergent bottle until dry. (The detergent bottles give shoulders to the figure.)

D. Leave the puppet for about a week to make sure it is absolutely dry. Then paint features and skin with tempera.

E. Use yarn for hair. Paint or paste on features. Felt cutouts make interesting eyes and mouths. Clothes can be made from crepe paper or scraps of cloth. Decorate with buttons, lace, and jewelry.

29. *Interesting Things To Do* Sheets

Distribute an *Interesting Things To Do* sheet once a week or once every two weeks.

Gather a variety of textbooks, workbooks, reference books, party and game books. Turn to their end-of-chapter lists of activities and jot down ideas. Fit their suggestions to your curriculum. The list can be as long or as short as you like; it can change completely each time or carry over some of the activities while adding on new ones. Here is a sample.

Interesting Things To Do

(For Those Who Finish Early)

1. Write a poem (about anything you suggest).
2. Paint a picture about (whatever you are studying).
3. Choose three worksheets to complete. (Keep a supply on hand.)
4. Review your geography facts (or any facts) with the flash cards.
5. Listen to the current selection in our Music Corner.
6. Make a puppet of (any person).

The ability to work independently, to continue to accomplish, whether or not the adult is physically present at one's elbow at all times, the ability to initiate work because one has had previous successful experience, are important learning skills for a child.

    —Nancy McCormick Rambusch

30. Culture Corner Quest

For the study of history, geography, language arts, art appreciation and nature, purchase a series of color or sepia notebook prints.

The 2¢ sepia and 4-5¢ color reproductions are designed for notebook study projects. Let students choose a print and find out all they can about the subject. Mount the print on their report.

Catalogs may be ordered from:

Perry Pictures   University Prints Catalog
Malden   15 Brattle Street
Massachusetts 02148   Cambridge 38, Massachusetts
35¢   50¢

Prints range from 3 x 3½ inches to 5½ x 8 inches at the 2¢-5¢ prices (minimum order is $1.00).

A partial listing of subjects:

Poets and Authors
Scenes in Literature
Historical
Famous People
Sculpture
Presidents
Mythology
Works of Art
Animals
Trees
Religious
Landscapes
Architecture

No. 21   BOYS IN A BOAT   HARVEY
True-Color Prints, Saugatuck, Conn.

Actual size of 4¢ Perry color print

Larger prints may be ordered for 5¢, 10¢, 25¢ and in specially priced sets.

Perry Pictures offers a series of art masterpieces with a leaflet guide for the teacher. The guides contain descriptive material to help teachers present paintings to students.

31. Make a Grammar Kit

a. Color code the parts of speech, phrases and clauses:

> Nouns—yellow
> Pronouns—pink
> Verbs—blue
> Adjectives—brown
> Adverbs—orange
> Prepositions—red
> Conjunctions—purple
> Interjections—green
>
> Prepositional phrases—red
> Participial phrases—blue
> Infinitive phrases—aqua
> Gerund phrases—yellow
> Appositives—pink
>
> Dependent clauses—grey
> Independent clauses—white

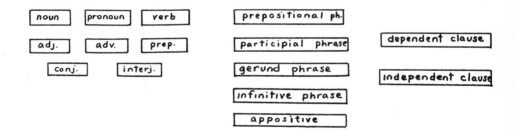

* Purchase your sheets of paper from a printing company and ask them to cut your cards to size.

b. Take sentences from their textbook or workbook. Print them on cards * according to the color codes. Keep all the cards from one sentence in one stationery envelope with the sentence written on the front. Give each student one sentence to work with. He can arrange the cards in order, list the parts of speech, and answer questions. As they finish with one sentence, let them swap envelopes and sentences with someone else.

c. Duplicate worksheets that can be colored in and written on according to the code. Take the sentences from their textbooks or workbooks.

d. Post charts showing the color coded grammatical parts.

Students will begin to *see* the way in which the different grammatical elements work together and to recognize specific words as being specific parts of speech.

32. Punctuating Conversation

As an exercise for punctuating conversation, let groups of three or four students gather to chat. As two or three of the members converse, let the others record the conversation. Limit the number of sentences to 8 or 10. Have the group check each member's written work for correct punctuation before turning in the assignment.

33. Perk Up Your Penmanship Program

Try the following:

- *Penmanship Scales for evaluating progress*

    Leonard P. Ayres Scale
        The Bureau of Educational Research and Service
        University of Iowa
        Iowa City, Iowa

    Freeman Scientific Evaluation Scales
        The Zaner-Bloser Company
        612 North Park Street
        Columbus 15, Ohio

- *Honor Rolls, Certificates*

    Joseph Dixon Crucible Co.
    Handwriting Research Dept.
    Jersey City 3, N. J.

    The Zaner-Bloser Company
    612 North Park Street
    Columbus 15, Ohio

    Wearever Handwriting Kit
    David Kahn, Inc.
    North Bergen, N. J.

- *Pen Pals for fun*

  Parker International Pen Friend
  Parker Pen Company
  Educational Department
  Janesville, Wisconsin

  Children's Plea for Peace
  World Affairs Center
  University of Minn.
  Minneapolis 14, Minn.
     (Ages 8-18)

  League of Friendship
  4 Ash Street
  Mt. Vernon, Ohio
     (Ages 12-19)

34. Arithmetic With the Cuisenaire Rods

The Cuisenaire Rods are now used by school systems in all fifty states to teach arithmetic and math at any grade level.

Write for the catalog of Cuisenaire Kits, texts for teachers, pupil texts, worksheets and supplementary aids. (All rods and kits are suitable for purchase under the National Defense Education Act of 1958.)

Write to:

> The Cuisenaire Company of America, Inc.
> 9 Elm Avenue
> Mt. Vernon, New York

CHAPTER 11

Projects, Displays, Exhibition Techniques

Whatever be the detail with which you cram your student, the chances of his meeting in after-life exactly that detail is almost infinitesimal; and if he does meet it, he will probably have forgotten what you taught him about it. The really useful training yields a comprehension of a few general principles with a thorough grounding in the way they apply to a variety of concrete details.

— *Alfred North Whitehead*

First find something to say and then find something to say it with.

— *Arnold Newman*

Students are eager to make things, to use tools, to experiment with materials, to create models, charts and displays.

The ability to secure information for these projects, to test ideas and put knowledge to work is the "really useful training" that equips your students to tackle problems in the real world outside of the classroom.

1. Project Work

Project work is significant only if the problems are significant, the planning carefully done, the representation authentic, and the completed projects serve as learning devices for all who view or work with them. This is not as hard to achieve as it might seem!

Do not hesitate to work closely with your students *at first*. Very quickly they will gain the skills that enable them to take a project from start to finish without your help.

2. What Sort of Projects?

From drawings on acetate sheets to model scenes in sandtables, we will discuss 17 various classroom projects, displays and exhibitions. To avoid the idea that any one is preferable to another, we list them alphabetically.

In planning their projects, students can be helped to:

a. *Pinpoint the problem*
   State the problem in a short, simple, arresting manner—a phrase from three to six words long.
b. *Organize the information*
   List the facts. Decide which are the main and which the subordinate points.
c. *Borrow ideas*
   Carry a notebook and jot down clever layouts, unusual presentations, catchy phrases, slogans. Ideas are everywhere: in store windows, magazines, newspapers, commercials, museums, books and packaged goods.
d. *Trial and error layouts*
   Make a rough sketch of all the elements to be included in the project. Cut them out and arrange in different positions. Choose the most effective layout or design. Paste it up and proceed.
e. *The presentation*
   Strive for a project that is simple, forceful, dynamic, dramatic. Check for:

   - accuracy
   - organization
   - clarity
   - simplicity
   - forcefulness

MEMO

Write for a catalog of

School Teaching Aids and Supplies

from

Models of Industry, Inc.
2100 Fifth Street
Berkeley, California 94710.

The catalog is itself a valuable teaching resource. It has a center section science guide and a cross reference index of equipment in the catalog. Books, aids, models, equipment, kits (Playground Geography, Model Oil Refinery, Story of Paint, and the like).

3. Setting Up a Project Period

Naturally, your classroom will have to undergo some changes for project work. Everyone will not be seated, there will not be absolute quiet—but confusion, clatter and clutter need not be part of the scene! Establish a few "ground rules" and insist that they are observed.

a. If one group is working on a project:

1. Reserve one section of the room as a work area.
2. Arrange the materials before class begins.
3. Give the rest of the class a seat-work assignment.
4. Meet with the group, go over the directions, and get them started before you turn back to the class.
5. Ask them to work as quietly as possible and to be courteous about interrupting for help.

b. If the entire class is taking part:

1. List all of the projects, arrange the materials, set up specific work stations around the room.
2. Assign every student to a specific project. Don't allow trading.
3. Be sure that the tools, materials and references are set up before class begins.
4. Discuss behavior standards with the class before work be-

127

gins. If any student should fail to be courteous and industrious, send him to his seat for the remainder of that project period.

5. Have seat work assignments prepared. As the different groups wait to be called for directions, let them work quietly at their seats. Students who finish their part of the project early can go back to their seats and work quietly.

—No idle hands!—

6. Call one group at a time for directions. Get them started before calling another group.

7. Never allow the noise or activity to get out of hand. If you cannot isolate individuals who may be causing confusion, send the whole class back to their seats and wait until the group is more settled and willing to try again.

8. Allow enough time to clean up. At least one hour should be allotted for the work session with 15 or 20 minutes beforehand for directions and 15 or 20 minutes afterward for clean-up.

9. If projects are not finished during the one session, let their completion be an individual activity for those who finish their work early in the next few days.

All of this, of course, takes time and involves noise and movement and personal relations and actual reading, and above all communication, one with another: the vital thing so often cut off in a schoolroom.
—Sylvia Ashton-Warner

4. Acetate Cover Sheets

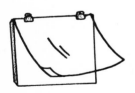

Cover charts, maps, pictures, drawings or graphs with an acetate sheet. Related concepts, notes, highlights and sequence studies can be drawn or written on the acetate without harming what is underneath. Special marking pens—black, red, blue and green—can be used and erased with a special fluid.

Acetate jackets can be purchased at office supply stores to exhibit single sheets or notebook pages. Exceptionally good papers, articles or pictures can be displayed and highlighted with your comments.

5. Bulletin Boards

If your classroom is cluttered with tiny chalk and bulletin boards and you have no large area for projects and displays, talk to your principal about the possibility of consolidating space with one large board.

GUIDELINES FOR EFFECTIVE BULLETIN BOARDS

a. If students are helped with initial projects, very shortly they can carry a project from start-to-finish by themselves. Do not hesitate to do a large part of the planning at first!

b. A preliminary *layout* is essential! Make several sketches and choose the most effective. Indicate:

> use of titles, labels, captions
> illustrative material
> use of color
> textures
> materials

c. Portray *one idea,* one theme, one situation.

d. Limit yourself to *three colors:* one background and one or two correlated colors for accents.

e. Keep all items *large* enough and *simple* enough to be grasped at a distance.

f. Keep material at the children's *eye level* wherever possible.

g. *Lettering* should be large, bold, easy to read.

h. Use different *textures:* burlap, corabuff, yarn, wood, acetate, cotton, and the like.

i. Keep a notebook of *ideas:* slogans, layouts, themes. Urge students to contribute ideas and materials.

j. Use straight *pins* instead of tacks.

k. *Change* the material frequently. Never let a display get stale. Always have a committee or an individual planning the next display.

k. Rate yourself and your students:

Points	Item	Points	Item
10	Organization	10	Illustrations
10	Accuracy	10	Captions, Titles
10	Originality	10	Color
10	Clarity	10	Textures
10	Layout	10	Lettering

a. The board itself

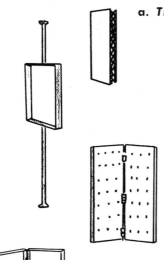

Make panels from heavy *corrugated* box cardboard.

Attach shallow boxes to spring-type divider or lamp poles.

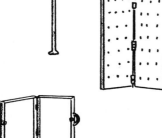

Pegboard panels can be hinged for standing, mounting or hanging.

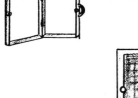

A portable bulletin board case is easy to make.

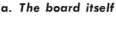

Cover a door or wall area with a coarse fabric, such as burlap.

Mount strips of molding along a narrow panel.

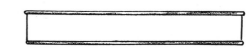

b. *Collect clever captions*

Ask your students to be alert for themes, catchy phrases, and ideas. Start a file of book titles, movie titles, headlines, magazine titles, display captions, advertisements.

Says Who?
Courage Was Their Watchword
Live Dangerously
Over the Top
When Time Stands Still
The Geography of Hunger
Trial By Fire
Up From The Rubble
Touchdowns in Type
Tales and Trails
Treasure Chests of Literature
They Conquered With Courage
It's a Matter of Fact
Literature Is Eavesdropping
Who Knows?
Bright Reading for Dull Days
Quite a Catch
Arm Chair Travel
Spooks and Sprites
Laugh a Little
Long Ago and Far Away
This Kind of Life
Around the World in 80 Books

MEMO

An outstanding collection of student, teacher and librarian work:

POSTER IDEAS AND BULLETIN BOARD TECHNIQUES:

For Libraries and Schools

by

Kate Coplan
Oceana Publications, Inc.
Dobbs Ferry, N. Y. 10522

1962 $8.50

Over 250 photographs of posters, boards, and displays which are easy and inexpensive to create.

c. Some samples and examples

Aa WORDS

A collage of pictures, words and phonics stressing "Aa".

Or

Bb

Cc

etc.

DID YOU KNOW THIS ABOUT COLOR?

A manipulative board! Use a white background and pipe cleaner circles covered with cellophane to show what happens when you mix colors.

Cover the table with newspaper. Have a jar of water, the paper, paints and brushes ready for use.

WHAT DO YOU KNOW ABOUT THAT?

A manipulative board. Library book card pockets are labeled with names, dates, facts, symbols, etc. An envelope of cards to insert in the proper pockets should be mounted on the board.

LET'S ALL BE FRIENDS

Use a pegboard panel. Various articles from countries of the world are exhibited on shelves. Dolls are cut paper-doll fashion and dressed in native costumes. The globe is a flat cutout.

HALL OF FAME

Use clippings, articles, magazine covers and pictures of famous people. Identify each one with a 3 x 5 card of information.

RED, RED, RED (OR ANY COLOR)

Concentrate on a color! How it is used, what does it represent, what does it do to us, where do we see it?

Bright, Bright, Bright
Sad, Sad, Sad
Hot, Hot, Hot

THE FEUDAL SYSTEM

Photographs of students portrayed the different levels of feudal society. Heads were pasted onto costumes and mounted on the board.

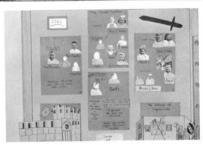

LET'S FIND OUT

Committees can plan the board to help initiate a unit:

Lists of questions
Photographs and realia
Sign-up sheets for committee
work
Envelopes for information
Experiments, instructions,
equipment

LET'S GET EMOTIONAL

A collection of words in one category—

Quiet, Please
Happy Talk
Tough Talk

HAVE YOU REALLY SEEN ME?

Objects are chosen from the world we pass by every day and often take for granted.

A magnifying glass or microscope is placed on the table. Question cards help students to take a good look.

THE ABOMINABLE SNOW MAN

MEMO

An excellent reference for math bulletin boards is the 11 page illustrated pamphlet published by the National Council of Teachers of Mathematics. It is already punched to fit a 3 ring notebook. Send 50¢ for "How To Use Your Bulletin Board"

—

NCTM
1201 Sixteenth St. NW
Washington, D. C. 20036

FACES AND PLACES TO NOTE

Mount newspaper sheets at an angle. Paste clippings, pictures and articles on black construction paper before pinning to the board.

MAN INTO SPACE AND BACK AGAIN

Clip photographs from magazines and mount on construction paper. Have students bring in clippings. A committee can select books on space (fact and fiction). Cut the globe from chart paper. Paste up the book jackets.

HERE AND THERE

Compare one area or one country with another: climate, geography, language, customs, people. Bins with soil, grains and realia from the two areas are very effective. Encourage students to handle the material in the bins.

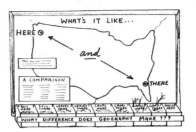

A WEEK LONG PROJECT

Place the aquarium on a table in front of the board. Post a list of questions to be answered during the week.

1. How many fins do our fish have?
2. Show our fish in a picture. Notice how the light shines through the water.
3. How do our snails move?
4. How do our snails eat? Try to find out by watching.
5. Does one fish seem to boss the others?
6. Draw a picture of the female fish, the male fish.
7. How many kinds of plants do we have? Draw and label them.
8. How many baby fish can you count? How many adults?
9. How many baby snails can you count? How many adults?

MIGHTY IMPORTANT TO US

Post pictures of students who have made outstanding contributions to the school or in the class: scholastically, athletically, in citizenship and through contests.

MEMO

Get a copy of

MAKING AND USING CHARTS

Alice Liechti & Jack Chappell

Fearon Publishers, Inc.
828 Valencia St.
San Francisco, Calif.

$1.50 paperback

Good for charts and for bulletin board ideas!

NAMES IN THE NEWS

TIME, LIFE and LOOK covers are excellent current events material. Let a committee identify each individual with a card of information or use this as a manipulative board and ask students to identify the personalities.

HIGHLIGHTS OF APRIL (or any month)

Current events articles, cartoons, bulletins, photographs, calendars . . . work on this board throughout the month, or collect the items and post them at the end of the month.

I CAN TIE MY SHOES

. . . or I can write my name.
I know all my number facts.
I have read 10 books.
I know all 25 abbreviations.
I know the 20 formulas.

• *Do something different to your bulletin board!*

Make a personal "field trip" to your local display materials center (look it up in the yellow pages of the phone book). Take a notebook and collect ideas, then re-assess your bulletin board.

Add an awning—

Add an awning!

a booth—
a bin—
patterns—
textures.

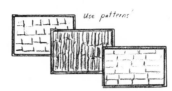
Use patterns

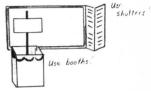
Use shutters

6. Charts

No doubt about it—one of the most useful of all teaching tools is the chart! Use it for—

Use booths.

RK STANDARDS

BEHAVIOR STANDARDS

ACHIEVEMENT

ATING EXPERIENCES

IMPORTANT FACTS

DIRECTIONS

VOCABULARY

LESSONS

SELF-TESTING

Songs, poems, paragraphs, stories, experiments, terms, projects, graphs, information, rules, standards—put it all on charts!

Guidelines For Charts

a. Sentences: short and to the point.
b. Lettering: easily seen by the student who sits in the last seat on the last row.
c. Illustrations: simple, bold, clear, large.
d. Margins: similar to the mat of a picture or format of a book.
e. Lined chart paper is available at school and office supply stores.

MEMO

John U. Michaelis'
SOCIAL STUDIES FOR CHILDREN IN A DEMOCRACY
is chock-full of chart ideas!

Prentice-Hall, Inc.
1956

7. Dioramas

Dioramas or scenes in perspective may be housed in any sort of container. Use dioramas to illustrate—

- social studies
- poems
- stories
- songs

- biography
- health
- nature
- geography

Titles and information cards are an important part of the assignment. Check for accuracy of detail. Assign committees or individuals to diorama projects.

8. Dwellings

Raising a cabin, building a post office, constructing a castle, setting up a grocery store, outfitting a covered wagon—all of these projects call upon many learning skills. Students must be able to locate and to apply information, to plan, to calculate, to measure, to select and to work responsibly with others.

Whatever unit your class is studying in Social Studies, Geography, History, Dramatics or Literature, the possibility for a dwelling exists.

PAUL'S BLACK SMITH SHOP

United States Post Office

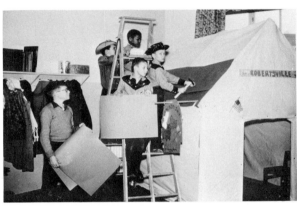

ROBERTSVILLE

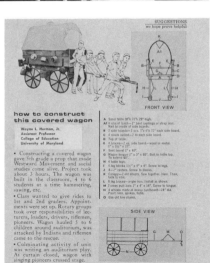

SUGGESTIONS
we hope prove helpful

FRONT VIEW

how to construct this covered wagon

Wayne L. Herman, Jr.
Assistant Professor
College of Education
University of Maryland

• Constructing a covered wagon gave 5th grade a prop that made Westward Movement and social studies come alive. Project took about 3 hours. The wagon was built in the classroom, 4 to 6 students at a time hammering, sawing, etc.

• Class wanted to give rides to 1st and 2nd graders. Appointments were set up. Rotary groups took over responsibilities of lecturers, loaders, drivers, riflemen, pioneers. Wagon hauled 5 to 6 children around auditorium, was attacked by Indians and riflemen came to the rescue.

• Culminating activity of unit was writing an auditorium play. As curtain closed, wagon with singing pioneers crossed stage.

A Sand table 30"x 72"x 29" high.
A1 2 sides of bed—12" peat saplings or strap iron. Nail to inside of side boards.
B 2 side boards—3 pcs. 1"x 6"x 72" each side board.
C 4 cleats nailed—3 to each side board.
D Top of table.
E 8 brackets—2 ea. side board—wood or metal. 1"x 31/2"x 27".
F Seat board 1"x 40".
G Wagon tongue 1"x 3"x 60". Bolt to table top. To extend 60".
H 4 table legs.
I 4 leg blocks 11/2"x 8"x 4". Screw to legs.
K 4—2" casters. Screw to blocks.
K Canopy—old sheets. Sew together. Hem. Then tack to ribs.
L 8 leg brackets—angle iron. Install as shown.
M 2 cross pull-bars 1"x 4"x 18". Screw to tongue.
N 4 wheels made of heavy cardboard—14" dia. Paint rims, spikes, hub.
O Use old tire chains.

SIDE VIEW

TONI'S CASH

GUARDIAN

9. Exhibits and Displays

Ideas and materials for exhibits are all about us: store windows, billboards, magazines, museums, fairs, grocery stores and department stores. Carry a notebook, and urge your students to do the same. Jot down clever presentations, creative approaches and imaginative themes. Use bulletin boards, tables, racks, chairs, bricks and planks to create display areas.

Heavy cardboard, plywood, beaverboard or chipboard cutouts of states, areas, countries and continents can be used in many ways. Photographs, clippings, drawings and cut-outs can also be used to highlight a display.

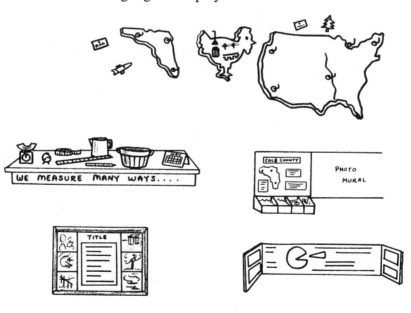

Glass cases can be built very inexpensively to protect work on display in the hall or in rooms used by many classes.

140

Use toy figures

Add scale model toys to exhibits.

Tiny motors and turntables can be purchased from hobby shops to give motion to part of a display.

Move desks from the center of the room and plan a floor exhibit for open house.

Our Visit to The Farm

The display area pictured here is 9' x 50'. Assignments for this area are rotated between classrooms.

One group of children painted the grass on the mural with large sponges. Others did the sky lightly with chalk. Some made clouds of white paper and cut trees to be pasted on.

One group made the animals of balloons and paper towel tubes (cut in thirds). The position of the animal was decided first: eating grass, drinking, or looking up, and the tubes were fastened on accordingly with tape. Paper maché strips and patches were used to cover the whole animal. After the first application has dried, a second "coat" will make the animals smoother and easier to paint. Masking or freezer tape holds better than scotch tape.

After painting the animals, add eyes, manes, tails and other details by gluing on with Duco cement. Use cut paper, leather strips, yarn, or dried beans for your materials.

A coat of shellac applied to the animals will make them sturdier and keep them cleaner.

A committee worked on the cardboard box buildings. The roofs were fastened with pins. Hay was put into the loft. The fence was borrowed from a yard but corrugated cardboard could have been used.

Chalk was used over the green sponged paint to make shadows, wheat fields, tall weeds, stonewalls and fences.

Christmas Cookies

A box of freshly baked cookies were enjoyed by the class as they heard the following poem:

Mix them and fix them
With sugar and spice—
Cookies for Christmas
Must look extra nice.

Cut them and shut them
In ovens to bake.
Fleck them and deck them
With frosting you make.

Dry them and tie them
To boughs of your tree.
But don't let your puppy
Come sniffing to see!

A committee of six made the figure from boxes and crepe paper and dressed it to look like Grandma.

A second group printed the poem on a sheet of 24" x 36" paper, decorated its edges and mounted it in the project corner.

A third group made the stove and a fourth, the curtains.

A tiny cuckoo clock was mounted in the kitchen and a stuffed puppy was placed beside Grandma.

Firm cookies were brought to be decorated with water colors. They were suspended from the ceiling around the project corner for a happy, festive atmosphere.

The most important devices then are those which encourage the visitor to participate in the exhibit, either with his eye, mind, or hand. In participating in some manner the visitor is apt to concentrate to a greater degree and to be less distracted by what is going on around him.

—James H. Carmel

MEMO

An excellent illustrated reference is James H. Carmel's

EXHIBITION TECHNIQUES—TRAVELING AND TEMPORARY

Reinhold Publishing Corp.
1962

10. Flannel Boards

Almost any lightweight, flat material can become a visual aid
with the flannel board at hand. Paper cutouts, pictures, letters,
cards and drawings will adhere to the flannel if strips or pieces
of sandpaper are glued to their backs. Many materials will hold
without any backing: yarn, corduroy, velvet, suede, blotting
paper, sponge and small pieces of balsa wood. Prepared flannel
cutouts are available at every school supply store.

If you make your own board, be sure it is large enough to be
seen by every student. Choose a firm material such as plywood,
celotex or masonite. Buy enough flannel to allow for overlapping
edges. Stretch the material tightly and smoothly so no wrinkles
can possibly appear. Tack the cloth to the board.

Use your flannel board for—

> new lessons
> reviews
> student talks
> story telling
> book reports.

Remember to practice placing and removing the cut-outs before you are involved in a lesson situation. Work from one side
of the board. Talk to the class, not the board. Arrange your cutouts in proper sequence before class. Since felt will adhere to felt,
several layers can be arranged and peeled off as a lesson
progresses.

Study the prepared materials for ideas of your own!

11. Graphs and Pictographs

Warm up cold statistics! Help your students learn to prepare
graphs which make the reader sit up and take notice.

A. *Use color*
Strips of tape make neater, more dramatic graphs than columns filled in with
ink, pencil or crayon.

B. *Repeat symbols*
Instead of using a bar or line, repeat a
drawing or photograph.

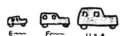

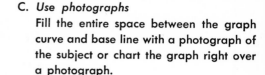

C. *Use photographs*
Fill the entire space between the graph curve and base line with a photograph of the subject or chart the graph right over a photograph.

D. *Add cartoons*
Cartoons always spark interest. They give emphasis to the story in the graph.

E. *Divide a representative object into parts.*
Split a coin, a bill, a pie, a house—any object into representative parts.

Averages and relationships and trends and graphs are not always what they seem. There may be more in them than meets the eye, and there may be a good deal less.

—Darrell Huff

MEMO

We highly recommend Darrell Huff's

HOW TO LIE WITH STATISTICS.

He best describes it himself:

"This book is a sort of primer in ways to use statistics to deceive. . . . The crooks already know these tricks; honest men must learn them in self-defense."

Part of your lessons on making and reading graphs should give students an awareness of how statistics can deceive.

HOW TO LIE WITH STATISTICS
Darrell Huff

W. W. Norton & Co.
New York
1954

Textbook material gains dramatic dimensions when expressed through pictographs, picture stories, pictorial maps and charts. The illustrations here are just a small sample of what you and your students can do.

Pictograph Corporation, which supplied the illustrations used here, makes a special offer to teachers. For $1.00 you may purchase series of ten 8½" x 11" charts (pictographs, time lines, maps, picture stories) covering subjects such as these:

- Agriculture and Science
- American History
- Business, Economics and Trade
- Communication and Transportation
- Geography
- Government
- World History

WORLD'S TELEPHONES

BILL IN CONGRESS BECOMES A LAW

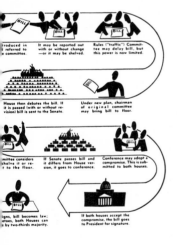

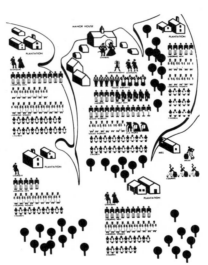

FEUDAL SYSTEM

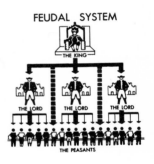

PRECIPITATION AND THE HYDROLOGIC CYCLE

WHAT ONE KILOWATT MEANS

WHAT ONE KILOWATT HOUR MEANS

THE CONSTITUTION

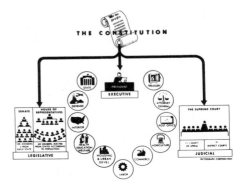

All of these charts include the very latest available information from reliable sources. Use them in bulletin board displays, as reference materials or for lessons!

12. Magnetic Charts and Boards

Magnetic boards may be purchased from school supply stores —or you can make your own by painting a piece of sheet metal with slate paint and putting a frame around the edges.

Magnets, magnetic strips and magnetic cutouts are all available from school supply dealers. Make your own cutouts by pasting or taping pictures and symbols to the single magnets or single strips.

Clip maps or charts to the board. Present your lessons, moving the symbols as you teach.

Have students repeat the steps as a review or independent activity.

Students can prepare reports, lessons and demonstrations with the board. As a manipulative chart, magnetic boards are wonderful:

      ✔ campaigns and explorations
      ✔ matching vocabulary
      ✔ locating products
      ✔ matching signs and symbols
      ✔ showing the growth of an area
      ✔ putting things in order
      ✔ time lines

For desk charts take a dime store checkerboard, have two pieces of sheet metal cut to fit the board and tape the metal or cover it with contact paper. If you tape the metal and paint it with slate paint, you can write or draw on the surface with chalk.

13. Maps

There are so many possibilities for learning through maps. Maps may show us:

- Boundaries, states, capitals (Political)
- Mountains, rivers, deserts (Physical)

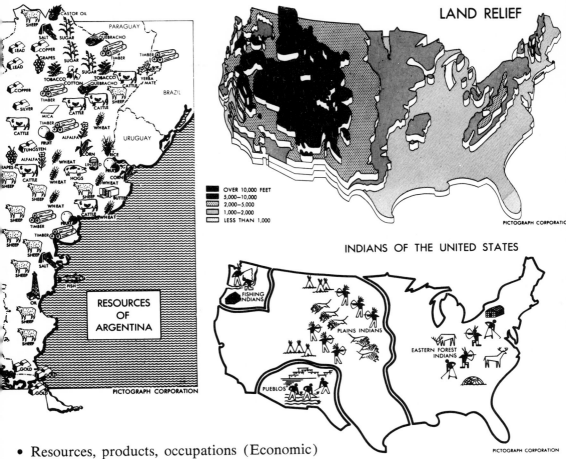

- Resources, products, occupations (Economic)
- Density of population (Population)
- Weather, winds, temperature, rainfall (Weather, Climate)
- Airways, waterways, highways, railways (Travel)
- Telephones, cables, radios, television (Communication)
- Changing frontiers, explorations, growth (Expansion)
- Historical points of interest (History)
- Scenic spots, tourist areas, parks, monuments (Special Interest)
- Local streets, buildings, important spots (Community)

And for attention-getters:

- Add acetate overlays to point up parts of the map.
- Mount specimens (rocks, grain, wood, seeds, etc.).
- Show the area in relief.
- Build the map in the sandtable.
- Add lights.
- Surround the map with pictures, articles and specimens.

147

GUIDELINES FOR MAP MAKING

1. Portray a few key ideas. Do not clutter your map with a mass of detail.
2. Lettering should be bold, clear, and easy to read.
3. Colors should be standard: blue—water
             green—lowlands
             yellow
             orange—higher altitudes
             brown
4. The scale should be clear and easy to use.
5. Symbols should be carefully chosen and explained.
6. The key or legend should be placed conspicuously in one corner. Title, symbols, colors and scale should be clearly shown. Bordering the key will help it stand out.

Spend a great deal of class time helping your students visualize the geographical features they will be representing by symbols on their maps. Pictures, films and field trips to observe actual surface features will give real meaning to their map work.

Charts and worksheets can be prepared to help develop map making and map reading skills. Prepare charts on directions, the key, symbols, colors, shading and relationships.

MEMO

"Using Globes and Maps Effectively"

and

"Making Maps"

are two chapters by John U. Michaelis which are outstanding for teachers at any level! Read Chapters 10 and 11 in

SOCIAL STUDIES FOR CHILDREN IN A DEMOCRACY
John U. Michaelis

Prentice-Hall, Inc.
1956

Let your students map an area in every possible way—from boundaries, physical features and resources to climate, travel, and special interest points! Let them discover how much can be said about an area through the symbols, colors and lines of a map.

14. Murals

First consider some general guidelines:

MAKING A MURAL

The First Day—Setting the Mood

a. Try to find something tangible to represent the theme of the mural:
 —a leaf, a branch, a shell to hold
 —a model to examine
 —a recording to listen to
b. Bring the whole class together and seat them in front of the mural area.
c. Ask them to close their eyes and picture the scene they will try to portray:
 —What time of day will it be?
 —What is the season?
 —Will there be people, objects, trees, water, animals?
d. Now look at the paper and the counter or table top. How will they be limited by available space? Sketch in the horizon.
 —Point out the difference in size as objects move from the foreground to the horizon.
 —Point out the change in color from bright to dull as objects move away from the foreground.
 —Point out the difference in morning, noon and afternoon shadows.
e. On newsprint or on the chalkboard make several sketches based on the group discussion. The class will choose the most effective mural plan.

The Second Day—Teacher's Preparation

a. Assemble all the materials that will be needed.
b. Plan something for every single child to do and know *who* will be doing *what!*
 —painting
 —drawing
 —cutting
 —lettering
 —preparing models
 —gathering realia
 —working on related projects
c. Plan seat work assignments for those who finish their part early or who must wait to start their part.

  d. Gather a variety of reference material. Display them close to the work area.
  e. Discuss behavior standards. Let there be no misunderstandings.
  f. Announce the committees and the individual assignments.

Second Day—Getting To Work

  a. Start one committee or group to work at a time. Other students should stay at their desks to work on assignments.
  b. Give directions, show materials and get the group started before calling another from their seats.
  c. If anyone fails to observe the established behavior standards, send him to his seat and do not allow him to participate until the next day.
  d. Allow time for a clean-up period.
  e. Judging by what is accomplished during the first work period, estimate how many more work sessions the class will need as a whole. Some parts of the mural can be finished by students who finish their work early and have time for independent activities.

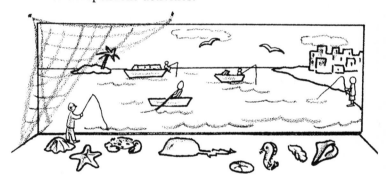

BY THE SEASIDE

1. The scene was sketched lightly on the mural paper according to layouts developed through class discussion.

2. Unusual shells, coral and pictures of seaside life were displayed in the classroom.

3. Fish netting was draped over the side and top of the mural. A long table was placed in front of the board, covered with yellow paper and sprinkled with sand.

4. One committee filled in the background before any details were added. A large sponge was dipped in blue for the sky and in blue-green-and-white paint to create the water.

5. Cloth, string, feathers, buttons, coral, twigs, shells and art equipment (paint, brushes, rubber cement, Duco cement) were placed on a Materials Table to the side of the mural. They were ready for individual assignments.

6. Assignments included:

- the background
- boats
- people fishing with real poles
- a distant city
- islands
- gulls
- shells modeled from clay
- a starfish modeled from clay
- preparation of a Beachcomber Test on different shells
- corals
- sea creatures placed on the sand shelf in front of the mural

Identify these shells.

7. Chalk was used for accent and highlight when the painting was completed.

8. Related assignments were:

- paper fish mobiles
- finger paintings
- choral poems about the seaside
- a puppet show of starfish dressed in net skirts, suspended by threads and dancing to an original song to the tune of "The Sugarplum Fairy"
- the Beachcomber Test

9. Two afternoons were devoted to the mural. Individual students finished the different sections during the rest of the week in their free time.

HAWAII

1. This mural was the culminating activity for a three week unit of study on the Hawaiian Islands.

2. Slides of the Islands were shown and a recording of Hawaiian music was played as part of the planning session.

3. The class was divided into five committees:

- Background
- City
- Volcano
- Pineapple Plantation
- Sugar Plantation

crepe paper →

4. Each child prepared something for the mural:

buildings	clouds
pineapple plants	birds
trees	boats
people	the island
sugar cane	the background
parks	the volcano
cars	

5. Materials were placed on a table beside the mural area. They included straws, pipe cleaners, cereal boxes, cotton, scraps of cloth, construction paper, crepe paper, paper maché, glue, paint, sponges, brushes, scissors.

6. A special committee assembled books, pictures, slides, Viewmaster reels and realia for reference materials.

7. During the week a resident of Honolulu spoke to the class about life in the Islands and checked the mural for accuracy.

8. Related activities included:

- an original play based on a legend
- a banquet of Hawaiian foods
- pen pal letters to children in Hawaii
- booklets about the Islands
- bulletin board displays
- charts of Hawaiian words and phrases

WINTER

1. The day of the first snow the lights were turned off in the classroom and children were asked to concentrate on the winter scene outside.

2. Stella Tuttle's poem, *First Snow,* was read quietly.

3. Winter and first snows were discussed. A scene was sketched on newsprint as the discussion continued.

152

4. Each child made his own picture expressing his feelings about winter and snow. The final mural represented a combination of several of these.

5. The background was gray-blue paper. Materials for both the individual pictures and the mural were:

> tempera paint
> cut paper
> cotton

UNDER THE SEA

1. The book, *Animals of the Sea and Seashore,* was read to the class. Interest was so keen that a second sea book, *The Whales Go By* was read.

2. Classroom discussion led to the development of the layout for the mural.

3. A committee of five painted the blue water with large sponges. Highlights were added with chalk. Greenish and purplish lights and shadows were added as the water grew deeper.

4. Islands were formed with chalk.

5. Each child made, cut out and placed a sea creature on the mural:

fiddler crabs	fish
hermit crabs	turtles
shrimp	whales
spider crabs	octopus and seaweed
lobsters	coral

lobster pots (complete with attached string and float)

6. "Coral" was made by mixing soap powder and water into a paste, then adding powdered paint and applying it to the paper using fingers with a dabbing motion (a brush won't work).

7. From the ceiling the students suspended imaginary colorful fish with white thread. (Everything in the mural was factual but the mobiles were fanciful.)

8. A committee lettered UNDER THE SEA above the mural in bright blue letters.

9. On the shelves beneath the scene, on dark blue paper, an exhibit of sea life was arranged. Students contributed:

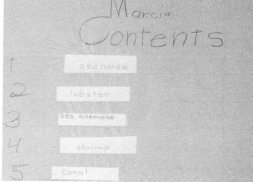

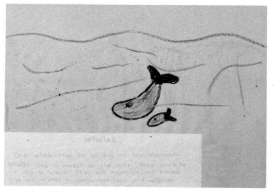

sand dollars	coral
star fish	crab shells
horseshoe crab shells	sea urchins
oyster shells	

10. On the library table a committee assembled a collection of books pertaining to the sea.

11. Each student made a booklet, "Under the Sea," illustrating ten things found under the sea with mimeographed factual material to paste with his picture.

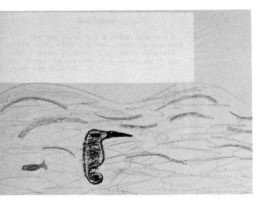

THE GREEN ELF MARKET

1. The Green Elf Market was a continuing project during a marketing unit.

2. The sections—produce, dairy, bakery and meat—were chosen by the students.

3. The fruit and vegetables in the produce department were cut from paper and pinned on. The dairy products were the same.

4. All baked goods and meat goods were wrapped in cellophane.

5. A scale hung in front of the produce department. It was made with oaktag and suspended by a ruler from the wall. Its black pointer was movable in order to add pounds as produce were "weighed."

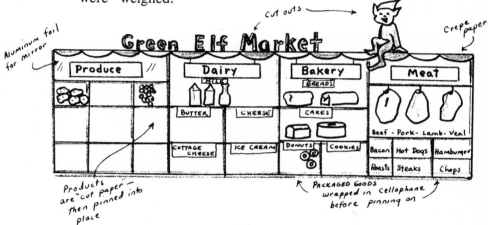

6. Each child prepared a marketing booklet with oaktag covers and accordion fold-out paper. It was completed as the different sections of the market were studied.

7. A unit on manners and telephone etiquette accompanied the study.

15. Posters

The successful poster flashes one theme, one thought, one message. A good poster is dramatic, vivid, uncluttered. It makes an immediate impact on the viewer. Teach your students to make them!

GUIDELINES FOR POSTERS

a. Simplicity is the keynote!
b. Use catchy slogans.
c. Use bold colors.
d. Use textured materials.
e. Use lettering which matches the theme of the poster.
f. Make lots of sketches and layouts.
g. Keep a file of outstanding layouts, posters and designs.

Assign many poster projects to your students. Can they sum up a book, a lesson, a theory or an idea in one dramatic illustration?

16. Sandtable Displays

Sandtables should be "Standard Equipment" for every classroom which includes project work with its assignments. Maps, scenes, experiments, models from all areas of the curriculum can be expressed in sandtable displays.

17. Prepare a Project Kit

Collect materials for use in project work. Ask your students to contribute from scrap material at home. Store the items in partitioned cartons.

☐ Aluminum foil
☐ Clear plastic wrap
☐ Tacks
☐ Screws
☐ Nails
☐ Crepe paper
☐ Construction paper
☐ Corabuff
☐ Oaktag
☐ India ink
☐ Pen staffs
☐ Pen points
☐ Small mirrors
☐ Cereal boxes
☐ Corrugated cardboard
☐ Tin cans
☐ Oatmeal boxes
☐ Clay
☐ Realia
☐ Toys
☐ Magic Markers

☐ Paints
☐ Water jugs
☐ Brushes
☐ Rags
☐ Sponges
☐ Airplane dope
☐ Pipe cleaners
☐ Buttons
☐ Spools
☐ Compass
☐ Protractor
☐ Ruler
☐ Yardstick
☐ Triangle
☐ Cotton
☐ Straight pins
☐ Safety pins
☐ Toilet paper rolls
☐ Paper towel rolls
☐ Wrapping paper rolls

☐ A pile of magazines
☐ Newspaper
☐ Wheat paste
☐ Dowling
☐ Lattice
☐ Pine
☐ Balsa
☐ Yarn
☐ Ribbon
☐ String
☐ Cloth scraps
☐ Hammer
☐ Saw
☐ Brace and bit
☐ Tin snips
☐ C-clamp
☐ T-square
☐ Masking tape
☐ Freezer tape
☐ Scotch tape
☐ Paste
☐ Glue
☐ Rubber cement

CHAPTER 12

Teaching Them to Draw and to Letter

The sensory and manual preparation for drawing is . . . an alphabet; but without it the child is an illiterate and cannot express himself.

—Maria Montessori

While in the primary grades children can do little but illustrate ideas; illustrations should not be confined to those grades alone. I am a firm believer in the plan of making drawing a part of every assignment that can be illustrated in every grade.

—W. W. Charters

Anyone can draw—and everyone should draw! You may never be a finished artist, nor may your students, but you can equip them with basic drawing skills—important tools for conveying their ideas quickly, clearly and imaginatively.

159

Drawing becomes art—personal expression—when it is taught by seeing, by discovering, and by increased sensitivity, but students first need an "alphabet," a knowledge of the "language of forms." Before we perfected our individual handwriting, we copied and learned the standard letter forms of the Roman alphabet. Likewise, students need to be taught the techniques which enable them to portray their personal ideas, feelings and interpretations on paper.

For the teacher who needs help in a hurry, for anyone who has wailed, "I wish I knew how to draw!" and for those who feel at a loss to competently teach drawing, we highly recommend two books:

EXPRESS YOURSELF IN DRAWING

Gerhard Gollwitzer

Sterling Publishing Co., Inc.

1962

and

A 75¢ BANTAM PAPERBACK — # S 3071

HOW TO DRAW

Edward H. Freedman

A 75¢ Bantam Paperback #53071

1965

MEMO

Get yourself a copy of both and start teaching!

These two volumes are the closest you could possibly come to having a teacher beside you—inspiring you, urging you on, scolding and schooling you.

Mr. Freedman proves that if you can write, you can draw. You don't need to learn special skills. With his approach to subject and form, you can teach your students and yourself how to draw as easily as you write your name.

Both he and Mr. Gollwitzer have provided you with a course of instruction. Adapt it to your grade level and teach your students to draw.

Learn how to write pictures—the solution for those who can't draw.

Throughout the book we have considered various aspects of school art. At this point we wish to emphasize the importance of the need for stressing *drawing* and *lettering* as a means of conveying ideas graphically, forcefully, skillfully.

> *Any artist would show his apprentice this; it seems a most justifiable way to free the child to express himself without any direct intervention on the part of the adult in the act of expression.*
> —Nancy McCormick Rambusch

1. The Proper Tools

Give your students the proper tools for drawing! It's easy to make a passable picture if your pencils fill in, accent and outline for you!

  a. See that each person has:
      An ordinary HB pencil—for outlining
      An ordinary 6B pencil—for accenting
      A flat 6B sketching pencil—for masses and filling in.
  b. Reams of newsprint can be bought for classroom practice sessions. Sketchpads are nice for walks and field trips.
  c. Primary black crayons—rounded or squared—and medium-soft charcoal are the only other materials you will need. Charcoal is messy; students should wear old shirt smocks when working with this medium.

2. The Basic Strokes

The pencils, crayons or charcoal sticks can be held in three different positions to obtain a wide variety of strokes. Give your students plenty of time to experiment, to discover just what *will* happen if they change their grip on a pencil.

No "drawing" yet—just strokes, lots and lots and lots of them. Circular, angular, wavy, straight, perpendicular, horizontal, vertical, thick, thin, flat and sharp.

1.　　　2.　　　3.

After these exercises, which are intended to make you relaxed and free, you are ready for some concentration and discipline.

        —Gollwitzer

3. Teach Shape

Teach the basic geometric forms which are fundamental to all objects.

The basic form of all objects can be traced to cylinders and rectangular solids.

        —Freedman

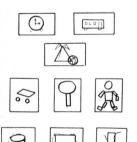

Start a search for geometric shapes. Clip magazine pictures and have the lines of the basic shapes superimposed with dark crayon or magic marker. Use these pictures in a bulletin board display.

Have students cut out circles, squares, triangles, rectangles, trapezoids and parallelograms from construction paper; mount them on additional sheets; add details with chalk, paint, magic marker or crayon. Basic shapes become objects!

Distribute sheets torn from coloring books (bold outlines and simple forms). Ask your students to find the basic shapes and color them in with a bright crayon.

Distribute outline maps of areas, states, countries or continents. Ask students to find the basic geometric shapes and trace their outlines.

4. Teach Form

Having outlined the basic shapes, go one step farther in the search. Now look for forms! The circle becomes the sphere; the square, the cube; the triangle, the cone; the rectangle, the cylinder. Every object can be reduced to one or a combination of these forms.

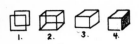

a. Draw the shape.
b. Connect the sides.
c. Erase the "inner lines."
d. Shade.

Make many studies of brightly lighted objects and then subtly lighted objects. Make sketches from every direction. Use the flat 6B sketching pencil or medium soft charcoal for shading the forms.

Art is something innate which exists and grows within each of us, of itself. Craft, however, is something you can learn. You can learn the language of forms, how to play with forms, and the many techniques which constitute the rules of this game.

— *Gollwitzer*

Note the direction of light and its effect on an object:

> the darkest part,
> the reflected light,
> the length of shadow,
> the sharp outlines,
> the blended lines.

Study and copy, study and copy!

5. Teach Simple Perspective

For their drawings to be convincing, your students must understand a few simple elements of perspective. All objects may be studied under two groupings: cylindrical and rectangular.

Cylindrical

a. Have your students roll a piece of manila paper and pin or staple it in the form of a cylinder.
b. Have each student hold his cylinder straight out at eye level. How does the bottom edge look? the top edge? Draw it.

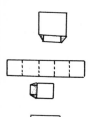

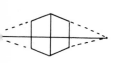

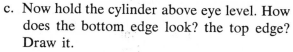

c. Now hold the cylinder above eye level. How does the bottom edge look? the top edge? Draw it.

d. Hold the cylinder below eye level. What do you see? Draw it.

e. Draw the cylinder in at least five different positions.

Rectangular

a. Point out the following: everything a person draws is related to an eye level. We usually speak of this as the horizon. Standing or sitting, the horizon is always at your eye level.

b. No picture can have more than one horizon. Take any point on the horizon: it is called the vanishing point.

c. Draw radiating lines in all directions from the vanishing point. Fill in the spaces for "perspective."

d. Have each student make a cube by folding and stapling a piece of paper 2 x 9 inches (or hold a child's block).

e. Hold the cube at eye level. What do they see? Draw it.

f. Hold it above eye level. How many sides can they see? Draw them.

g. Draw the cube in at least 5 different positions.

h. Now hold the cube with one *edge* toward the eye and the sides turned away. Can they see the diamond shape? Draw it. Notice the slant of the side lines. If extended they would go to two vanishing points.

i. In one point perspective the lines all lead to one vanishing point. When you can see two sides of an object, you have two sets of lines leading to two different vanishing points.

j. To put a circle in proper perspective, put it in a square.

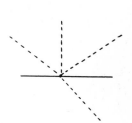

    k. To put a cylinder in proper perspective, put it in a rectangle.

6. Teach the Human Figure

The average human figure is divided into eight equal parts or eight "heads."

Children are 6 to 7 heads high.

Babies are about 4 heads high.

Clip magazine illustrations and outline basic shapes in the human figure.

Draw figures with cubes, rectangles, spheres and cylinders.

See what lines determine attitudes and action.

Practice drawing stick figures in different poses.

    a. Establish a line of action.

    b. Add the rib cage, pelvis and head.

    c. Add the arms and legs.

    d. Check for balance. (The weight of the body is always balanced on either side of an imaginary vertical line.)

7. Teach the Head and Face

Teach the "egg" shape and these general proportions:

the eyes are placed halfway between the top of the head and bottom of the chin

one eye space *between* the eyes

the nose is ½ the distance between the eyes and chin

the mouth is ⅓ to ½ the distance between the end of the nose and the chin

ears fit between the eyebrows and the bottom of the nose

the end of the mouth should line up with the center of the eyes

Teach the basic shapes of

 the eye
the ear

 the nose
the mouth

Have each child do several self-portraits and portraits of his friends.

a. Take a 9 x 12 sheet of manila paper.
b. Cut out an egg shape (or the shape that most nearly matches the student's face).
c. Fold in half or measure for eye placement.
d. Measure for the eyes, nose, and mouth. Draw them in.
e. Take a second sheet of 9 x 12 paper—any pastel color. Cut out a body shape (shoulders and neck). Paste behind the chin. Mount on a third sheet of paper.
f. Add eyes, hair, collar and name.

Have students make quick portrait sketches of student models with charcoal and newsprint. Aim first for accurate *placement* of features, *then* for resemblance.

Time the sketches: 5 minutes, 3 minutes, 2 minutes. Stress that students are not working for finished portraits but to practice placing features, analyzing basic shapes and catching expression.

8. Teach Expression

To emphasize the subtleties of expression, use cartoon forms. Cartoons are simply an exaggeration of basic forms and will give students an immediate awareness of what makes the face look sad, happy, or frightened.

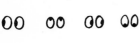

Name the expression. Ask students to act it out and to look carefully at each other to see what happens to the face. Let them practice with crayon or charcoal on newsprint—bold and exaggerated forms at first, subtleties later.

a. First let's look SAD at each other—what do we see? Everything seems to go down.

b. Now look happy at each other—everything goes up!

c. Suppose I handed you a million dollars. Would you be surprised? Show a lot of the white of the eye.

d. What do our eyes do when we look around?

e. When we go to sleep or simply get sleepy, what happens?

f. How can we keep from staring? Put on a top eyelid.

g. What if we are afraid?

h. What happens if we are angry? furious? just perturbed?

i. What if we are skeptical?

j. And if we are sitting quietly and peacefully, how do we look?

9. Teach the Hand and Foot

Emphasize the basic forms of the hand and foot in many different positions. Let them use their own or a neighbor's as models.

10. Teach Familiar Animals

They should be familiar with the basic shapes and forms of the animals they are likely to include in their paintings and drawings:

dog   horse
cat   bird
rabbit   elephant
cow   bear

11. Teach Standard Symbols

There are specific lines which represent motion, power, action and reflection. Students should be taught all of these.

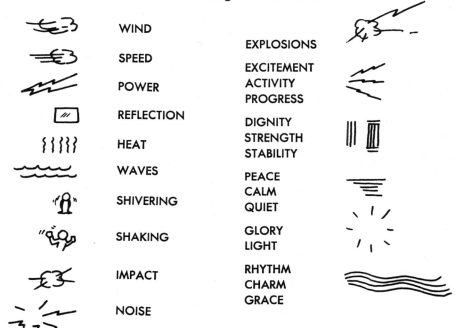

	WIND
	SPEED
	POWER
	REFLECTION
	HEAT
	WAVES
	SHIVERING
	SHAKING
	IMPACT
	NOISE

EXPLOSIONS

EXCITEMENT
ACTIVITY
PROGRESS

DIGNITY
STRENGTH
STABILITY

PEACE
CALM
QUIET

GLORY
LIGHT

RHYTHM
CHARM
GRACE

12. Teach Them to Cartoon

Cartoons are simply exaggerations of the basic shapes. The circle, oval and pear are the most important for students to learn. Begin by having your students fill several sheets of newsprint with these three shapes.

Progress to the stick figure:

a. Exaggerate the line of action.
b. Use the circle, oval or pear.
c. Add arms and legs.
d. Check for balance.

Expression is important! Accentuate, exaggerate!

Hands and feet are very important in cartooning. Note that cartoon characters do NOT have five fingers.

A few strokes of a cartoonist's pencil produces a stronger editorial than could be put into a column of type. . . . it tells amazingly much in an amazingly small space.

—Harlan Tarbell

13. Teach Composition

The camera duplicates a scene exactly but the artist may be selective. Help your students see that rearrangement and selectivity are a must in planning a composition.

Take students on a sketching hike around the classroom, the schoolyard and the neighborhood. Each student should carry a

- ✔ picture finder (a piece of cardboard with a ¾" square opening)
- ✔ small sketchpad
- ✔ soft pencil

Each person should bring back to class at least a dozen miniature compositions which he found through his picture finder:

- close ups
- unusual perspectives
- silhouettes
- interesting lines

Teach students that the eye should travel easily and naturally through a composition. The picture should have a definite *eye pathway*—through, in, around, back through the composition. It should never lead out of the picture!

Bring reproductions of famous and familiar paintings, advertising art and magazine illustrations. Cover them with acetate sheets and trace the eye's pathway. Can the students determine what kept the eye moving? Was it line or color? What keeps the eye from leaving the picture?

14. Sketch Sessions

Schedule as many sketch sessions as you possibly can. Use

newsprint (inexpensive) and soft pencil, charcoal, or crayon with chiselled and rounded points.

Practice with still life and student models—

- Studies in light and shade
- Action
- Still life composition
- Portraits
- Details of texture

Time the sketches: 10 minutes, 5 minutes, 3 minutes, 1 minute. Sad results *at first* but students quickly learn to catch a basic line and get it on paper. Don't grade these! No pressure—just an opportunity for practice.

Take them on *Sketching Safaris.* You will find a wealth of material right around you:

- The Waterfront
- The Zoo
- The Park
- Farms or ranches
- A construction area
- The schoolyard
- Neighborhood streets
- The seashore

Assign a minimum number of sketches. Use these as the basis for finished drawings or paintings back in the classroom.

Ask them to bring in "homework" from their own neighborhoods:

Sketches showing:

- ► the height of their house as compared to a tree
- ► A tree silhouetted
- ► Unusual cloud formations
- ► A flower from the garden

15. Teach Them to Letter

An often neglected but all important area is *Lettering*. Sloppy, crowded, run-away captions and titles should be unacceptable on student exhibits, posters, scrapbooks and art work.

Just as we are not striving for finished artists, we do not expect professional letterers from our classroom. But learning to use the proper tools and recognizing the importance of careful lettering should be definite goals.

> *Lettering is so largely a matter of design and a feeling for what is right and proper in its place, that it is very difficult to lay down hard and fast rules, but in the beginning it is very necessary.*
>
> —*Russell Laker*

Cardinal Rules for Classroom Lettering

1. Always use a straight edge.
2. Always balance the letters and space them correctly.
3. Always sketch the message in pencil before attempting to letter in ink.
4. Always choose the correct tool to express the message: one which makes light lines, bold lines, firm or free lines.

a. Lettering tools

Proper equipment is neither costly nor difficult to obtain. The dime store can meet many of your requirements.

T-Square: For your purposes the plastic 12″ T-Squares in the dimestore are sufficient.

Triangle, or *Ruler:* A good straight edge is essential.

The Zaner-Bloser Company has a clear plastic ruler with lines and squares for lettering and layout projects. A 1" x 6" ruler costs 30¢.

The Zaner-Bloser Company
612 North Park Street
Columbus, Ohio 43215

Pen Staff and Points: Get a #170 for all-round regular work. Speedball sets have variety and are reasonably priced.

Magic Markers: In a variety of colors.

India Ink: In a variety of colors.

Slick-Surface Newsprint: For practice sessions.

Remember that India ink will NOT wash out. Insist that students wear a smock or some sort of protective clothing.

b. Practice sessions

Lots and lots and lots of practice sessions! Let your students discover what can be accomplished with the tools at hand.

- Draw lines with the straight-edges.
- Use a variety of pen points.
- Practice different hand positions to achieve different strokes.

After students are familiar with the basic lettering tools, give them practice sessions in spacing, choosing a style and actually lettering words or slogans.

c. The alphabet

The manuscript alphabet your students learned in Penmanship should be the beginning alphabet for your lessons in Lettering.

MEMO

Rand Holub has published a lettering manual for beginners. His alphabet has the basic strokes of manuscript printing. The dialogue and explanatory text with the many illustrations would provide you with a wonderful lesson plan. Just what to say, just what to do!

LETTERING SIMPLIFIED
Rand Holub

Watson-Guptill Publications, Inc.
Watson-Guptill
Publications, Inc.
1957

d. Spacing

Good spacing is NOT measuring each letter and giving all letters equal space. Good spacing IS adjusting letters according to their weights and the white space surrounding them.

Nothing takes the place of the letterer's eye in judging good spacing.

Sketch the letters in pencil; squint through one eye and judge for yourself how well the letters are spaced along the line.

e. Personality in print

All manner of ideas, feelings and emotions can be conveyed through hand lettering. Dignity, boldness, speed, charm, grace, historical periods, fear, climate, awkwardness—the letterer is limited only by his imagination and his ability to handle his tools!

Type faces are highly individual. They give character to the printed page. Type may be delicate or brutal, refined or baudy, conservative or aggressive.
—William Longyear

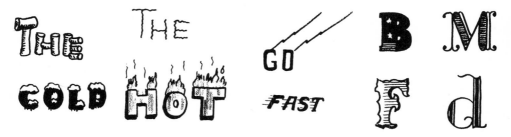

Scrapbook collections, charts and bulletin boards will give your students an awareness of personality in print. Let them design their own alphabets in character letters. Ask them to print a slogan or a statement in character letters. See how closely they can portray a mood, an idea or an emotion through lettering.

CHAPTER 13

Far-Reaching
Field Trips

*The world is a country which nobody ever
yet knew by description: one must travel
through it one's self to be acquainted with it.*
—Chesterfield

The following questions were asked of Ruth Gross whose
unusual and interesting field trip excursions were famous throughout North Florida and were often the subject of *Florida Times-
Union* feature articles.

1. What Can You Expect From a Field Trip?

A very special kind of learning! Firsthand knowledge is always exciting for the students, and there are many opportunities in and around every community for significant excursions.
They don't have to be formal—many times a walk around the
block will produce the very information needed in the classroom.

And remember, the trip does not have to include the whole

class; often one person or a small committee can do the job effectively.

Nor is it necessary for all trips to be made on school days or during school hours—evenings, holidays, and late afternoons offer many possibilities.

When your students have carefully prepared themselves for the trip, they are ready to use a dozen or more of the skills you are teaching in the classroom. They must plan, study, listen, observe, record and question. They must organize and review their material, then put it to work in reports, projects, discussions and displays. So, wherever you go, you can *and should* expect a lot from a field trip!

2. Where Should You Go on a Field Trip?

Anywhere and everywhere the textbook or classroom discussion can safely lead you! Don't overlook short walk field trips in the neighborhood. Be alert to opportunities around the playground.

I have taken my students to the airport, to restaurants, to the water works, churches and synagogues, banks and stock brokers, museums, homes, foundries, mines, the fair, gardens, to hear choirs and to watch artists at work. There is always somewhere wonderful and interesting to go!

MEMO

*More details on field trips can
be found on pages 213-222 of*

SOCIAL STUDIES FOR
CHILDREN IN A DEMOCRACY

Second Edition

by

John U. Michaelis

Prentice-Hall, Inc. 1956

and

pages 479-493 of

AUDIO VISUAL MATERIALS
AND TECHNIQUES

Second Edition

by

James S. Kinder

American Book Co. 1959

3. What Advance Preparations Must Be Made?

We form committees to help handle the details of planning. Then we write and request permission to visit, making an appointment for a specific day and time. In our letter we indicate the size of the group, the purpose of our visit and the grade and age level of our class.

We search for films, recordings and other reference materials which relate directly to the trip. Committees plan displays and give reports which help prepare us for what we will see.

Finally, we send a list of questions to our host which will show what we are hoping to learn from the trip. We send these, with an outline of our classroom study, several days before the visit.

4. How Many Trips Should the Class Take Each Year?

Many schools allow only two formal trips a year. But there's nothing to stop you and the parents from organizing a trip after school, in the evening, on Saturday, or during a holiday period.

5. What Do You Do for Transportation?

We usually engage a school bus but sometimes parents drive.

6. How Much Do the Trips Cost? Does the Student Pay His Own Way?

Transportation costs vary, but the children pay their share of the fare and for entrance fees and soft drinks. Funds are collected ahead of time to avoid embarrassing children who cannot pay.

7. Are Most of These All Day Excursions?

Yes. We usually leave right after school starts and try to be back as school closes. Sometimes we make arrangements for parents to pick up children after school is out.

8. How Do You Keep Track of All the Children?

We use the "buddy system" and each child knows he is responsible *for* and *to* another child. We never assign more than six to a single adult.

9. How Many Chaperones Go on the Trips?

Enough to separate the class into groups of six. Children wear name tags and each chaperone is given a sheet of our rules, standards and procedures well in advance of the trip.

10. What Safety Factors Have to Be Considered?

Children cannot buy bottled drinks. We observe silence at all stops. Hands must be kept inside the bus or cars. The rules of safety and behavior are discussed before we leave.

11. What Behavior Standards Are Set?

The group must stay together. Children must keep their voices regulated. Courteous attention must be paid to the host. If discipline problems arise, the children involved are isolated and deprived of the next field trip.

12. What Do You Do About Meals?

We carry sack lunches and thermos bottles, or arrange to buy soft drinks in cups. If we are still traveling at lunch time, we stop the bus before we eat. No eating while the bus is in motion.

13. What About Bathroom Facilities?

We locate a sanitary and attractive service station beforehand and get permission to use it.

14. Do the Students Have a Specific Assignment on the Trip?

Absolutely. We take notes and we sketch. Some carry cameras. Everyone makes a written report. Nothing should be left to chance. I tell them things to look for; they list questions they will want to ask; we discuss data which can be gathered and pictures which can be sketched or photographed. Sometimes we collect specimens. We prepare a "briefing sheet" beforehand:

Our Visit To _____

1. Our reasons for making this trip are:
   a.
   b.
   c.
2. We will be looking for:
   a.
   b.
3. We should pay particular attention to:
   a.
   b.
4. We should be able to discuss:
   a.
   b.
5. Our whole class assignment is:
6. My committee assignment is:

15. Do You Have Standards for Dress?

We do not allow shorts or slacks. The girls always wear dresses and the boys their regular school garb.

> *Students must be made aware that they are representing* their *school on an* educational *trip; therefore, they must look like school children and* not *like picnickers.*
>
> *—Stockton School*

16. Do You Refer to a Check List as You Plan the Trips?

I use a dittoed form which I file for future information:

1. Field Trip To: _____
   Contact _____
   Phone: _____
2. Distance From School: _____
   Transportation: _____
   Cost: _____
   Travel Time: _____

3. The Tour:
   Time Involved: _____
   Comments: _____
4. Eating Facilities: _____
   _____
5. Bathroom Facilities: _____
   _____
6. Interesting Sights En Route: _____
   _____
7. Chaperones:
   _____   _____   _____
   _____   _____   _____
8. Permission Slips:
   Filed in Office: _____
                              (date)
9. Thank You Notes to: _____
   _____   _____
10. Activities Relating to the Trip:
    _____
    _____

Also, every school has its own policy sheet. I file a carbon of ours with the above form. That gives me a complete record and a good basis for planning a future trip.

17. What Do the Students Do While They Are Traveling?

They sing, chat and play observation games. Sometimes I ditto a sheet of sketches showing the landmarks we will pass en route. They cut these up, reassemble and paste up their own individual "Bingo" sheets. They mark their papers as we travel, using the familiar Bingo rules to determine the winner.

18. Are the Follow-up Activities Planned Before the Trip?

Yes. Reports, projects, dramatics, poetry, art and music are outlined before we leave. Committees and individuals have their assignments in mind.

I also ask each child to critique the trip on the illustrated ditto form:

Field Trip To: _____
Date: _____
Name: _____

1. Do you think we were well prepared for what we saw?
2. Did you think the trip was interesting?
3. Were your questions answered?
4. What did you like best?
5. What did you like least?
6. What problems, projects or activities were suggested to you by the trip?
7. What did you feel about our class behavior?
8. Was there any way in which you felt we could have improved the trip?

19. What Do You Feel Are the Most Important Ingredients of a Successful Trip?

Planning and purpose make the difference! The class must know that the trip fits some part of a unit which they are studying. Every step must be thought about *before* starting out. All the persons who are to be a part of the trip should know his or her part in the venture. Children should be prepared to take notes, make sketches, and come away with material for classroom activities.

20. How Did You Handle Publicity?

The newspaper is usually interested in school activities. If your principal will notify them that the class is making a field trip, the paper will take it from there!

Have You Considered . . .

☐ Taking A Short Trip By—
   —Excursion Boat
   —Ferry
   —Tramp Steamer
   —Train
   —Bus
   —Bicycle
   —Hiking
☐ Dining—
   —Aboard ship
   —Aboard plane
   —In a foreign restaurant
☐ Searching For Specimens—
   —Soil
   —Rock
   —Agricultural
   —Plant life
   —Industrial
   —Fuel
   —Building material
☐ Photographing or Sketch-ing—
   —Land formations
   —Trees
   —Plant life
   —Construction sites
   —Unusual structures

☐ Touring an Area As—
   —Early Explorers
   —Early Settlers
   —Indian Scouts
   —Soldiers
☐ Visiting a Battlefield
☐ Touring a Fort
☐ Camping Out As—
   —Indians
   —Early Explorers
   —Settlers Traveling West
☐ Attending A—
   —Film
   —Musical
   —Opera
   —Recital
   —Play
   —Concert
   —Lecture
☐ Mapping an Area For—
   —Historical Events
   —Soil Conditions
   —Land Formations
   —Monuments
   —Trees

What's in Your Vicinity?

Airport	Craft exhibit	Fort
Bakery	Dairy	Gardens
Bank	Dam	Government offices
Battlefield	Department store	Grocery
Bottling plant	Excursion boat	Harbor
Bridges	Factory	Hatchery
Bus terminal	Farm	Highway Patrol
Cannery	Farmer's market	Historical sites
Cemetery	Ferry	Hospital
Churches and	Fire Department	Hotel
Cathedrals	Foreign restaurant	Laboratory
College campus	Forest Ranger	Library
Construction sites	Hqrs.	Livestock show

Lumber yard
Meat packing plant
Military installation
Mill
Mine
Monuments
Moving Company
Museums
National shrine
Newspaper
Nursery
Oceanarium
Oil rig
Parks

Planetarium
Police Department
Post Office
Power plant
Printing company
Radio station
Ranch
Refinery
Sanitation Dept.
Shipyard
Synagogue
Tannery
Taxidermist
Telegraph company

Telephone
  company
Television studio
Theatre
Train terminal
Travel bureau
Truck farm
Truck line
University campus
Veterinary hospital
Warehouse
Water works
Zoo

CHAPTER 14

Teaching Through "Make Believe" Trips

Through my coming to an understanding of other thought, my own became clearer.
—Albert Schweitzer

Many classes have suffered dull, informative, geography lessons on journeys across Canada. How few have shared, in imagination, the exploits, dangers, hardships, hopes and fears of the pathfinders and railbuilders, in traversing the forest and swamps and cutting their way through rocks and mountains to lay, mile by mile, the great Canadian Pacific Railway.
—L. Wilkes

Don't ignore the fascination of travel when you're planning your lessons! Students never tire of taking trips, be they real or imaginary—and arm-chair travel can be amazingly realistic. The most exciting way to become acquainted with one's state, coun-

184

try and world is through a trip. Take your students on a First Class Tour . . .

1. Making Plans

Arm-chair travel should be as accurate in detail, experience, and atmosphere as you can possibly make it. Many text books cover too much territory and go into too much detail. Students tend to bog down, to lose the excitement and adventure of learning about new places, new people and new ways of life.

There are people and agencies to contact, materials to gather, and committees to organize as you and your students begin the search for information that will make your trip come alive!

MEMO

Pan American Airways offers the teacher a bi-monthly publication, CLASSROOM CLIPPER. Each issue (free!) includes a study unit with text, pictures, a bibliography, list of audio-visual materials and a suggested teaching plan on one of the countries served by Pan American.

Write to:

> Educational Services
> Pan American Airways
> Pan Am Building
> New York 17, New York

Pan American also offers an inexpensive series of

> WORLD ROUTE MAPS
>
> and
>
> TRAVEL POSTERS

Write for the correct order form:

> Pan American Airways
> P. O. Box PAA
> Jamaica, New York

• Contact your local and state Chamber of Commerce, travel bureaus and transportation agencies. All of these people are in the

business of promoting what is worthwhile in an area. Ask them
for bulletins,
    brochures,
       pamphlets,
          folders,
            posters,
              speakers,
                slides,
                  films,
                    and

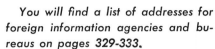

MEMO

You will find a list of addresses for foreign information agencies and bureaus on pages 329-333.

Write to them for information, brochures and posters about the countries you are studying.

       realia. They will be happy to help you with your
planning and to refer you to the agencies and individuals who
can help you the most.

• If you are traveling in this country, contact several filling
stations for road maps—one for each student—on which the
trip can be plotted.

• Ask your librarian for help with travel guides. The authors
of these highly interesting volumes spend a great deal of time and
money gathering pertinent and vivid material for their readers.

    ✔ Check out several guides for the same area.
    ✔ Use these books with their up-to-date information
       to add color and excitement to the facts and details
       in your textbook.

Take advantage of "the personal experience of a staff of editors
and writers whose exciting coverage of the world annually lures
tourists to foreign shores."

• Locate folk music, mood music and sound effects from the
area you will be visiting. Write to Folkways Records, Inc. for
their catalog of recordings. A few titles will give you an idea of
the scope of their catalog:

             Sounds of Steam Locomotives
             Sounds of American Southeast
             Lappish Folk Songs
             Songs of Four Continents
             Music of South Arabia
             Indians of the Canadian Plains
             Who Built America
             Eskimos, Alaska & Hudson Bay
             Man of the Whole Wide World

Russian Choral Music
Tribal Music of Australia
Finnish Folk Songs

Folkways Records, Inc.
117 West 46th Street
New York City 36, N. Y.

• Show as many films, slides and pictures of the area as possible. Re-run films without sound and discuss the picture in relation to the textbook.

2. Student Committees

Prepare a LET'S GO TRAVELING bulletin board with maps, pictures, clippings, folders, lists of questions and sign-up sheets for research committees:

- The Itinerary
- Best Routes
- Transportation
- Baggage Requirements
- Language
- Sightseeing
- Entertainment
- Budget & Financing

- Climate
- Food
- Lodging
- Cultural Aspects
- Industry
- Agriculture
- Customs of the Area
- Physical Features

Travel is an investment in yourself. If you put your money in stocks and bonds, you expect to get it back with earnings and, if you're lucky, with appreciation. But travel is an investment which, whether business is good or bad, pays dividends as long as you live.

—Strong-Runyon

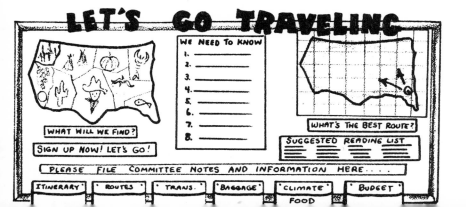

3. A Brief Case for Documents

Let each student prepare his own folder or "brief case" to carry the papers and documents you will be making and collecting in class:

Tickets	Booklets
Passport	Pamphlets
Shot records	Prints
Itinerary	Maps
Customs Forms	Pictures
Baggage tags	Notes

4. The Passport

If your trip takes you out of the country, have your class apply for passport information. Write to Passport Division, Department of State, Washington, D. C.

Have each student make his own passport and affix postage stamps from the different countries as each "border" is crossed in your studies.

5. Shot Records

Contact the Board of Health for immunization forms and information as to which shots are required and which suggested for the different countries. Let each student complete a form and attach it to his passport. Initiate a health unit on immunization!

6. Planning the Itinerary

With your textbook as a guide and a specific number of days or weeks to cover the material, work out an itinerary for your trip. Meet with a student committee in the classroom first and then ask for advice from an interested travel bureau.

The committee should determine:

    a. The number of countries, states or towns to be visited.
    b. The number of days in each place.
    c. The material to be covered, places to see, things to do at each stop.

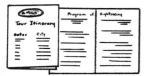

Have them ditto an itinerary for each member of the class. It can serve as an outline, an advance sheet and a souvenir!

As you go visiting and sight-seeing take some knowledge with you so you will "see more than stone and brick and mortar, and clammy corridors and musty corners and ancient sarcophagi."
          —Enid Evlin

7. Planning Transportation

There are at least six different ways of transporting yourself from one spot to another—trains, planes, cars, bicycles, boats, busses and on foot. Let your student committee plan for some of each in their journey—and then try to arrange some way for them to experience simulated or actual travel.

By Plane	By Ship
Visit an airport.	Visit a military ship.
*	*
Board an airplane.	Visit a transport vessel.

By Plane

Try to arrange for students to have a meal in the grounded plane.

*

Create an airline cabin in your classroom. Choose stewardesses to serve a meal to passengers. (TV dinners on pillows.)

By Bus

Make a short trip from your town to a neighboring town.

*

Tour the bus terminal.

By Train

Make a short trip from your town to a neighboring town.

*

Eat a meal in the diner. Have a coke in the Club Car.

*

Tour the train station.

*

Visit the different railroad cars: Pullman, day coach, etc.

By Ship

Visit a luxury liner.

*

Make a short trip on an excursion boat.

*

Make a crossing by ferry.

*

Try to arrange for students to have a meal on board a ship.

*

Create a ship's dining room in the cafeteria or a local restaurant for a *Captain's Dinner*. Talk to a Travel Agency about the details.

By Bike

Contact the Youth Hostelers Association for information on bike travel in this country and abroad.

*

Make a short trip by bicycle.

On Foot

Take a hike!

8. Financing the Trip

Let a committee exercise its skill in math by budgeting and financing the trip. With information from travel guides, the travel bureau and trip brochures, have a report prepared giving the approximate cost of travel, food, lodging and touring. If the trip is to be financed, let them explain the "Go now-Pay later" plans, pointing out the extra costs involved in financing.

(Number of) Weeks to *(Destination)*

By *(Means of Transportation)*

a. Passport:	$10.00
b. Round trip fare (Tourist Class, First Class)	_____
c. Rail travel (Eurailpass)	_____

d. Bus Travel　　　　　　　　　　　　_____
e. Automobile　　　　　　　　　　　　_____
f. Taxi　　　　　　　　　　　　　　　_____
g. Bicycle　　　　　　　　　　　　　_____
h. Living Expenses ___ days at $___ a day　_____
　　　　Youth Hostels　　　　　　　　_____
i. Miscellaneous expenses:
　　　　Snacks, postage, souvenirs, etc.　_____
j. Fare from home to port　　　　　　_____
k. Tour expenses, fares, during trip　　_____
l. Recreation: theatre, sports, museums,
　　　　dances, festivals　　　　　　　_____

MEMO

Check with your library—
Get a copy of

SO YOU'RE GOING ABROAD
Enid Evlin

Comet Press Books
New York
1958
and

TRAVEL ABROAD AT LOW COST
William A. Strong
A. Milton Runyon

Doubleday & Co. Inc.
1960-61

for an orientation to traveling out
of the country. Excellent!

Americans are worried about their overseas performance, and our friends abroad are worried about it too. The general sense of frustration on the subject has produced an intense desire to improve American education so that Americans are better prepared to assume international responsibilities.
                    —The Overseas Americans

9. Packing for the Trip

One committee should prepare information on baggage allowances, customs regulations and suitable wardrobes.

Have one suitcase for boys and one for girls packed by the committee. Weigh the luggage and check it through Customs. As each country or state is visited, paste a travel sticker on the cases.

10. Set Up a Ticket Counter in the Classroom

Include scales, time schedules, ticket booklets, customs policies, and the like. Have each student purchase the necessary tickets as shown on the itinerary: ship, plane, train or bus. Make up ticket forms on ditto stencils.

11. Sightseeing

Let one committee set up a detailed sightseeing program for each city, area, state or country visited. Their information would be gathered from the textbook, travel guides, pamphlets and brochures.

> **MEMO**
>
> *Eugene Fodor's*
> *Jet Age Travel Guides*
> *published by*
> *David McKay Co., Inc.*
> *of New York*
>
> *have organized the facts and fun of cities and countries in a most delightful manner. Have students refer to these as they prepare charts and reports.*

a. *The geography of the area*

Help students to see the inter-relatedness of geography, history and economics, the influence of geography upon the major activities of society. See that they understand and can visualize geographical features, that they build a vivid *mental* collection of pictures of the world.

1. "Home" Geography: The geography of the community offers the best concrete illustrations of forms, terms and features which students will meet in their textbooks.

Local springs, brooks, rivers, beaches, swamps, hills, valleys, meadows, and surface features furnish first hand knowledge of geography.

2. "Foreign" Geography: Films, models, maps, slides, pictures and charts will help to build concepts of geographical features far from home.

3. Physiography: Develop a simple outline of physical features and apply it to the study of each area:

> Country, state or county
> Capital
> Mountains, plateaus, plains
> Rivers, Seas
> Gulfs, Bays
> Capes
> Islands
> Peninsulas, Isthmuses
> Lakes
> Comparison of the area to local area

Only important and significant names should be listed in the outline. If they are important enough to be included, they should be memorized as part of the permanent body of geographical facts the student is learning.

4. Maps and Globes: Detailed and precise maps are important but so are sketches designed to show the shape of an area and the location of its important physical features. Give students lots of practice reading maps and globes and making maps of their own—physical, political, weather, special interest and historical.

> *Better that your students sketch one*
> *map ten times in 20 minutes than spend*
> *20 minutes on one sketch.*
> —*W. W. Charters*

Philadelphia should not be a mere dot, but a great city, throbbing with life and containing many spots of historic interest. Pike's Peak should be a great mountain, lifting its summit above the clouds and having its sides covered with loose, irregular fragments of rock. The black line crossing the United States from north to south should be the great river, with its changing banks bordered by fertile fields and bearing upon its bosom the commerce of great states.

—Public School Methods

b. Famous landmarks

Show films, post pictures and study textbook and guidebook illustrations of the famous landmarks in each place you visit. Review with flash cards and with sketches on worksheets. Students should be able to identify these important features without hesitation.

c. The cultural arts

Visit the museums, theatres and concert halls of the area through slides, prints, recordings and tapes.

Panorama, a division of Columbia Records, offers a monthly art program of slides showing paintings and art pieces in world famous museums.

The Instructor, Perry Pictures and *University Prints* offer inexpensive reproductions of paintings, sculpture and architecture.

d. The industry and agriculture of the area

Prepare product displays, charts and maps. Make still life drawings of the displays for notebooks and scrapbooks. Make dioramas showing the major occupations of the area.

12. Food on the Trip

By discussing, copying recipes and trying a few of the foods and favorite menus of other lands, other sections and other periods, students can begin to understand that—

foods and food preparation grow out of and reflect the living conditions of peoples.

Send a committee to the library and to their mothers' pantry shelves for a collection of cook books of regional and national dishes.

MEMO

We highly recommend

THE FOUR WINDS COOKBOOK

Cyril von Baumann

and

Beulah Phelps Harris

Thomas Y. Crowell Co.
New York
1954

It includes Latin American, Pacific Island, Far and Near Eastern, European and African cookery with recipes for soups, salads, meats, poultry, sea food, specialties, sauces, breads, pastries and desserts!

MEMO

Write for a copy of

BARTH'S
COLONIAL GARDEN
Valley Stream, N.Y.

It's a wonderful catalog of reasonably priced food specialties, seeds, candies, teas, accessories, toys and gifts from other countries and other historical periods. Authentic American regional foods, gifts and accessories!

Appreciation and adoption of the foods and cookery of many peoples is progress. In a world where attitudes have been determined chiefly by reactions to differences, what people eat and the way they eat it has long been one of the factors of prejudice.

—*U N Cookbook*

Split the class into groups of from 4 to 6 students. Let each prepare a different dish (or the same dish) of a country, section or period. These snacks and meals can be prepared on the playground, in the classroom, in the cafeteria or in the home with the help of room mothers.

If you aren't inclined to start from scratch with a recipe, let the grocery store help you. On its shelves you will find packaged, canned, mixed and bottled samples of the world's famous foods —spaghetti, pizza, New England chowder, chop suey, French bread, French onion soup, snails, Swiss cheeses and Dutch cheeses.

ADD SEVERAL COOK BOOKS TO YOUR CLASSROOM REFERENCE SHELVES

Don't be afraid of trying "foreign" dishes. They are neither mysterious nor peculiar. Every dish that has ever been cooked anywhere had a logical reason for its ingredients and method of preparation, and it is "foreign" to us only because we weren't raised on it.

—Beulah Phelps Harris

196

Whoever said that bread is the staff of life was an occidental isolationist, since most of the people in this world hardly touch the stuff. They lean on rice, which has four times the nutritional value of bread.

—Beulah Phelps Harris

Since the earliest settlers were equipped only with spoons and knives (forks came later), much of their menu was in the form of thick stews and soups made with chopped vegetables and meats.*

—Redbook

Long ago when the 20th Century was still young, Cuban bread was delivered in a horse-drawn bakery wagon, and the delivery-man, swinging the loaf of bread like a bat, would impale it on a nail hammered to the side of a customer's house.

—The Gasparilla Cookbook

Frontier people preferred sour milk to sweet, which was just as well, since there was no way to refrigerate it. Tea and coffee were not only scarce, they were also despised as "slops that don't stick to your ribs."

—Edwin Tunis

In every region of the United States we find foods that beg to be cooked and consumed outdoors. Culled from the generous yield of land and sea that provides us with some of the finest raw materials in the world, many of our alfresco feasts have remained virtually unchanged since the days when the pioneers first served them forth.

—Helen Evans Brown

Everyone knows that the feature of cooking in the Indian Ocean area is curry. What everyone doesn't know is that there is no curry in "curry"; that is, there is no curry powder in the dish called Curry.

—Beulah Phelps Harris

The gracious ritual of gathering for tea and conversation before a cheery fire has long been a favored English tradition.
—Elaine Ward-Hanna

13. A Taste of the Language

Learning a few phrases is no substitute for formal foreign language instruction but it does add real interest and flavor to the

* Quoted from "Festive Foods from an Early American Kitchen," from December, 1963 issue of *Redbook* magazine, © McCall Corporation, 1963.

textbook study of another country. And although not *foreign,* don't forget colloquial expressions, language patterns and distinctive vocabularies of different regions and different historical periods of our own country!

a. Phrase books, charts and flashcards

Libraries, book stores and travel agencies will help you find phrase books. From these you can make up charts, flashcards and even simple reading exercises.

Include a few words and a few phrases that deal with:

Courtesies
Numbers
Food and Drink
Directions
Colors
Dimensions
Common Nouns
Common Adjectives
Money
Shopping

b. Language records

Most libraries have several language courses on records and tapes. Tape sections that fit the needs and interests of your class and let them practice hearing and speaking correctly.

c. Simple reading lessons

Ditto simple paragraphs or conversations to be read and acted out in class. These can be used in short skits at the end of the unit.

d. Worksheets

Give the students a chance to practice recognizing and using their new vocabulary. Prepare simple completion and matching (with pictures) exercises on worksheets.

e. Sing-a-long

Learning the popular folk songs of a land is always fun. Music books, record shops, libraries and Folkways Records, Inc. catalogs can help you gather material.

f. *Play-a-long*

Learn and play one or two games from the country you are studying. Give simple directions in the language.

g. *Dance-a-long*

Learn one or two of the folk dances of the country. Dress in native-like costume and have a folk festival!

14. Have a Good Time on the Trip

Children are always interested in the games of other lands. They want to link themselves with others—what do these children play? Do we like the same things? Are they different from us?

Often the games are very much like their own—but the flaunting of a scarf or sash and the substitution of different words does give one the feeling of a far-away place! Play the folk games and national games of the countries or areas you are visiting.

> *Play in its many varied forms is universal and, like good music or a cheery smile, requires no interpretation. Games are a round-the-world passport, because the spirit of fun and play soon breaks down all barriers of misunderstanding, language, and creed.*
> —*Allan and Paulette Macfarlan*

Your library will have collections of games from regions of this country and the world.

And don't forget folk dancing!

> *Most of us know that folk dancing is a universal expression of social enjoyment with participation its keynote!*
>
> *We also realize that the heart of folk dancing lies in the reflected gaiety of*

the dancers reacting to the bubbling good spirits of the music.

So, let's put aside our degrees,—let's relax our dignity for just a bit and have a really good time with our children as we explore this true spirit of folk music and movement combined.
                    —*Dr. Kurt R. Miller*

15. How Can You Tell if They're Learning?

Tests are important but there are many other ways to check on how much your students are learning as they travel through these imaginary trips. Of one thing you can be sure—they will *never* forget these journeys, and quite possibly, if they find themselves exploring new lands in the future, they can trace their interest straight back to your classroom.

If the situation in which learning occurs is one in which pupils are having fun, the chances are greater that they are more nearly learning what the teacher hopes they will learn.
                    —*Kimball Wiles*

a. Notebooks and scrapbooks

Have each student keep a detailed record of the trip in a notebook and scrapbook. These can be graded at the end of the unit. Include:

Textbook notes
Guidebook notes
Lecture notes
Maps
Drawings
Pictures
Clippings
Reports

Take the best pages from individual books and use on the bulletin board.

b. *Letters home*

Just as any traveler sends cards and letters to the family, have your students write home throughout the trip. The correspondence should reflect both the facts and the fun of the trip. Postcards and snapshots add special interest. (Cut out snapshot figures of your students and paste them on an appropriate background.)

Munich, Germany
March 21, 1966

> Mom and Daddy,
I'm having such a good time! People
~ings differently here; They even sleep
~ntly. They have big funny blankets
feathers inside. The landlady gave
a red one. It sure keeps me warm.
Mrs. Träger took her children to
~nich and invited me to go along.
went for a walk in the mountains
we saw a beautiful flower called
~weiss. It reminded me of a daisy
it is much prettier.
They have signs that hang over shop
~ telling what each shop owner does.
doll maker next door has a little
~mer and a doll on his sign. I think
~ are called guild emblems. You don't
~ to read a word to know what the
~ is.
I am sending you a snapshot
~me in Garmisch.
Tomorrow we are driving to
~nberg. I will write you about
~ experiences.

STUDENT LETTER

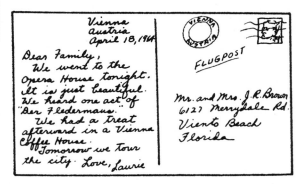

Vienna
Austria
April 18, 196?

Dear Family,
We went to the
Opera House tonight.
It is just beautiful.
We heard one act of
"Der Fledermaus."
We had a treat
afterward in a Vienna
Coffee House.
Tomorrow we tour
the city. Love, Laurie

FLUGPOST

Mr. and Mrs. J.R. Brown
6127 Merrydale Rd.
Viento Beach
Florida

c. *Diaries*

Have each student keep his own Diary of the trip—a paragraph or two summarizing each day's travels and sights, or use a group compilation for Experience Charts or Penmanship lessons. Illustrate the pages with drawings, prints and stamps.

d. *Projects*

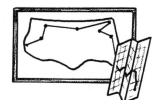

Chart the trip on a large wall map.

Let each student plot an individual map at his desk.

* * *

Ask students to prepare many types of maps as the trip progresses: historical, product, relief, special interest and the like.

* * *

Cut out a wallboard or plywood shape of the area you are traveling. Insert cuphooks at major points of interest. Prepare cardboard cutouts: symbols for cities, products, landmarks, geographical features. Add them to the "map" as they are visited. Use them for review purposes.

* * *

Assign models, dioramas, sand table displays, posters, bulletin boards, murals, movies and puppets.

The accuracy with which these projects are completed will indicate as clearly as a written test just how much your students are learning.

Open your treasure chest and relive every enchanting moment. Was it fun? You bet it was! Did it really happen to you? It certainly did! Will you ever go again? And how!

—*Enid Evlin*

CHAPTER 15

The

Activity Day

*True physical education is not only education
of the physical but also education through
the physical.*

           —Kathleen Tiemersma

*Any materials or techniques which make
learning more dynamic and more realistic will
undoubtedly foster better learning.*

           —James S. Kinder

    Physical activities often spark interest in an academic lesson
that is dragging. The children themselves like to work a new
angle on an old favorite—history, science and literature through
mimetics, story plays, folk dancing and sports! This can be the
basis for an Activity Day: a morning, afternoon or evening devoted to restaging a textbook event—turning paragraphs and
pages into a dynamic classroom experience.

Activity Days offer children a chance to participate in the customs, games, contests, hardships and festivals which have been a part of Man's life throughout the ages. Reading about the Olympics is one thing; participating in your own is quite another. Knighthood? A covered wagon journey? A land rush? Afternoon tea in London? Sharing fish with the Eskimos? Arguments and debates from the Continental Congress? Putting a bill through the House of Representatives? Choose your event and plan an Activity Day around it!

PLANNING AN ACTIVITY DAY

1. Choose your theme.
2. Assign committees to research every aspect of the event.
   a. Locate every visual aid
      > biographical sketch
      > anecdote
      > story
      > recording
      > article
      > quotation
      > illustration
      > and
      > bit of regalia that will bring the event into sharp focus.
   b. Prepare a reading list.
   c. Set up a special corner with reference books. Urge the students to read as widely as possible: excerpts or whole selections of poetry,
      > stories,
      > biography,
      > folk tales
      > and
      > reference works.
3. Plan a definite program of events based on the committee findings.
   a. Plan for every single minute. No time lags.
   b. Plan so carefully that you can move from one activity to another without confusion.
   c. Keep the activities energetic.
   d. List more activities than you will have time for. If interest begins to wane, switch to another.
   e. Every child should take an active part in the program of events.
4. Draw a plan of the area (playground, classroom, gym) in which the events will be held.

  a. List props and equipment.
  b. Be sure all items are collected a day or two before the event.
5. If the activities are to be indoors, consider
  a. Noise factors
  b. Safety factors
  c. Breakable objects
6. If the activities are to be out of doors, consider
  a. Noise factors
  b. Safety factors
  c. Substitute plans in case of rain
7. If costumes are to be worn, check two days before the event to be sure each student has prepared an outfit.
8. If events are competitive, consider:
  a. Teams
    1) Divide class by age, height, weight, size, energy, endurance, strength and spirit.
  b. Ground Rules
  c. Scoring
  d. Prizes and Awards
  e. Safety
    1) For any game involving possible contact, have students wear soft shoes.
9. Establish definite behavior standards for observers and participants. Post the list. Halt all "horse play" at once. If any child becomes too boisterous, remove him from the group.
10. Use a whistle and demand prompt obedience to it.
11. If you will need assistance, ask parents well in advance of the event. Be sure they are given a copy of the ground rules and behavior standards.
12. If food is involved, arrange for:
  a. Storage
  b. Preparation
  c. Cooling or heating
  d. Cooking and serving utensils
  e. Serving committee
  f. Clean-up committee
13. Keep notes on all phases of the Day. Use a ditto form to help you plan.

PLAN SHEET FOR ACTIVITY DAY

Theme:
Date of Event:
Number of Students:
Time of Event:

Research Committees

Activities

Schedule
:00
:15
:30
:45
:00
:15
:30
:45
:00

Special Equipment

Costumes

Safety Rules - Work Rules

Competitive Events
Teams:
Scoring:
Awards:
"Ground Rules"

Food
Cooling/Heating:
Utensils (Cooking-Serving):
Serving Arrangements:
Storage:
Clean-Up:

Sun   Mon   Calendar for Planning   Thur   Fri   Sat

Adult Assistants   Evaluation   Thank You Notes

1. The Oklahoma Land Rush: An Activity Day in Detail

During a study of the Southwest one 5th grader wondered, "What's a Sooner and why is Oklahoma called The Sooner State?" The ensuing discussion so stimulated the class that a project lasting several weeks was developed. Study of the period was correlated with all areas of the curriculum:

- *Language Arts:* Reading legends and stories of the period.
  Writing an original play.
  Composing poetry about the West.
  Compositions on the joys and hazards of the period.
  Special vocabulary studies.
- *Arithmetic:* Old methods of measure.
  Areas, perimeters, liquids and solids.
- *Science:* Indian lore.
  Pathfinding.
  Trail blazing.
  Fire building.
  Shelters.
  Food value of wild edible plants.
- *Art:* Paintings.
  Drawings.
  Dioramas.
  Scenery for the play.
- *Music:* Songs and dances of the period.
- *Phys. Ed.:* Square dancing.

The class worked together on maps, the history, geography and government of the period. Special committees researched ways of cooking and common recipes of the period, costumes, transportation and colorful personalities.

Reference materials were gathered from home, school and public libraries. Among the resource people who spoke to the class, some had taught among the Indians, some knew Indian crafts, some knew Indian tales which had come down for generations from "tongue to tongue."

The final day of the unit work the class staged a Land Rush:

a. A day as close to April 22 as possible was selected.

b. The school playground was divided into 80 foot squares (one square foot represented one square acre).

c. Fathers drove stakes at intervals within the play areas. These were used as starter points for the rush.

d. The class was divided into family groups. Equipment for each group was arranged at the starter line.

e. The class presented an original play telling of a family on the trail heading for the Oklahoma Land Rush. The last line of the play was the signal for each family to leave the stage and gather behind their wagons on the playground.

f. At 12:00 noon the rush signal was sounded and the rush began.

g. Each family had a scout whose duty it was to locate one of the stakes. When he discovered one, he and his family were to "lay off" the surrounding land (80 sq. ft.) and pitch their camp.

h. A prize was awarded the family who pitched the most comfortable camp in the least time.

i. When the camps were finished, Mothers served lunch from a Chuck Wagon in the field.

j. Girls wore sunbonnets, billowing skirts, and blouses. Boys were dressed in cowboy hats, plaid flannel shirts and dungarees.

MENU

Corn Bread
Brown Beans
Western Stew
Gingerbread
Apple Juice

k. Wagons were children's wagons and wheelbarrows with wire frames covered by sheets and cloth. Equipment included:

> Shovels
> Hoes
> Water barrel
> Tents
> Log piles
> Cooking equipment
> Quilts
> Rope

l. A staff writer and photographer from the Jacksonville *Florida Time's Union* were on hand to give full newspaper coverage to the event.

2. Schedule of a Pioneer Activity Day

2:30   Leave school on bus
2:45   Arrive at Settlement for a snack of punch and buttered bread
3:00   Pioneer Children's Games
3:30   Dunk for apples
Begin Contests
    a. Spoon and potato race
    b. Sack race
    c. Two-on-a-log race
    d. Log rolling
    e. Hand wrestling
    f. Foot wrestling
    g. Relay race
    h. Leap frog relay
    i. Wheelbarrow race
5:00   Wash up for supper
5:10   Bidding for Box Suppers
5:30   Eat supper
6:00   Spelling Bee
6:20   Square Dancing
6:30   Pioneer songs around the fire
6:40   Square Dancing
7:00   Leave for homes

Competition was by family groups —10 students to a family.

Bidding was with packages of dried beans. Each boy drew a packet out of a hat. He could only bid as high as the number of beans in his packet (15 to 40).

3. Schedule of Olympic Games Activity Day

11:30 Greek Banquet served by the girls

11:50 Greek Tragedy presented by the 6th graders

12:00 Selections from The Illiad for Story Hour

12:20 Division of teams:
      Athens vs. Sparta
    Discussion of events
    Discussion of rules and standards
    Gathering of equipment
    Preparation of Olympic Field

12:50 Beginning of competition
    a. Javelin throw
    b. Discus throw
    c. Hand wrestling
    d. Chariot race
    e. 50 Yard dash
    f. Relay race
    g. Marathon

2:00   Gather in Amphitheatre to hear scores announced.

Captain of winning team awarded Crown of Leaves

All students were dressed in sheets.

In each event an Athenian competed against a Spartan. Winners received 5 points and the losers 2 points.

Every child competed in every event.

4. Schedule of Middle Ages Activity Day

10:30   Hour long program for parents and friends including the Knighting of A Squire and presentation of Shakespeare's MACBETH

11:45   Ten course banquet for the whole class in the classroom

12:30   Stories of King Arthur for Story Hour

1.00   Tournament on the Lists
    a. Horse races
    b. Sword fights
    c. Jousting
    d. Knights spear Rings

2:00   Best Knight receives Jeweled Sword as a trophy

5. Schedule of a Revolutionary War Activity Day

10:00	Poems and a film in the classroom
	Student reports
11:00	Gather equipment and move to points shown on maps drawn in class
11:05	Lantern signal given
11:06	Revere and Dawes start their rides
11:10	British troops begin their march
11:20	Skirmish at Lexington
11:30	British march to Concord
11:40	Battle at Concord
11:50	The Retreat
12:00	All troops gather in Colonial and British Camps for Field Mess

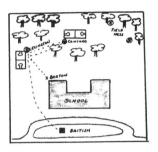

6. Schedule of a House-Raising—Sewing Bee

1:00 The girls gather in a decorated corner of the classroom to piece a small patchwork quilt.

A parent led the sewing session.

At the same time the boys gathered in the other end of the room to raise a pioneer cabin.

The framework had been cut by parents. Students assembled and covered the frame.

> 2:30   Refreshments were served by the girls
>
> 2:45   The "Throwing of the Quilt"

7. Early Days Antique Show

Following a unit on the early days of Ithaca, New York, students raided attics and basements to gather a collection of early American clothing, utensils, tools, maps, paintings and furnishings.

After considerable research on each item, guests were invited to view the displays and read the information cards. Children were by each display to answer additional questions about the articles.

Tea and cookies were served to the guests.

8. A Yurt on the Khirghiz Steppe

Students built a round felt yurt for their Activity Day on the Khirghiz Steppe, the treeless grassy plains of Russia.

Cheese, bits of fried dough and kumis (milk) was the Kazak meal for these nomads.

The strange dwelling, food and clothing of their day on the Steppe brought another part of our world into sharp focus for middle graders.

9. Baffin Island Afternoon

Igloos were constructed by draping sheets over desks and chairs. Children wore coats, boots, parkas, hoods. Windows were wide open on a cold winter's day and the atmosphere was authentic. Raw fish (sardines) and hot tea were served while stories, games, songs and dances of the Eskimos were enjoyed. Recordings of a Folkways album, *Eskimos, Alaska and Hudson Bay,* gave the excitement of sound effects.

10. Covered Wagon Journey

One wagon was constructed and packed according to textbook and reference book research. Students made an hour's trek through the snow with their wagon. The trail included a steep hillside and it was no easy task to get the loaded wagon to the top. Midway through the journey the boys pitched camp and the girls prepared and served a meal. Another hour from the camp site and the wagon and travelers were back at school.

11. Knighting a Squire

The squire's preparation for Knighthood was studied in detail. One member of the class was chosen to be the Squire and he prepared himself as directed. The ceremony was part of a program to which parents and other guests were invited. A banquet and tournament followed the Knighting.

12. Safari

Following a study of the African continent, children made a field trip safari to the zoo. Sketch pads and notebooks were their "ammunition." There were specific assignments for pictures and reports. A plaque was awarded to the student whose "hunting" was most accurate.

13. An Afternoon in Paris

Cheese, French bread and champagne (ginger ale) were served in a sidewalk cafe while French songs and French music were enjoyed. Ladies modeled Paris fashions. Artists painted scenes of the city. Slides of France and a travel film were shown.

14. Afternoon Tea in England

Scones, muffins, tea cakes and hot tea with cream were on the Tea Table. Nursery rhymes with their historical significance were recited, a recording of Queen Elizabeth II's coronation was heard, Drury Lane and selections from "My Fair Lady" were part of the program and a travel film on England was the final activity.

15. Along the Amazon

Coarse twine, bamboo poles, dried grasses, raffia, real and paper leaves were the basic materials for an Indian dwelling in the make-believe rain forest.

Patterned Corobuff gave an authentic background to the scene. The waters of the Amazon were added with tempra.

A parrot and several parakeets visited the class for a few days to add to the tropical atmosphere.

Sweet potatoes, fruits, fish and a bubbling meat stew were washed down with coconut milk on the Activity Day.

Girls wove baskets, created simple dishes out of clay and ground kernels into corn meal; boys practiced dart blowing skills and worked on a dugout, blow guns and fish nets.

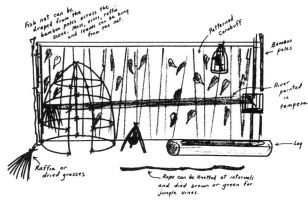

16. What Can You Do?

✔ Spend a day as an Indian tribe.

✔ Turn your classroom into the Mediterranean Lands.

✔ Become a Conquistador exploring for Spain.

✔ Get involved with politics—a two party election with banners, platforms, speeches, slogans, posters and promises.

✔ Plan a Classroom Congress with special committees, the introduction of bills, debates and voting.

✔ Plan an Old South Barbecue, a New England Clambake, a Hawaiian Luau.

✔ Go panning for gold in Alaska, gather sap for a sugaring off in Vermont, wage a campaign from the chronicles of military history.

✔ Dine with chopsticks in a Chinese restaurant, try smoked eel with the Dutch.

✔ Flip through the pages of your textbooks and readers for "any materials or techniques which make learning more dynamic and more realistic!" Choose your event and plan your Activity Day around it!

CHAPTER 16

Putting on a Program

Our task is to provide enough direction to give the pupils a sense of security but not enough to discourage initiative.

—Kimball Wiles

Dramatization adds realism, interest, and zest to instruction, and, if kept within reasonable bounds, makes learning more vivid and intense. It is a type of activity that breaks down barriers to co-operation.

—James S. Kinder

Classroom programs can be about *anything* your students are learning! History, English, Math—there are dramatic possibilities, related folk tunes, rhythms, poetic notations, pop tunes and dances which can give depth and dimension to all of your lessons.

Let your students put on the show! From start to finish, the programs should reflect *their* ingenuity. Elaborate planning, costuming, stage setting and equipment are unnecessary.

Take your themes from current lessons and every rehearsal will serve as a review.

Of course, there *are* some things you must tend to—and here is a check list to help with the planning. Science Fair, Open House, Operetta or Play—we urge you to attempt something grand and extravagant!

PLANNING A PROGRAM

☐ 1. Try to plan for an hour of entertainment.

☐ 2. Audiences enjoy variety: dramatics, music, singing, reports, poetry, choral reading and films all on the same program!

☐ 3. Keep things moving. Fill every minute. Pay attention to transitions—avoid long pauses between selections.

☐ 4. Plan "relief drills" as part of the program: have the audience stand for patriotic songs or the pledge to the flag. You may need an intermission.

☐ 5. Strive for audience participation: singing, clapping, responses.

☐ 6. Advertise. Send invitations, put up posters, mail out a bulletin.

☐ 7. Prepare the guest list carefully. Make certain that invitations are issued early enough for guests to plan to attend. Try to avoid conflicts with other important activities. Pick your date after checking the calendar.

☐ 8. Give a dress rehearsal. Invite another class. Ask for a critique. Welcome suggestions.

☐ 9. Check equipment just prior to guests' arrival. If films are being shown, make sure an extra bulb is available for the projector.

☐ 10. Prepare souvenir programs.

☐ 11. Choose a host and hostess to greet guests and distribute programs.

☐ 12. Discuss good manners and courtesy with the whole class.

☐ 13. Keep the room cool. Open the windows before the guests arrive and lower the temperature. Be sure of adequate ventilation. A hot room causes restlessness. Performers and guests are not attentive.

☐ 14. Plan a few minutes after the program for parents and guests to visit with the students.

☐ 15. Be sure to write thank you notes to everyone who assisted.

☐ 16. Once the program is underway, relax and enjoy yourself!

1. Writing an Original Play

a. THE LEGEND OF THE CHEROKEE ROSE was written and produced by a 5th grade class after a social studies unit on Oklahoma and homesteaders.

b. The script was prepared after several weeks of textbook study and committee research.

c. Round table discussions, based on the classroom lessons and the special research reports, led to the development of

    1) a situation, and

    2) a plot.

d. More discussions led to the elimination of extraneous material and a tightening of the plot.

    1) The Writing Committee took notes during these discussion periods.

e. The Writing Committee worked up the preliminary dialogue.

    1) More class discussion led to a refinement of the dialogue.

f. When the class was satisfied with the script, parts were assigned and copies of the play were distributed.

g. Props, costumes and scenery were worked out by committee groups as the rehearsals progressed.

Excerpts from
THE LEGEND OF THE
CHEROKEE ROSE

—5th Grade, Stockton
Elementary School

Time: April, 1889

Setting: An open spot on the prairie

Opening Scene: The Indian Chieftains of the five civilized nations are holding a pow-wow. They sit in the rank of their nation's importance, with Great Eagle, the Cherokee Chief, in the middle.

GREAT EAGLE: For many moons, my brothers, we have been friends. We have carried the tomahawk together. We have hunted the buffalo and we have smoked the Pipe of Peace. Today we meet; Great Eagle brings bad news from the Great White Father.

FIRE FACE: Great Eagle speaks wise words—Red Man listens.

GRAY HAWK: Great Eagle, our brother, Thunder Cloud of the Choctaw Nation, is not among us. We cannot start.

GREAT EAGLE: Sun sets soon. Evil gods cast long shadow. Great Eagle no longer can wait for slow friends. All Indian nations have waited many moons for Great Eagle's return.

———

GREAT EAGLE: Great Eagle sorrowful—Great White Father say to tell my brother chieftains that Indian hunting grounds, all Indian plains and prairies must go to white man. Indian must move over. Great White Father say Indian must be peaceful—no "trail of tears" as when our fathers came across Great Smoky.

BRAVE BULL: When white man come? Brave Bull see many white men on horses, in wagons on the trail. Make much dust.

FIRE FACE: Fire Face see great fire wagon on steel tracks make much smoke, go fast like wind.

GREAT EAGLE: The white man comes from the north, the south, the east, the west. He comes on horses, in wagons, by train, anyway to reach the middle of our Red Land. It will go to the ones who reach here first.

BRAVE BULL: What day do they race for our land?

GREAT EAGLE: On the third sun, after the first full moon, in the month of showers. When shadow shortest, the white man runs. That will be what white man calls April 22 at the hour of 12 Noon.

The play continues with the settler's point of view. The closing lines were a signal for the students to leave the auditorium and gather on the playground for the 12 Noon signal of their own Land Rush.

Fifth Grade Homesteaders Scramble for Claims as Land Rush Opens

IN OKLAHOMA

34 Fifth Graders Stage Land Rush

By RICHARD A. MARTIN
Times-Union Staff Writer

A band of land-hungry homesteaders carved up an empire yesterday in South Jacksonville.

In a half-pint Oklahoma land rush that was exceeded only in physical dimensions by the original thing, 34 fifth graders of Mrs. Ruth Gross' class at John N. C. Stockton Elementary School, demonstrated how learning can be fun.

The boys and girls, decked out in frontier garb, stood at a starting line beside their covered wagons on the school grounds, waiting for high noon and the signal to race for their claims.

By order of President Benjamin Harrison, the original Oklahoma Territory was opened to settlers at high noon on April 22, 1889. Some 20,000 took part in the rush for 180-acre homesteads, but the many who slipped in ahead of the gun instigated the name Sooner State.

No Sooners This Time

There were no Sooners in the small-scale re-creation of that event yesterday, as the Oklahoma Territory of nearly two million acres was whittled down to fifth grade size to fit into the Stockton School grounds.

The boys and girls went at the land rush with a spirit that would have done a Sooner proud. And why not? At stake was a box of candy for the winning team with the best camp.

The event culminated several weeks study of the Southwest, including Oklahoma, and was preceded in the morning by a play complete with cowboys and Indians, naturally.

As a result, many of the girls were decked out in sun bonnets and billowing skirts of "homespun," while the boys tried to look as much like 19th Century clod-breakers as possible.

One little girl, Mary Ford Barnett, 11, took the homespun idea literally, and made her own costume complete with bonnet. Michael Anchors—whose crew won the candy prize—even sported a handlebar mustache to top off his convincing characterization of an 1889er.

But it was the covered wagons that took the most imagination. Mary Barnett, whose dress was white with a blue apron, decked a toy wagon with a cover in the same colors. Mike Anchors' outfit was complete with a water barrel, and at least one wheelbarrow with a cloud of white sheet hovering above it was in the starting line.

Claims Staked Out

The kids staked out 80-foot square claims, put up tents and even had log piles for their cooking fires nailed together so they could be set up quickly.

Looking on from windows were children of other classrooms. A line of mothers whose children were taking part in the land rush stood discreetly to one side watching the doings.

A chuck wagon dinner prepared by the moms, rounded out the program—with beef stew, cornbread, gingerbread and apple juice on the menu. It was a meal typical of the Western frontiersmen.

Said one 11-year-old pioneer between gulps of his mouth-watering stew. "Look at it." He leaned back against a pine tree and pointed out over the field where other boys and girls worked at their claims.

"Frantic. But fun," he said, probably echoing the sentiments of many a settler in the original land rush.

2. Adapting a Play From a Story

Any story from a reader or a library book can become a class-room play. Students can go through the text and turn the narra-tive into speeches.

HASTY PUDDING was prepared by a 3-4-5 grade combination class after one of the reading groups had been enchanted with the story in their Scott Foresman reader.

HASTY PUDDING

Time: Pioneer Days
Setting: Living room of a log cabin

PA: I'm all ready, Ma. The horses are hitched up. Come along, now.

MA: Just a minute, Pa. Now don't for-get, Betsy—you're in charge. Uncle John and Aunt Hilda will be here by dusk so you won't be alone tonight. You other children do exactly what Betsy says.

PA: I'm counting on you children to be-have. And don't forget to keep the fire going and to bar the door when it be-gins to get dark.

BETSY: I won't forget a thing, Ma and Pa. And I'm going to make Hasty Pud-ding for supper as a special treat!

ANNOUNCER: (Reads a paragraph taken directly from the book.)

BETSY: Oh my goodness—look how late it is and I haven't started my pudding. I'll hurry and do the milking. Tom, you and Martha finish your chores. The sun is already sinking in the west.

TOM: I'll do the milking, Betsy, so you can start the pudding. Gosh, it takes forever to make it and I don't want you to be so late we can't have any.

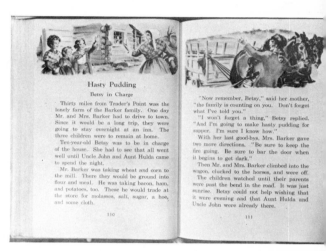

> Choose a story with dramatic possi-bilities! The children have an excit-ing visit from a wild bear before their aunt and uncle arrive.

* From *Child Life* magazine, Copyright 1936, 1964 by Rand McNally & Company, story by Cornelia Meigs.

3. Adapting a Play From the Classics

Teachers at any grade level can adapt the themes and stories of our great literature for simple classroom dramatizations. Follow the sequence of events in the original. Use as much of the original language and as many of the original speeches as possible. Transitional speeches should be written in the same style as the original.

A 4-5-6 grade combination class became intrigued with Shakespeare and adapted his MIDSUMMER NIGHT'S DREAM and MACBETH for classroom programs.

MACBETH

Time: Medieval Days

Setting: A lonely heath in Scotland

ANNOUNCER: Our story opens in ancient Scotland during time of war. The king has sent his trusted captains to defeat some rebels. Three witches meet on a lonely heath not far from the battle and plan to speak to Macbeth when he returns from the fighting.

1st WITCH: When shall we three meet again—in thunder, lightning or in rain?

2nd WITCH: When the fighting's done—when the battle's lost and won.

3rd WITCH: We'll meet Macbeth: fair is foul and foul is fair—through the fog and filthy air.

MACBETH: Well, Banquo, home we go to the king to report the details of the battle.

BANQUO: Macbeth! What are these? These creatures in such wild attire! They are so horrible . . . are they alive?

1st WITCH: All hail, Macbeth. Hail to thee, Lord.

2nd WITCH: All hail, Macbeth. Hail to thee, lord of two lands.

3rd WITCH: All hail, Macbeth. Hail to thee that shall be the king.

MACBETH: What? What is this these fiendish creatures say?

BANQUO: Macbeth, you look so pale. What has happened?

MACBETH: (aside) I cannot let him know I had a sudden vision when the witches spoke. I saw myself the King. But that's impossible. I cannot be the king. Unless . . . . unless . . . . but that is too horrible to consider.
Nothing is wrong, Banquo. Let us forget these strange witches. Let us hurry to the king to report our battle.

4. Adapting a Play From an Article

Did the Vikings leave this stone in Minnesota before Columbus?

Minnesota's Vikings

Hjalmar J. Holand, who was born 56 years ago in Norway and has lived since 1899 in Ephraim, Wis., where he now raises apples and cherries, was a happy man last week. Experts of the Smithsonian Institution had at last accepted a 31-inch slab of rock, carved in Norse runes which Holand first translated in 1908, as almost certain evidence that Norse explorers reached Minnesota 130 years before Columbus left Europe.

Known as the Kensington Stone, the carved slab was found in 1898 by a farmer named Olof Ohman when he was clearing some brush on a hilltop near Kensington, Minn. Its language was that of the Viking. It carried its own date—1362. Its brief message indicated that a party of 30 Norsemen had traveled deep into the American Continent and lost ten members as a skirmish with Indians. The survivors wandered whither they would ever get back to their own land.

Scholars, of course, knew Norsemen had colonized Iceland and Greenland and penetrated the northeastern fringe of the American Continent as early as the eleventh century. But an exploration as far west as Minnesota seemed fantastic. For half a century scientists tended to dismiss the carved stone as a rather crude hoax.

Sticks and Stones: But Holand, as curator of archives of the Ephraim Norwegian Society, took it seriously. For years he prowled through Northeastern Minnesota in search of supporting evi-

dence. Along lake shores he found steep-deeply chiseled for ring bolts to which the Vikings might have tied up their boats. In the same area he collected halberds, battle-axes, and swords of fourteenth-century style. He wrote three books on the story of the fourteenth-century Vikings. Meanwhile the Kensington Stone rested in local glory in the window of the Alexandria, Minn., chamber of commerce.

Last week it was conspicuous in the foyer of the National Museum in Washington. Archeologists of the Smithsonian Institution, while not completely convinced of its authenticity, called it "one of the most significant historical objects ever found in the New World." Evidence provided by Holand and others led them to reconstruct this story of the stone:

About 1362 the king of Norway sent an expedition of picked young men to reestablish contact with a lost colony in Greenland. Not finding the settlers there, the party went on, to Canada, traveling by boat through Hudson Bay and southward to central Minnesota.

For Posterity: "There is a very high probability," the Smithsonian statement said, "that the Kensington Stone was the despairing message to posterity of a party of doomed white men and Christians who had penetrated almost to the center of this continent more than a century before the first voyage of Columbus."

Holand's version of the event is less tragic. After some members of the party returned from a fishing trip to find ten of their companions "red with blood and dead" (in the words of the inscription,

50

A two column article in the Science section of Newsweek was the basis for a play written by a class of 6th graders. The play, THE KENSINGTON STONE, had three scenes: the farm of Olof Ohman in Kensington, Minnesota, the Ohman home, and the Smithsonian Institute in 1948. Characters, the story plot and situation were developed from the article. The dialogue was worked out by student committees.

Given the opportunity, most children will perform with sincerity and dignity. The amount of creative ingenuity which they display will be in proportion to the artistry with which the teacher inspires the pupils.

—N. F. Ryan

THE KENSINGTON STONE

Scene 1.

Place: Kensington, Minnesota
The farm of Olof Ohman.

Time: Noon about fifty years ago.

Setting: The Ohman family is working in the field.

HALVOR: Father, let's stop and eat.

OLOF: No, son, you know we must finish this row.

KARI: (who has been running up and down) Oh, oh, I stubbed my toe. Halvor, help me.

INGRID: Oh, Kari, why don't you look where you are going.

OLOF: Halvor, move the stone out of the row for your little sister.

HALVOR: I can't, father. It is too heavy. Can you come?

OLOF: Well, Halvor, it is heavy and queer, too. Look, there is strange writing on it.

HALVOR: Can you read it, father? What does it say?

KARI: Read it, read it; I want to hear a story!

HALVOR: Oh, Kari, you only think of stories.

KARI: Oh, I know the Wagtails left it—they did, they did!

OLOF: Come, Son, let us finish our work. There are many strange things in this land.

INGRID: Yes, finish your work and let's go to dinner. I have made fish cakes and coffee.

After the father and mother go to the house the children hang behind.

KARI: Listen, Halvor, this evening let's bring our sled up and take the rock to the house—the Wagtails would not like us to leave it out here.

HALVOR: It's awfully heavy, Kari, but I guess we could do it.

We've had some rather exciting times exploring ways of bringing children into the heart of this powerful force called music. Let's hope that possibly as they threw their heads back and really sang, or as they stomped out the downbeat of a fine folk dance, that each of our young people rediscovered the fundamental truth, namely: this music is their very own—their true heritage, and that as we all make music together each of us becomes America in the finest cultural sense.

—Kurt R. Miller

5. Plan and Produce a Classroom Musical

A musical play should be presented during the second half of the year. It should be the culmination of a year of working together as a class group and should measure the extent to which children have learned both responsibility and the use of their talents.

Preparation begins early in the school year. First, the songs are learned during music class. About mid-year the class should discuss The Theatre and plays. Operas and operettas are discussed as "plays set to music."

a. If possible, they should listen to professional recordings of the opera, operetta or musical they will produce.
b. Then, the story is studied apart from the music. (You might use an abridged and simplified version of the original production—or your students can make the adaptation themselves.)

It should be clear from the beginning that the musical is a student project, that your role as teacher is one of consultant.

The Planning Committee: An over-all planning committee should meet with you to set up other committees and to establish standards for the production.

The Writing Committee: An editor and four other good writers can divide the play into parts and each take one portion to develop the script and relate the music. When all the writers have submitted their work, the scenes can be pieced together and the final script written. The writers are concerned solely with dialogue and incorporating the music. Action is worked out by narration and direction.

MEMO

You will find words, songs and music for a production of "Hansel and Gretel" in

Singing Together,

the 5th Grade music book of Ginn & Company's OUR SINGING WORLD series.

Try-Outs: When the script is complete, a dittoed copy is given to each member of the class. It is read through once by the whole class and try-outs are scheduled for the next day. Every child is allowed to try out for a role. If he is not chosen for a part, he may continue to try for others.

The Cast: The cast is chosen by the class. They are cautioned to choose the player who is best suited for the part, rather than their friend or a popular individual. Almost invariably, the choices are excellent. Everyone has some role in the play, although they may not have a solo speaking or singing part.

The Director-in-chief: When the cast is selected, the class chooses the Director-in-chief. This person is *responsible for* the action in the play and will have final decisions during rehearsals. The class is encouraged to make suggestions but the director has the final word.

Practice Sessions: During rehearsals those who are not interested in working out the action begin to design the SCENERY AND PROGRAMS. A chairman is picked for each of these committee groups.

Early Rehearsals: Early rehearsals are conducted in the classroom. Actual practice takes only about 2 weeks with 3 rehearsals on stage.

Since all committees are working at the same time, it is absolutely necessary that each student respect the rights of others.

DISCIPLINE and self-control are stressed and rigidly enforced. A person who cannot participate constructively must leave his group for that day and sit by himself. He is given several chances but if the Discipline Committee feels that he cannot work responsibly, he can no longer be a committee member. (So far, no one has ever had to be removed from a committee for lack of self-control!)

Costumes: Costumes are handled by each individual player.

Props: Props are brought in by anyone who has them. A SCENERY COMMITTEE is assigned the task of collecting the props and staging them. They are also in charge of lighting.

Action: Some of the action is planned to take place outside of the curtain—or to the side when there is no curtain—while scenes are being changed. This makes the action continuous. There is no delay between acts.

Scenery planners prepare no more than three main scenes. They should be simple in design and structure.

Absence of Principals on Opening Night: Since the class is writing and directing the play, most of the students know the lines and actions of every player very well. They become familiar with what actions are dramatically effective and how important vocal inflection is. If a player is absent, a member of the directing committee fills in for him. There is no fear of the star being sick on opening night.

Pride in Performance: It is always amazing when the musical is presented, to see the stage presence of the class. During curtain call, all of the students take a bow—they can honestly feel that is has been *their* production.

Music: If you do not play the piano, turn to an interested parent, member of the community, the music teacher, tape recordings or records.

Productions: Rewrite stories in musical form, adapt themes, purchase simplified and abridged published versions which are suitable for your grade level. Present scenes from Grand Opera, parts of Broadway favorites, any of the Gilbert & Sullivan operettas. *Hansel and Gretel* is an excellent way to introduce opera. *The Nutcracker of Nuremberg* is fine for a Christmas theme. *Oklahoma* when studying the west, *Carousel* when studying New England, *Camelot* and *My Fair Lady* for England past and present, *Li'l Abner*'s comments on politics and government, *The Sound of Music* for family fun, *Kiss Me Kate* as a taste of Shakespeare. Look to these for patterns and procedures! By the time your students adapt and rewrite, cast and direct, the production will have a flavor all its own—one that reflects the creativity and ingenuity of your class!

"H. M. S. PINAFORE"

W.S. Gilbert   Arthur Sullivan

presented

by

The Seventh & Eighth Grades of

PONTE VEDRA-PALM VALLEY SCHOOL

8:00 P.M.   25 April, 1963

Cast in Order of Appearance

Boatswain   Ramsey Huston

Little Buttercup   Stephanie Peterson

Dick Deadeye   David Thames

Ralph Rackstraw   Tom Ellis

Captain Corcoran   Rod Henson

Josephine, the Captain's   Patti Reed
Daughter

The Rt. Hon. Sir Joseph Porter, K.C.B. - Ivan Browning

Hebe, Sir Joseph's first cousin - Charlotte Haymans

SIR JOSEPH'S SISTERS, COUSINS & AUNTS

Patsy Beckford, Nimi Bradford, Mimi Brewer, Joyce
Cason, Edna Haworth, Robin Hicks, Brenda Mickler,
Kathi Sheridan, Judy Tribble, Merry Trumble, Janet
Brooker, Jean Brooker, Nancy Brown, Peggy Cason,
Mary Haworth, Darlene Hunter, Linda Medders, Faye
Rawson.

SAILORS

Tommee Carr, Ricky Devereux, Dick Draper, Bill
Harrison, Robbie Hruska, Gus Kroner, Dave Parrish,
Jack Beckford, Bobby Bridges, Kent Buckley, Ronnie
Hawks, Ken Hutchison, Alex Juhan, George McLatchey,
Nelson Sayford, Eric Searcy, Sandy Stout, Jim Tinsley
Joe Jerner, Todd Harris, Dell Richardson.

SCENE

Deck of H. M. S. Pinafore off Portsmouth

ACT I Noon   ACT II Night

SYNOPSIS OF MUSIC

ACT I

We Sail The Ocean Blue	Sailors
Little Buttercup	Buttercup
The Captain of the Pinafore	Captain
Over the Bright Blue Sea	Girls
Sir Joseph's Barge is Seen	Sailors
I Am the Monarch of the Sea	Sir Joseph
When I Was a Lad	Sir Joseph
Finale	Ensemble

ACT II

Things are Seldom What They See - Buttercup & Captain	
Bell Trio Josephine, Captain & Sir Joseph	
The Merry Maiden and the Tar	Captain & Dick Deadeye
Carefully on Tiptoe Stealing	Chorus
HE is an Englishman	Chorus
Farewell, My Own	Ralph Rackstraw
A Many Years Ago	Buttercup
Finale	Ensemble

It is well for the teacher to keep in mind that in school dramatics it is always what is gained along the way that counts, not the perfection of the final performance.

—N. F. Ryan

6. A Panorama of History Through Song

Restage the pages of your history textbook in a panorama of song—American music from the Indians and early settlers to today's Broadway musicals. Plan a program of:

- Tableaux
- Skits
- Readings
- Poems
- Reports
  and
- Music:

> Indian chants
> Madrigals
> Ballads
> Sea chanteys
> Cowboy songs
> Songs of the mountain men
> Logging songs
> Canal boat songs
> Songs of the homesteaders
> Songs of the riverboat era
> Mining songs
> Sagas of battles, wars, heroes, villains
> Political laments, lullabyes, carols, rounds
> Spirituals
> Field songs
> Minstrel songs
> Vaudeville numbers
> Camp meeting hymns

7. A Concert and Community Sing

Prepare a Rhythm Band concert with the whole class participating. Alternate band selections with songs sung by the class and the audience. Ditto song sheets with 10 to 20 well known campfire and community songs. Plan enough for an hour long program.

What this country needs, in addition to a good five-cent cigar, is a lot of bad piano players, accordion players, harmonica players, ukulele players, guitar players, and possibly saxophonists and trumpeters.

—Sigmund Spaeth

8. Produce Your Own "Telecast"

Taking a cue from Leonard Bernstein's *Omnibus* television scripts, let your students work up a similar production explaining some phase of music. Bernstein's THE JOY OF MUSIC contains seven of these scripts which can serve as a guide for your student committees.

    a. Let students read them, absorb them, digest them.
    b. Choose a theme.
    c. Research the theme, organize the music, write the script, work out the staging and the acting.
    d. Tape record the music.
    e. Have many, many narrators.
    f. Plan on group and solo work.
    g. Work up charts to accompany the narration.

Possible "telecasts" include: *The World of Jazz, What Makes Opera Grand, Our American Musical Comedy, Great Men of Music, Music's Part in History, The Instruments of the Orchestra, The Musical Styles of Various Periods, The Symphony—What Is It?, The Concerto—What Is It?*, and the like.

9. A Poetry Assembly

Plan a program of classical, modern, humorous and religious poetry to be presented by the students. Each member of the class is responsible for learning and delivering one poem.

Work out choral readings of one or two selections. Ask the students to dress to fit the mood, period or subject of the poem. Print a souvenir program of the selections.

PITT ELEMENTARY SCHOOL

4th, 5th, 6th
Grades

POETRY ASSEMBLY

CLASSICAL POETRY

"The Years At The Spring". . . . . .Robert Browning
                    Elizabeth Cook

"On His Blindness". . . . . John Milton
                  Jan McGurran

"I Wandered Lonely As A Cloud". . . . . **William Wordsworth**
                    Tracy Prater

"The Raven". . . . . Edgar Allen Poe
                  Frankie Burdges

"Lady Macbeth's Sleepwalking Soliloquy". . . . . . .William Shakespeare
                  Margie Saunders

MODERN POETRY

"Trees". . . . . .Joyce Kilmer
                  Linda Medders

"There Will Be Rest". . . . . Sara Teasdale
                  Catherine Logan

"Little Boy Blue". . . . . Eugene Field
                  Charles Easaw

"The Night Has A Thousand Eyes". . . . . .F. W. Bourdillion
                  Molly Devine

"Fog". . . . . .Carl Sandburg
                  Jason Schroeder

HUMOROUS POETRY

"Belinda and the Pet Dragon". . . . . Ogden Nash
                  Kaye Stanley

"Sneezles and Measles". . . . . A. A. Milne
                  David Braddock

CHORAL READINGS

"O What Is That Sound?". . . . . .W. H. Auden
                  The Class

"Danny Deever". . . . . Rudyard Kipling
                  The Boys

"Daniel Webster's Horses". . . . . Elizabeth Coatsworth
                  The Girls

ORIGINAL POETRY
Recited by the Author

Haiku. . . . . The Class

"An Artist's Canvas". . . . . .Sandy Stout

"Thanksgiving". . . . . .Peggy Cason
----
Music: Janet Brooker   Special Effects: David Thames   Props:
Costumes: Jean Brooker Scenery: Robin Christiansen   Nan Sexton
                  -COMMITTEE CHAIRMEN-

10. Produce a Movie

Shoot your own movie! If you don't own an 8mm camera yourself, borrow or rent one for the filming.

a. Choose the book, play or story situation you wish to film.

b. Work out the number of scenes necessary to cover the story.

c. Group the scenes so that all from one location can be shot at the same time. They can be spliced in proper sequence when editing the film.

d. Read the scene, discuss it, ask for suggestions. Act it out once and then shoot it.

e. Be sure that everyone in the class appears in at least one scene.

f. Use the tripod for all the scenes. The camera will be much steadier and you will be much happier with the final results.

g. Plan to shoot a title and author card for the beginning of the reel and a "The End" sequence for the end. Let students prepare the title cards.

h. 400 feet of film will give you a full half hour show. Each roll of 8mm film is 50 feet. (You will probably lose some footage in splicing and editing your final reel.)

i. A camera with a Zoom lens adds great interest to the final product.

j. Let students write a script to go with the film. It can be taped or narrated as the movie is shown.

k. Sound effects can be recorded on tape.

MEMO

An excellent reference for planning, shooting, editing and projecting a movie is:

THE AMATEUR'S 8MM MOVIE GUIDE
Sid Norinsky

Universal Photo Books
1957

11. Sound Effects and Slides

Present a program of narrated slides. Black-and-white slides can be made from any snapshot or negative. Color slides can be taken of any illustrative material in color. Supplement your own slides with travel slides borrowed from the school audio-visual center, the library, families and friends of the class.

Record sound effects on tape. Include music, songs and actual sound reproductions of events in the slides.

Let the students prepare the script and narrate each slide:

CHARLES: We also learned about Italy as a great art and music center. Many of the world's treasures are here, such as Raphael's *Madonna of the Chair.*

CHRISSY: Meanwhile, 5th graders have been studying the beginning of American history—from the days of the Vikings to the Revolutionary War.

KENNY: Here you see Father Marquette, who with Joliet explored the upper Mississippi. In the center is Queen Elizabeth I. She encouraged exploration and settlement in the new world. On the right is Magellan, the first man to circumnavigate the world.

MEMO

Projection Slides, Inc. will make 2 x 2 slides from black and white negatives (15¢ ea.) or black and white prints (35¢ ea.). Use snapshots of your class, or drawings, magazine cutouts, postcards. Turn them into slides for your program!

Projection Slides, Inc.
P. O. Box 26072
Indianapolis, Indiana 46226

12. Open House

Invite the parents to an Open House. Collect and display projects, exhibits and samples of the students' work. Post students beside each project or display to answer questions, give demonstrations and conduct experiments.

Include posters, charts, bulletin boards, models, experiments, dioramas, sand tables, maps, scrapbooks, folders of written work and special exhibits.

Chapter 11 covers projects, displays and exhibition techniques in detail.

13. The Science Fair

Any single classroom, single grade level, or entire school can sponsor its own Science Fair! Simply set less rigid standards for entries than those in national competition. Here are detailed suggestions for planning a fair. This same procedure has been followed in setting up a fair for First Grade to High School.

THE CLASSROOM SCIENCE FAIR

At the Beginning of the Year

a. Post or display a list of projects suitable for Science Fair competition. Include both individual and group projects.

b. After classroom discussion, ask each student to sign up for at least one project. The sign-up list should be available all through the year.

c. Each time a student selects a project, ask him to turn in a brief report outlining his plans:

> The project
> Time involved
> Materials needed
> Sketch of the display

d. Post a schedule of "conference" times when you, or outside resource people, can be available to help students with their projects.

MEMO

Professional training in science and nature is available through:

THE AUDUBON CAMPS

in

> *Connecticut*
> *Maine*
> *Wisconsin*
> *Wyoming.*

There are one-week and two-week courses for teachers, youth leaders, and parents who have a professional or hobby interest in nature and conservation.

For brochures and information, write:

> *Audubon Camp Department*
> *National Audubon Society*
> *1130 Fifth Avenue*
> *New York, N. Y. 10028*

A certificate, recognized in many school systems for salary increment, is awarded upon satisfactory completion of the two week program.

e. At the very beginning discuss the standards which should be met by the projects and displays. Encourage uniform display cases—constructed from cardboard cartons.

f. Have the students keep careful records of their research and experiments so that the information can be converted into displays at the time of the fair.

A Week or so Before the Fair

a. Set a deadline for turning in the projects.

b. Start planning your display space. Will projects be shown in the classroom? the hall? the auditorium?

c. Arrange for publicity: invitations, posters, the classroom or local newspaper, bulletins, flyers. Draw up a guest list and be sure that special guests are personally invited.

d. Select your judges. Give them a list of the standards you and the students have agreed upon. Set up some sort of point system for them to evaluate the projects:

                    Accuracy
                    Originality
                    Scientific Method
                    Presentation

e. Decide on awards: How many will be given?
                      Will there be group and individual awards?
                      Will awards be made by grade level?
                      Will displays be separated into subject area groups?

f. Purchase or prepare the awards: certificates
                                   ribbons
                                   cups
                                   plaques

g. Make a blueprint of your display space. Indicate which exhibits will go on which tables, desks, shelves, floor spaces and wall spaces.

A Day or Two Before the Fair

a. Check each project as it is turned in to see that information cards and title cards are properly and neatly lettered and that the exhibit meets the established standards.

b. If the project will require a student demonstration, make definite arrangements for the student to be present for the judging and during the fair.

The Day of the Fair

a. Discuss behavior standards with the class.

b. If students are helping arrange the rooms, have specific instructions about *which* students and *what* they are to do.

Plan classwork which can be done quietly and without the use of desks: music, reading, films, oral reports.

c. After the exhibits are on display, prepare a set of questions which will require each student to look at each project. Ditto the questions and distribute one sheet to each member of the class. Use this as a daily assignment.

d. Have the awards ready for the judges.

During the Fair

a. Ask students to stand by the projects to answer questions.
b. Choose a host and hostess for each display room.

After the Fair

a. Keep a master plan of the projects: Name of Student, Project, Category, Size, Rating. File this for future fairs.

b. Take photographs of outstanding exhibits. Take notes on outstanding exhibits.

c. Ask each student to turn in a final report on his project or projects: Statement of the problem, Time involved, Experiments, Materials, Cost, and a sketch or photograph of the project.

d. Have students write thank you notes to each individual who assisted in preparing and presenting the fair.

SUGGESTIONS FOR PROJECTS

How A Flashlight Works

Materials Found in a Bird's Nest

Plants Seek Light

Air Has Weight

The Jet Principle

Simple Machines at Work in a Complicated Machine

What Makes an Earthquake

The Effects of Vitamins on Animal Life

How Erosion Wears Away the Soil

Phases of the Moon

What Causes the Seasons

A Simple Telescope

An Exhibit of Fuels

A Geologic Time Clock

Models of the Earth in Different Geological Periods

Soil and Its Effect on Plants

Observations of an Ant Farm

Simple Weather Instruments

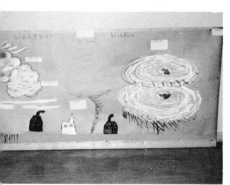

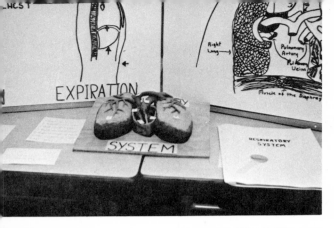

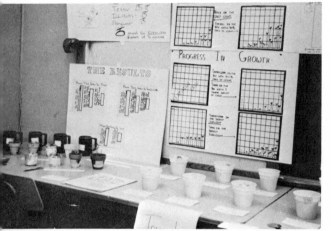

What Happens When We Get Shots
The Telephone
Simple Electrical Currents
Several Months in the Life of a Tree
Nature on the Rampage
Science in the Kitchen
The Body Fights Disease
Reproduction of Plants
A Study of Evolution
The Effect of the Slanting Rays of the Sun
The Earth as a Time Keeper
A Study of Navigation
Stories Told By Rocks
The Earth Makes A Mountain
Storms: What Causes Them
The Importance of Weather Prediction
Science and the Pilot
The Work of the City Water Department
Photosynthesis
Food Storage in Plants
We Digest Our Food
Nature's Jewelry Box
Man Makes Paper
Man Creates New Materials
What Is Television?
How the Radio Works
The Body Is a Complex Machine
Environments of the World
Camouflage in Nature
Captures on Film
Trapping Sounds on Tape
What Are Things Made Of?
Why Solid Water Floats
Heat As A Traveler
Smaller Than Atoms
The Fastest Thing in the World
Mold and Medicine
Explosions That Help
How Does Your Garden Grow?
Animal Food Makers
Science Builds A Bridge
Science Builds A Road

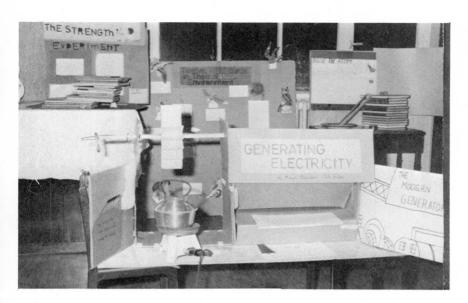

14. The Book Fair

If you are interested in stimulating interest in reading, plan a fair!

a. Appoint committees to plan:

        Exhibits
        Program and entertainment
        Publicity
        Hospitality

b. Require each student to submit some type of exhibit connected with his reading:

- charts
- displays
- puppets
- dolls
- dioramas
- models
- exhibits
- maps

Encourage group projects as well as individual efforts.

c. Plan a program of reading experiences for the guests:

- skits
- book reviews
- songs
- flannelboard talks
- chalk talks
- films

MEMO

Write to the National Children's Book Council, Inc., 175 Fifth Avenue, New York, N.Y. 10010 for a list of films.

d. Decorate the room with:

- student exhibits
- booths
- bulletinboard displays

e. Invite other classes as well as adult guests.

Third Grade
BOOK FAIR

JANUARY 24 - 2:30

Please enjoy our exhibits and displays before and after the program.

"Somewhere Over The Rainbow" . . . . The Wizard of Oz
Janet Brooker, pianist

"Huck and Tom Visit The Graveyard" . . . . . Tom Sawyer

Cast: Alex Juhan   George McLatchey
       David Thames   Jack Beckford
       Frankie Burdges

"The Honey Pot Song" . . . . , Winnie The Pooh

"How Doth The Little Busy Bee" . . . . . . Our Poetry Anthology
Nelson Sayford

"Autumn" . . . . Our Poetry Anthology
Jean Brooker

"Jo Gets In Trouble" . . . . Little Women

Cast: Peggy Cason   Linda Medders
       Stephanie Peterson   Kathy Jones
              Darlene Hunter

"We Whistle While We Work" . . . . Snow White and
The Seven Dwarfs

"In The Apple Barrel" . . . . Treasure Island

Cast: David Thames   Alex Juhan
       Sandy Stout   Kenny Stanley

"I Never Want To Grow Up" . . . . Peter Pan
Janet Brooker, Pianist

"Zip-a-dee-do-dah" . . . . Uncle Remus Stories

15. Open an "Art Gallery"

One of the most exciting and challenging projects you and your students can attempt is an art exhibition—a gallery of paintings and prints in the classroom and the school.

243

Plan early in the year to hold your exhibition near the close of school. All year long collect, sort and mount the prints, drawings, paintings and art pieces which will be displayed.

Decide whether or not your exhibition will carry one theme or whether pictures will be grouped to express a variety of themes such as:

> Student art work
> Art reproductions
> The World We Live In
> Our Community in Art
> English Painters
> American Artists

Ask the local art dealer or museum director to speak to your class and discuss the exhibition. Organize committees to handle the mounting and framing, the publicity, invitations and Catalog. Prepare a Catalog of the selections which each guest can carry through the exhibit. Let students write the information notes. Invite parents and friends to visit "the Gallery."

16. Creating Costumes

Many parents dread the announcement of a forthcoming program since it often means expensive and elaborate costumes. Classroom productions are actually more interesting and exciting if the pupils are given very little direction about their costuming and are asked to create their own outfits from scrap material at home.

Red shirts, blue jeans, a squashed cowboy hat and a girl's white sash—*a British Redcoat*

Part of a Cub Scout uniform, the sash of a smoking jacket, a cowboy hat, and sword—*General Grant*

Bath towels, paper mail, cardboard swords, rubber boots—*Medieval Knights*

A wooly winter coat and loud snarls—*a bear*

Mother's house dress, sashes, jewelry and a cardboard crown create —*a Medieval Queen*

Sheets, draped and hiked at different lengths, and ribbon lacing— —*Greeks, Romans, Angels*

Rubber rain boots, blue jeans, wide belts and sashes, white shirts and army fatigue hats—*Russians*

Hair tied in a top knot, a patterned blanket, bathing trunks, a broom handle and a cardboard spear—*Queequeg from Moby Dick*

Mother's pillbox hat, Daddy's khaki trousers stuffed into souvenir wooden shoes, with a long sleeved shirt—*a Dutch boy*

Mother's house dress, a shawl, cardboard hat, uncombed hair—*a witch*

A waistcoat, white blouse, pedal pushers, knee socks, pasteboard buckles and a pony tail—*a Colonial gentleman*

17. Scenery and Props

> *Materials for properties are found everywhere—in attics, surplus stores, junk heaps, and other strange places which are usually overlooked.*
>
> —Gail Plummer

Scenery and props need never be elaborate. Ask the pupils for suggestions as you plan your sets . . . . they usually come up with the simplest but most effective ideas.

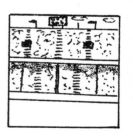

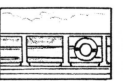

Investigate the corrugated display materials COROBUFF and REYTRIM. These papers are rigid enough to resist bending and sagging but are flexible enough to conform to flat or curved surfaces. There are guide lines printed on the back side for accurate measuring and cutting. They come in a variety of colors and patterns. The rolls are 4 feet wide and 25 feet long. They are easily stored and can be used again and again.

For less than $5.00 a roll, this display material is more economical and more effective than a surface painted with tempera.

CHAPTER 17

Ten Units
to Try

*A state's story is geography, history, current
events, and biography. It is interesting places,
folklore, music, art. It is the way people work
and play and govern themselves. It is yesterday, today, and the future.**

The successful unit takes a series of clearly stated purposes
and brings them to life. In unit work, school subjects fit together—It is "geography, history, current events and biography.
It is interesting places, folklore, music and art." It is students
planning, sharing, doing, discussing—and actively, busily, eagerly
learning. Everything matters; everything helps!

Here are ten units to try. This is what *we* did—where can
you go with bells, bridges and spice? Pick anything! Spend as

* From *Helping Children Study a State, a Teaching Guide,* © F. E. Compton & Company.

248

long as you like—one day, one week or all year. You will rarely exhaust the possibilities!

1. Bells Are To Ring

An entire school year was spent tracing music through the curriculum with a study of bells. The ten month project was called *Bells Are To Ring*.

On the first day of school the classroom was filled with bells: school bells, bicycle bells, cow bells, ship's bells and the many bells of Sarna. The bulletin boards carried pictures of world famous bells: the Czar Bell of Russia, the Bell of Notre Dame, the Taboo Bell of Canton and the Bell of Nara Japan. The walls were decorated with flower bells, Canterbury bells and bells of Ireland.

The class was intrigued. They had not dreamed there were so many bells. The list grew as they added others and immediately they expressed the desire to learn more about the subject. A project was thereby planned!

Its purpose was to trace man's joys and sorrows, his triumphs and defeats as expressed through bells. The project was correlated with every area of the curriculum. Together, the class and teacher developed this outline:

I. *The History of Bells*—Social Studies, Geography, Art

A. Bells were traced back to the Stone Age.
B. Bells have been and are still used in every country on earth.
C. As various countries were studied, the class found certain bells important to history and to the customs of each country.

ACTIVITIES:

1. The students searched school, public and home libraries for information on bells.
2. They visited an old church in Mandarin, Florida to sketch the stained glass windows and the bell tower.
3. They made blotter prints from these sketches for Christmas cards.

II. *Uses for Bells—Social Studies, Art, Music*

A. The class discovered for themselves the ancient uses for bells:

1) Worship
2) Battle
3) Signal
4) Music

B. They compared them with modern uses:

1) Worship
2) Alarm
3) Music
4) Decoration

ACTIVITIES:

1. They made a field trip to listen to the rehearsal of a bell choir.
2. They attended a lecture on the history of bells and their use in music.
3. They attended a bell choir concert.
4. They made an all bell Christmas tree.
5. Each child brought his own bell to the classroom where it was swung from a beam. He learned his own bell tone and was able to answer when this tone was rung.
6. Each child learned to play the melody bells.
7. The class constructed a three-dimensional church with bells called "Poetry of the Steeples" for the bulletin board.

III. *Construction of Bells—Art, Math, Science, Physical Education, Social Studies*

A. Materials from which bells are made and locations of the materials were investigated.
B. The class learned how metals were fused and shaped into bells (alloys and heat).
C. They learned the various values of weights and measures in the process of casting a bell.
D. They looked for and discovered bells in nature.

ACTIVITIES:

1. They visited the Hammond Foundry and observed the actual casting of a ship's bell.
2. They made ceramic bells.

3. Nature walks were made into the woods to collect bells of seed pods and flowers.
4. A trip was made to the seashore to hunt for sand dollars and other bell shapes in sea shells.

IV. *Bells in Literature and Music—Music, Art, Social Studies, Physical Education, Language*

A. The class found many references to bells in poetry, prose and song.
B. In reading they found reference to a bell collection in the north Florida area.

ACTIVITIES:

1. They wrote stories about bells.
2. They wrote poetry about bells.
3. They wrote letters of inquiry and arranged to visit bell collections in the area.
4. They wrote an original play about a gypsy tribe and a lost bell: "The Bell of the Kaldoras."
5. They made a field trip to Daytona Beach to see a bell collection.
6. They constructed the scenery for their play.
7. They dyed materials for costumes in the play.
8. They learned to play the songs in the play on the melody bells.
9. They created dances to gypsy music used in the play.

V. *Final Activities in the Bells Project Were:*

A. A production of the original play with the songs and dances:

> Kipling's *Gypsy Trail*
> *The Bells of St. Mary's*
> Song of the Open Air
> Wandering   Music Around
> On the Camel's Back The World
> Gypsy Song   Silver Burdett
> Wraggle Taggle Gypsies

B. A lunch of Zuni Stew served by the mothers
C. A treasure hunt using gypsy signs
D. Listening to the Hungarian Rhapsody
E. Working out original dances to The Turkish Dance

> **ZUNI STEW**
>
> A Favorite Meal of the Gypsies
>
> 5 fryers or 3 hens
> 2 quarts of water
>   Boil the chicken until tender. Pour off the broth. Add—
> 4 onions
> 3 green peppers
>   Simmer the vegetables until tender. Add—
> Rice or
> Noodles to thicken to the desired consistency.
>   Tomatoes may also be added, if desired.
>   Combine chicken, broth, vegetables and serve.
>   Feeds 16–20

2. Water Is To Draw From

On the opening day of school the bulletin board carried the caption: *Water Is To Draw From.*

There were many pictures showing the uses of water in industry, recreation and every-day living. A discussion arose regarding man's need for water, his constant search for it, and the present need for its conservation.

From this beginning water found its way into every area of study throughout the school year.

I. *Historical World Wide Importance of Water—Social Studies, History, Health*

    A. The class became familiar with the lakes, rivers and seas of Europe, Asia, and their own state of Florida.

    B. They came to know the sacred wells, spas, and watering places of history and modern times:

        1. Beersheba   5. Green Cove Springs
        2. Bethlehem   6. Mineral Wells
        3. Thermopolae   7. Saratoga
        4. Wormwell   8. Bad Aibling

C. They observed the importance of water in battle.

D. They saw how the conservation of water could serve nations.

ACTIVITIES:

1. They drew sketches of wishing wells.
2. They made clay cities centered around a well.
3. They built an oasis.

II. *Sources of Water—Math, Science, Health*

A. They studied the natural sources of water: lakes, rivers, springs, seas, oceans, water tables.

B. They studied the man-made sources of water: dams, reservoirs, wells.

C. They observed and studied the water cycle.

ACTIVITIES

1. A field trip was made under the supervision of the County Extension Department. The class visited springs, watersheds, artesian wells, reservoirs and dams.
2. They experimented with a "witching rod" or divining rod for the purpose of locating water. The superstition is that a stick of hazel shaped like a fork will point to a water hole. In this case the boy brought a stick of sumac rather than hazel! For several days the science talk and learning was the diagnosis and treatment of sumac poisoning!
3. The class measured rainfall and water depths.
4. They estimated the rise and fall of tides.

III. *Uses of Water—Science, Art, Physical Education*

A. Industrial uses of water were studied.

B. Home uses were observed.

C. Recreational uses were listed and discussed.

D. Useful chemicals were found in water.

ACTIVITIES:

1. A manufacturing plant was visited and the amount of water used was estimated.
2. Individual and home uses of water were estimated.
3. Amount of water and health requirements for recreational areas were investigated.
4. Tests were made on gardens with and without water.
5. A project was submitted to the local Garden Club.
6. Students participated in the local Flower Show.
7. The class planted and cared for the school garden.

IV. *Conservation and Protection of Water—Science, Health, Art*

A. The class studied ways of conserving water in the home.

B. They studied ways in which industry can conserve water.

C. They studied ways in which water can be protected from contamination.

D. They became familiar with local projects such as The Cross Barge Canal and the Green Swamp Area.

ACTIVITIES:

1. They made a field trip to watch a well being drilled.
2. They collected materials for building a water collage.

V. *Water in Literature—English, Physical Education, Art*

A. They discovered and noted many references to water in their reading of prose, poetry and songs.

B. They found a new and different vocabulary connected with water.

ACTIVITIES:

1. They collected poems about water.
2. They collected and wrote stories about water.
3. They wrote a play about the flight of the Dali Llama of Tibet

across the various waters down the "Giant Staircase" to India.
4. They made murals of great watering places.
5. They made a trip to Marineland to observe marine life and to draw it.
6. They learned songs about water.
7. They made costumes for a play on India.
8. They made all the scenery for the play.
9. They made a vocabulary booklet on the specialized vocabulary of water.

VI. *Final Activities on Water*—Language Arts, Social Studies, Physical Education

A. The class produced their original play, "Jewel of the Lotus," a story of the watering places of Tibet and India and the ghats of Benares.
B. They created Indian dances.
C. They took part in a well dressing, as practiced by the ancients, using flowers from their own gardens to decorate the well.
D. Indian curry was prepared and served by the mothers.
E. The theme song for the unit work was *Peace of the River,* published by Silver Burdett. It was part of all activities.

3. A Gem Is To Cherish

The bulletin board carried the caption, *A Gem Is To Cherish,* and was covered with pictures of birth stones and famous gems. Interest and curiosity was so keen that intensive research was begun on the subject of gems: their composition, their location, their history.

I. *Locations of Gems and Other Important Minerals*—Science, Geography

A. Places where gems are found were located and studied:
   Natural—such as the Amethyst of Siberia
   Artificial—such as the pearl beds in boat ballast
B. A study was made of the geographical characteristics of these locations.
C. Other valuable minerals and metals in the same area were identified.

ACTIVITIES:

1. The class made a field trip to Fernandina Bluff to dig for semi-precious stones in the old ship ballast there.
2. They enjoyed an oyster bake, hoping a pearl might be discovered.
3. An expert on stones and stone cutting came to the school to help the class identify their finds.
4. The class returned his visit with a trip to his gem cutting shop.

II. *Chemical Composition of Gems*—Science, Art

A. The chemical composition of precious stones was analyzed.
B. The precious stones were compared with semi-precious stones and other minerals.
C. Interest was directed toward the stones which are not "stones"—pearls, amber, opal.

ACTIVITIES:

1. The class made a field trip to Humphries Gold Mine where they observed the processes involved in separating dross from valuable products, such as:
    a. Rutile
    b. Zircon
2. A visit was made to the Children's Museum for a lecture on rock formations.

III. *Marketing of Gems*—Science, Math

A. The processes of getting gems from the mines were studied.
B. Methods of cutting and polishing gems were observed in real stones, photographs and films.

ACTIVITIES:

1. The class viewed a film on marble cutting which had been made in Italy by one of the parents.

IV. *The Value of Gems*—Math, Art

A. Gems were evaluated according to weight, color and cut.

B. The changing value of gems in various periods of history was observed: jade, opals, diamonds.

C. Values relating to fashion and scarcity were studied.

ACTIVITIES:

1. Math work sheets covered:

   Problem solving in carats
   Problem solving in price fluctuation
   Problems in cost of getting a gem to market

2. Paintings were made of *gems from the spectrum*

   and

   Flowers of gem colors
   Fruits of gem colors
   Windows of gem colors

V. *Uses for Gems—Art, Health, Math*

A. The aesthetic values were discussed.

B. Gems for adornment were discussed.

C. It was discovered that gems were thought to have mystical and medicinal values. Superstitions were studied regarding the Opal, the Amethyst and the Moonstone.

ACTIVITIES:

1. Room mothers brought collections of jade and pearls so the children might feel the difference in temperature and see why pearls are worn in winter and jade in summer.

2. The class drew designs each month depicting the jewel of the month in some artistic setting.

VI. *Gems in History—Social Studies, Art*

A. As the countries of Asia, the Middle East and Europe were studied, gems associated with important figures were also studied, such as:

   1. Cleopatra's emeralds
   2. Catherine's rubies
   3. Josephine's emerald
   4. Mohammet's carnelian
   5. Edward's sapphire

B. Special collections associated with special events were noted:

    1. The Peacock Throne of Persia
    2. The Opals of Victoria
    3. The Crown Collections of Imperial Russia

C. Special stones were studied because of their size or unusual color:

    1. The Kohinoor Diamond
    2. The Shah of Persia Diamond
    3. The Cross of Pearl
    4. The Emerald Ungent Jar of Austria

D. Attention was given to the religious significance of precious stones:

    1. The amethyst symbolizing the sacrifice of Christ.
    2. The ruby in Hindu and Christian religions as the most precious stone.

ACTIVITIES:

1. A leading jeweler spoke to the class and showed them samples of jewels.
2. The class made a field trip to the County Fair to observe a collection of precious and semi-precious stones.
3. Parents and friends brought collections to the classroom.
4. The class made individual visits to jewelry stores.
5. They made murals of famous gem stories.

VII. *Gems in Literature*—Social Studies, English, Art

A. Gems, as they appeared in literature, were recognized as principal factors in story-telling and historical incidents.

    1. *Moonstone*—Wilkie Collins
    2. *Anne of Gierstein*—Sir Walter Scott
    3. *Acres and Acres of Diamonds*—Russell Cromwell
    4. *Beau Geste*—Percival Wren
    5. *The Necklace*—Guy de Maupassant
    6. *The Pearl*—John Steinbeck

B. Gems were recognized as symbols of traits of character as they appeared in literature:

    1. The stones of the Apostles.
    2. The favored stones of the Greek Gods: a. Tuesday —Day of Mars—rubies, garnets; b. Friday—Day of Venus—emerald.

C. Poetry with references to precious stones was examined:
           1. The Bible
           2. Kipling
           3. Alfred Noyes
           4. Christina Rossetti

ACTIVITIES:

1. The class learned many lines of poetry about gems.
2. They wrote poetry and stories about gems.
3. They dramatized parts of stories which dealt with gems.
4. They made miniature flower arrangements with jewel-like seeds and flowers.
5. They wrote a 40 minute play about the people in the opal mines of Coober Pedy, Australia.
6. They made booklets covering their studies and activities.
7. They chose and learned the following songs to be used with their play: Cockles and Mussels, Botany Bay, Greensleeves and Lord Lovel, published by Silver Burdett.

VIII. *Final Activities on Gems*

A. The class produced the play "Coober Pedy—Where A Road Turns Back." It was accompanied by original dances and songs which would probably have been used by the British in such a situation. All of the scenery was designed and painted by the class.
B. The mothers served a lunch of Yorkshire pudding and British tea.
C. The chief entertainment was the throwing of boomerangs—and one really did come back!

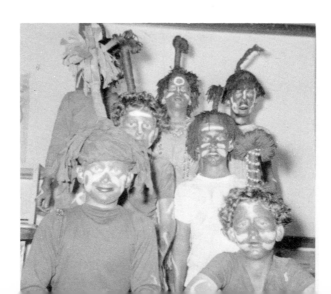

4. The Goodness of Grapes

As the door opened on the first day of school a basket of fresh fruits greeted the students' eyes. The basket was topped with large bunches of purple grapes.

During the mid-morning nutrition break the fruits were divided among the children. As the grapes were of a different variety than those on the market, they aroused the children's curiosity. What kind were they? Were they the same as Welches? Would they make jelly? Would they make wine? Could the class make jelly?

A project began to take shape. The students would soon learn of the influence grapes have had upon the lives of men around the world. First, the questions were answered—the grapes in the classroom were of the Scuppernong variety, native to the woodlands of the south. They would make wine and they would make jelly, though not the Welch type. It would be possible to make jelly in the classroom but it was agreed that "jelly making" would follow the exploration of some other areas of information.

An outline was developed. Students listed the mainheads and the subheads grew with the project.

I. *Locations Favorable for the Growing of Grapes—Geography*

    A. It was discovered that grapes grow all over the United States.

    B. Grapes grow all over the world.

ACTIVITIES:

      1. The discovery of this information served as a method of review of United States History previously studied, and as an introduction to World Geography which was coming up.

      2. Many maps were studied and made.

II. *The Culture of Grapes—Science*

    A. The structure of the grape was studied.

    B. Soil and growing conditions were investigated.

    C. The harvest was fascinating to the students.

ACTIVITIES:

      1. Field trips were made around the playground to observe wild grapes.

    2. Seeds were planted.

    3. The county agent came to school to talk about grape culture in Florida.

III. *Varieties of Grapes—Math, Science*

A. Native species were named, located and evaluated.

B. Commercial varieties were studied with regard to weights, measures, shipping qualities, prices.

    1. Individual students made trips to markets to discuss quality and price with grocers.

    2. Many students visited the Farmer's Market to obtain their information.

IV. *The History of Grapes—Social Studies, Art*

A. As the class moved from country to country, they found traces of the grape in the social life of each.

B. They found grapes in the economic structures.

C. They found grapes in art.

ACTIVITIES:

1. They built their own Hanging Gardens of Babylon.
2. They made blotter prints of grapes.
3. They drew murals on walls and windows.
4. They made string paintings of grapes and arbors.

V. *Grapes in Literature—Language Arts, Physical Education*

A. The class explored the Bible for references to grapes.

B. They found many grapes in Greek and Roman literature.

C. References were found in the Jataka Tales.

D. Many references were found in modern stories and poems.

ACTIVITIES:

1. A dramatization was made of the "Grapes of Canaan," of "Midas and the Golden Touch" and of "The Fox and the Grapes."
2. Original dances were created to accompany these dramatizations.

VI. *Uses for Grapes—Science, Health*

A. Many uses were found for grapes, the most important product being wine.

B. It was discovered that grapes may be used in many kinds of jellies, jams and preserves.

C. Grape sugar was discovered.

ACTIVITIES:

1. The class went to a vineyard and gathered grapes for making preserves. They prepared the grapes by cleaning and pulping (separating the pulp and skins).
2. Grape preserves were made in the classroom.
3. A Syrian merchant came to class and talked about Syrian foods. He brought Syrian bread on which they ate their preserves. He showed the class how the Syrians use grape leaves to roll certain mixtures of food.
4. Some students went for a meal at a Syrian restaurant.

VII. *Final Activities with Grapes*

A. At the end of the year the class produced a play which they had written: *The Secret of Chateau Jacquard,* the story of a French family who had lost the wine recipe belonging to the family.

B. The class made their own costumes and stage sets.

C. Their dances were original and were based on harvesting the grapes.

D. The mothers served the students crepes, chicken croquettes and grape juice.

Toward the end of school one of the girls selected a grape print for a dress. She said, "It seems like everywhere I go and in everything I do now, the grapes keep popping up!" —which was exactly as intended!

5. Sugar, Spice and Everything Nice . . .

"Sugar and spice and everything nice . . ." was the phrase which started a detailed study of spices. What was so great about spice? Wars have been fought over spices, the students found; and new worlds discovered. Countless lives have been enriched by the spice trade. So much interest was generated in this precious substance that an outline of study and activities was developed:

I. *History and Spice*

A. Early man and the spices

B. References to spice in the early cultures:

    1. Arabia   3. China
    2. Egypt   4. India

ACTIVITIES:

1. Maps of early spice users were drawn.
2. Clay figures were modeled and pictures drawn of men first finding spice.
3. Stories were written about the discovery of spice.

II. *The Influence of Spice on World Trade*

A. The establishment of water routes across the Mediterranean:

    Venice   Diaz's trip
    Portugal   Holland

B. The search by Europeans for new routes to:

    Africa   Malayan States
    India   China

C. The establishment of the East India Company by the British
D. The story of Columbus

ACTIVITIES:

1. Maps were drawn showing the first efforts to obtain more spices.
2. Maps of salt and clay were modeled.
3. Pictures of ships used in the transportation of spices were drawn.
4. Paper ships and boats of the period were constructed.

III. *Homes of Spices—Near the Sea*

A. India—Coriander
B. Ceylon—Pepper, Cardamon, Cinnamon
C. Malay States—Nutmeg, mace, cloves, tumeric, ginger
D. China—Cassia bark
E. Africa—Grains of paradise
F. American tropics—vanilla, red pepper
G. Northern climates—Cumen, caraway seed, mustard

ACTIVITIES:

1. The class made a mural with the actual spices attached to its

map. Routes to various markets were shown with different colored strings.

IV. *Uses for Spices*

A. Flavoring—all spices
B. Preservative—clove, allspice, pepper, mustard
C. Perfume—vanilla, cloves
D. Confections—cinnamon, cloves
E. Incense—cinnamon
F. Medicine—cardamon, ginger, nutmeg, cloves
G. Pickling—dill, mace
H. Dyeing—tumeric, majoram (wool)

ACTIVITIES:

1. The class made cookies using nutmeg, cinnamon and cloves.
2. They made a milk drink using nutmeg which they grated themselves.
3. They made pickles using cinnamon bark and cloves.
4. They tasted and tested the stems, leaves, seeds, bark and flowers of the spices.
5. They found traces of spice taste in some of the medicines they used.
6. A father who was a chemist came to the classroom and set up the apparatus for extracting the oil of cloves.

V. *Ancient Uses for Spices*

A. Chinese—held clove in mouth when talking to sovereign
B. Ceylon—death penalty to sell spices on the common market
C. Around the world—gifts to rulers

VI. *The Culture of Spices*

A. Growing conditions
     1. Soils
     2. Climate
     3. Required time for production
B. Treatment for harvest
     1. Bark
     2. Flowers
C. Expected yields

VII. *Price Values*

A. Ancient World
  1. One pound of pepper was a gift for the king.
  2. One pound of ginger was equal to one sheep in Rome.
B. Today
  1. An exhibit of modern spices was prepared and each spice container was marked with the current prices.

6. Bridges Are To Cross—A Regional Winner

This unit was entered in national competition in the *John Gunther's High Road* Teacher Awards Program and received a Regional Award for its excellence.

John Gunther's High Road was a weekly after-school documentary film series presented by the Ralston Purina Company over the ABC television network. In Jacksonville, Florida the program was shown Saturday evenings at 6:30. Teachers who built their social studies program around these televised travels spent part of Friday afternoon preparing students for what they would see:

- Longitude and latitude of the country were noted.
- Other countries of similar longitude and latitude were noted.
- The location of the country was compared with Florida.
- A glossary was written on the board and copied by the students.
- Encyclopedias and textbooks were reviewed for pertinent information.
- The class was asked to look for specific things during the program:

✔ "The lay of the land"	✔ Foods	✔ Government
✔ Language sounds	✔ Recreation	✔ Industries
✔ Vegetation	✔ Religion	✔ Mutual needs

- Students took notes on the program.

On Monday morning a discussion was held. The class voiced opinions on the pros and cons of living with the citizens they had visited Saturday on *The High Road*.

Interest often led into special projects: clay modeling, special maps, interpretive dances, music, folk dances and folk songs.

The program served as a splendid health resource. As children are always interested in the foods and recreational pursuits of children in other lands, it was easy to note the influence of climate and geography on food and recreation.

The program was easily correlated with current events: news articles, magazine articles and other television broadcasts.

Whenever it was possible to combine the lessons in the social studies text with the week's presentation on *The High Road,* special units were developed.

With the knowledge that *The High Road* would be part of the curriculum throughout the year, on the first day of school the students were greeted with the chalkboard notation:

BRIDGES ARE TO CROSS

Bridges of many kinds were displayed on all bulletin boards. Books and magazines with the theme of bridges had been assembled. The first discussion of the year developed the idea that in the next few months there would be many bridges—real and imaginary—which the students would cross.

Through *The High Road* came many bridges!

- Language
- Science
- Food
- Social customs
- Mutual needs of man

The class arranged their study of Japan to coincide with the High Road presentation of the country. Special emphasis was placed on the beautiful bridges of the country. An original play based on a Japanese legend was written and presented by the students. A Japanese meal was prepared and served by the mothers. A kite flying contest was held.

As Jacksonville is known as *The City of Bridges,* the theme of bridges was chosen for the state PTA convention. The class was asked to make place cards for the banquet. Their cards were imaginative sketches of bridges.

Field trips were made to sketch the many bridges that span the St. Johns River. Prior to the trip the class built their own bridges with clay, wood and paper maché. They read many poems and stories with the theme of bridges.

A classroom dinner featuring "Food Bridges of the World" was another activity.

The *Florida Times-Union* ran a Sunday feature article on the interesting work and learning experiences of this class which found beyond any doubt that bridges *are* to cross.

At the end of the year in evaluating *The High Road* and their experience of learning through television, the students commented that no matter how well prepared their textbooks were, the televised pictures were worth 10,000 words.

7. Early Days in America

Detailed plans of this unit were kept from year to year, making it a simple matter to adapt the work for single or multiple grade use from one grade level to another, and to shorten or lengthen the time involved.

In each case the unit developed an appreciation for and understanding of life in the early days of this country. The work began in grade level readers and extended to social studies, science, math—all areas of the curriculum.

At no time did the daily schedule give way completely to the unit work. Rather, the lessons were further enhanced because within the unit a real need existed for the skills of reading, writing, arithmetic and language. Project work was scheduled for afternoons and a few activities were held after school with the cooperation of the parents.

The unit work ranged from a three week session to a full semester to the whole year.

I. Reading Activities:

A. Stories and units in grade level and supplementary readers
B. Workbooks and special worksheets
C. Social studies textbook assignments
D. Research projects through encyclopedias and special reference works
E. A reading list of books and poems with early days themes

II. Physical Activities:

A. House raisings in the classroom
B. Quilting bees
C. A box social
D. Square dances

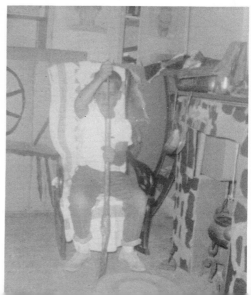

E. Community sings
F. Husking bees
G. Covered wagon journeys from the schoolhouse
H. Skill contests (races, log rolling, throwing)
I. Spelling bees
J. A day of old-fashioned school
K. Farming a garden

III. *Language Activities:*

A. Essays and compositions
B. Research papers and reports
C. Poems
D. Letters to parents
E. Thank-you notes
F. Newspaper articles
G. Interviews
H. Writing plays and producing them

IV. *Math Activities:*

A. Measuring and planning for the house-raising
B. Planning and packing the covered wagon
C. Working with recipes
D. Setting up contest areas
E. Marking off the garden
F. Special worksheets about early day life

V. *Social Studies Activities:*

A. Social studies texts were used to check the accuracy of the stories in the readers
B. Additional details were gained and put into effect in each activity

VI. *Science Activities:*

A. The students prepared a garden in the schoolyard.
B. The problems of watering, preparing the soil, fertilizing, sowing and harvesting were studied through the garden.

VII. *Music Activities:*

A. A study of early American folk songs and composers
B. Community sings

C. Original songs

D. New words for familiar tunes:

The People from McLatcheyville

Tune: Turkey in the Straw

We're the people from McLatcheyville
We sure have fun
Though we start our chores at the rising of the sun.
Oh, we're cooking and we're sewing and we're chopping down
    the trees
And for fun we sing and dance and have a lot of spelling bees.
We have a grist mill and the Thames Inn too—
It serves the world's best chicken stew!
Back in time one hundred years
You'll find the best three families of pioneers—
            Beckford, McLatchey and Thames!

VIII. *Art Activities:*

A. Dioramas
B. Scrapbooks
C. Murals
D. Drawings and paintings
E. Models
F. Charts
G. Exhibits
H. Handicrafts
 I. Boxes for the Box Social

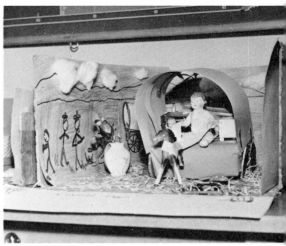

IX. *Study Skills:*

A. Research papers
B. Note taking
C. Outlining
D. Maps, graphs and charts

PLAN SHEET FOR
PIONEER UNIT

■ **Major Reference Materials:** Singing Wheels Manual
Days and Deeds
World Book Encyolopedia
Growth of America

■ **Study Areas:** (Class, Committees, Individuals)

Buffalo	Hunting	Schools
Clothing	Inns	Soap
Covered Wagons	Medicine	Stageccach
Dying	Mills	Stores
Foods	Postal Service	Traders
Guns	Recreation	Trapping
Houses	Religion	Travel
House Raisings	Roads	Weaving

■ **Projects:**

Bulletin Boards	Models	Demonstrations
Travel	Flatboat	Sap to Sugar
Clothing	Covered Wagon	Spinning
	Grist Mill	

Maps		Exhibits
Expansion	Dioramas	Tools
Main Routes	The Store	Soap
River Travel	The Mill	Weapons
The Town	The School	
	A Cabin	Displays
Murals		In The Peddlers Pack
Our Town	Charts	Packing A Covered
A Box Social	The Buffalo	Wagon
	Postal Service	
	Early Schools	
	Hornbooks	

■ **Activities:**

1.	Raising the Cabin	8.	Day of Pioneer School
2.	Furnishing the Cabin	9.	Covered Wagon Journey
3.	Quilting Bee	10.	Farming the Garden
4.	Box Social	11.	Original and Period Songs
5.	Square Dance	12.	Three Plays
6.	Field Trip to Museum	13.	Open House
7.	Spelling Bee	14.	200' Movie – written and produced

▲ ACTIVITY DAY	▲ OPEN HOUSE
Skill Contests	Reports (4)
Pioneer Games	Songs (4)
Box Supper	Square dances (2)
Square Dancing	Plays (3)
Singing	Movie (200' – 15 min.)
Spelling Bee	Projects and exhibits
on display

X. *Culminating Activities:*

A. Open House of projects, charts, bulletin boards, handicrafts and the furnished cabin.
B. An hour long program of plays, songs, essays, reports and narrated slides of the early days activities.
C. An Activity Day of skill contests, spelling bees, square dancing, singing by the campfire and enjoying a Box Social.

8. Multiple Grades Look at the Middle Ages

A 4-5-6 grade Combination Class spent four weeks studying life in the Middle Ages. Daily lectures were given from the material in three textbooks and two encyclopedias. Children took notes in outline form from the board. Essays and special reports were written by each individual. Daily pop quizzes of 10 questions were given over the previous day's material. Weekly tests were given to gauge progress.

The outline of topics was:

    I. The Barbarian Peoples Who Over-Ran Europe
   II. The Fall of the Roman Empire and the Rise of the Catholic Church
  III. The Way of Life
   IV. Trade
    V. Amusements
   VI. The Feudal System
  VII. Town Life
 VIII. The Crusades
   IX. Development of the Arts

Activities included the election of a king and queen to rule over the classroom kingdom, choosing a squire to prepare for knighthood and the building and furnishing of a castle 6' x 8' x 6'.

Projects included bulletin boards, sand table displays, dioramas, charts, models, maps, reports and scrapbooks. A special bulletin board on the Feudal System was prepared with photographs of the students as members of the system—from serf to king.

The culminating activity was a program of essays, reports, narrated slides, the knighting ceremony and a presentation of

Macbeth. This was followed by a 10 course medieval banquet at noon with a tournament on the lists in the afternoon. With flags flying, ladies tossing flowers as favors, riders with gay sashes, heralds, knights and trumpeters, the playground was turned into a festival of knighthood.

MEMO

In a fascinating book,

THE WRITING ROAD TO READING
Romalda Bishop Spalding with Walter T. Spalding

William Morrow & Co.
New York
1957

Romalda Bishop Spalding describes her approach to a project on the Middle Ages. She secured 17 copies of six different story books on the period—two students per copy. With these texts the class built a common background of knowledge. Mrs. Spalding scoured book shops for illustrations of life in the Medieval period. She took a museum course and an industrial arts course. She learned how monks made ink and paint, how to bind a book, weave a small rug, weave a tapestry, work in metal and leather, work with natural dyes and stained glass. Then she took this knowledge back into the classroom.

Her 6th grade students formed guilds, made banners, wrote laws, became journeymen and master craftsmen in weaving, dyeing, leatherwork and metalwork. They each wove a tapestry 5 x 8 inches. They wrote, illustrated and bound a book. They made field trips to the Metropolitan Art Museum and to the library. They embroidered. They wrote and produced a play using as props the articles they had been making in class.

Some of the students read 50 books on the Middle Ages during the project. They learned dozens of our finest poems on Medieval life. They wrote copiously of this period in world history.

Mrs. Spalding's was a come-alive classroom!

9. A Portable Unit for Dental Health Week

Fourteen second graders participated in this "portable program." The children visited eight classrooms with their ten minute illustrated Dental Health hints.

Seven pupils held large illustrations of what the speaker beside them was telling his audience. Each speaker held a large tooth— bright and shiny or decayed, depending upon his speech.

A classroom mascot, a hen piñata named Henny Penny, was used to introduce the message. The illustrations were done on 24 x 36 white oaktag with tempera paint. Music was "Scraping Up Sand" from the Grade 2 California songbook and the teacher accompanied the children on the autoharp.

1   Henny Penny is our friend.
    She lays eggs each day.
    Because it's Dental Health Week
    She has come to say . . .

2   How often do you brush your teeth?
    Only once a day?
    No! Right after I eat something—
    That's the better way.

3   Which foods make our teeth strong?
    Soda? Candy? Cake?
    No! Milk, fruit, meat and vegetables
    Good strong teeth will make.

4   Which foods are the scrubbers
    When your toothbrush is not around?
    Raw celery, carrots and apples,
    These help keep teeth sound.

5   We'll not forget the dentist.
    He is our teeth's good friend.
    Let him check them over;
    You'll be happy in the end.

6   Here you have a choice to make—
    Which one will it be?
    Sad Sally who forgets these things
    Or Happy Harry, as you can see?
                        (this poster illustrated on both sides)

7 Now Henny Penny says, Thank you—
   You've been so very nice.
   She knows you're all smart people
   And will take her good advice.

Chorus: Do you want teeth all shiny and bright?
         Brush them, brush them,
         Up and down both morning and night,
         Brush them every day.

         Go see your dentist
         Eat what you should.
         You'll feel so happy
         And your teeth will look good.

10. The Wonderful Miracle Machine

The first goal in health education should be an awareness and
appreciation of the human body as a miraculous machine—which
must be cared for as any machine. One of the quickest ways to
arouse interest in the subject is to personalize the different parts
of the body.

> *Much teaching consists in explaining.*
> *We explain the unknown by the known,*
> *the vague by the vivid.*
>
> —*Gilbert Highet*

The Brain........computer
               filing cabinet
The Eyes.........cameras
The Ears.........drum
               anvil
               stirrups
The Nose ....filters
               strainers
               vacuum cleaners
The Teeth........knives
               grinders
The Voice........stringed instrument
The Joints.......hinge
               ball-and-socket

The Heart........pump
pipes
valves

The Lungs .... balloons
bellows

The Muscles...... sunpowered engines
elastic
rubber bands

The Blood........ red cells—construction workers
white cells—the health department
blood platelets—seamstresses

The Nerves....... computer networks
telegraphic system

The Stomach ..... factory
refinery

The Intestines.... garbage disposal

The Kidneys..... filter system

The Arch .... basic arch used in bridges and
aqueducts

Tendons .... suspension bridge cables

MEMO

*The American Medical Association has published an entertaining
and educational booklet about the anatomy and physiology of the
body,*

THE WONDERFUL HUMAN MACHINE

American Medical Assoc.
535 N. Dearborn
Chicago 10, Illinois
$1.00

*It relates the skeleton to the engineering marvels of our modern
buildings and machines, the muscles to sun-powered engines, the
nerves to radar and computer networks, and so on.*

Teach simple anatomy as you would teach geography. Drill
with charts and models until your students can locate the vital
organs without hesitation.

Stage contests, prepare worksheets, ask Mystery Questions:

1. How strong is bone?
   (Generally, as strong as cast iron.)
2. Solve the Case of the Missing Bones.
   (At birth we have about 270 bones; by adulthood some of them have fused—eventually we have only 206!)
3. What do you have in common with an aqueduct?
   (The nearly perfect arch in your foot.)
4. Where are your own personal stirrups?
   (In the inner ear.)
5. What part of you can move at nearly 200 miles an hour?
   (Your nerve impulses.)
6. The human body has approximately 70,000 miles of sealed "pipe line." What are these pipe lines and what is carried through them?
   (Blood vessels; blood.)
7. Where is your own personal air conditioner?
   (The nose—it controls the temperature and humidity of the air entering the body.)
8. How much does your skin weigh?
   (About six pounds.)

Make yourself a---

MASTER PLAN FOR THE UNIT			
Outline of Material	Major Concepts	Special Vocabulary	Calendar
Textbooks	Library Books	Pamphlets-Bulletins	
Visual Aids	Recordings	Special Materials	
Resource Persons	Field Trips	Activities	Comments
Projects		Special Assignments	

Keep your plans on file to use again or to adapt for a similar unit.

A Unit . . . or More Than a Unit

That ours is a nation of economic il-
literates is a grave problem that only
the schools can solve.
        —Professor Lawrence Senesh

Grade School finance? Economics with the ABCs? Professor Lawrence Senesh developed just such a program for 1st, 2nd, and 3rd graders in Elkhart, Indiana. It has since been published by Science Research Associates, Inc. as a series of social studies materials for the primary grades. The SRA program (OUR WORKING WORLD) covers 28 weeks of classroom work—obviously much more than a unit.

Perhaps your school has already adopted or is considering this series. If not, or if you teach in the upper grades, what sort of unit could you develop to introduce your students to the basic economic principles that govern their lives?

ACTIVITIES ARE THE CRUCIAL ELEMENT

■ Begin gathering ideas for activities and projects—ways to transform the abstract principles of economics into real-life situations.

■ GRADE TEACHER published a series of articles on the subject by Anne McAllister, Coordinator of Elementary Education in Elkhart. Look to these for guidelines.

Economics is the subject of a new ele-
mentary school curriculum in Elkhart,
Indiana, that brings social studies into
sharp focus. Ingenious pupil activities
are the key. Clear thinking is the goal.
Understanding is the result. It all adds
up to an old truth: Learning—true
learning—can be fun.
        —School Management

Ask SRA for their sampler materials (no obligation) on OUR WORKING WORLD. Write to:

Science Research Associates, Inc.
259 E. Erie Street
Chicago, Illinois 60611

Study the articles, pamphlets and bulletins that show how the teachers in Elkhart worked with Professor Senesh to give their students an economic education.

READING LIST

Business Week, March 21, 1964, "Economics with ABCs." (Available through SRA)

Darby, Edwin, Financial Editor of The Chicago Sun-Times, "A Giant Step Forward: Social Studies for the Primary Grades." (Available through SRA)

Hodges, Luther, "Grade School Finance," LOOK, January 28, 1964.

McAllister, Anne, "Economics for 8-Year-Olds," *Grade Teacher,* October, 1964.

————, "All About Money," *Grade Teacher,* December, 1964.

————, "Helping Children Understand the Workaday World of Adults," February, 1965.

————, "Teaching Profit to Second Graders," March, 1965.

Rueff, Joseph A., "A Synopsis of the Elkhart Experiment in Economic Education and Related Social Sciences," General Electric Summer Institute on Economic Education, Purdue University, July, 1963.

School Management, "How One District Teaches Economics in Grade School," June, 1964. (Available through SRA)

Science Research Associates, Inc., "An Overview of Our Working World." (Available through SRA)

Senesh, Lawrence, "The Organic Curriculum: A New Experiment in Economic Education," Purdue University School of Industrial Management, Reprint Series #22.

We have found that every single big idea in economics can be related directly to the everyday life of the child at every grade level, down to the first grade.

—Professor Lawrence Senesh

CHAPTER 18

The Culture
Corner

*. . . we will have acquired models of high
thought and feeling. We will feel buoyed up
by the noble stream of Western civilization
of which we are a part.*

—Clifton Fadiman

*The teacher's own appreciation and ability
to influence the pupils in their appreciation
plays a very important part in developing the
proper attitude.*

—W. W. Charters

Mr. Fadiman was referring to the Lifetime Reading Plan in
the above quotation, but *models of high thought and feeling* may
include much more. Today's teacher has every opportunity to
provide such models for his students.

Establish a Culture Corner for your class—a small portion of
your daily schedule dedicated to the noble stream of music, art
and literature which is our heritage.

Encourage your students to get started on a lifetime adventure with greatness!

1. Featuring . . .

Prepare a "theater marquee" for a prominent spot in the classroom. Post the title of each day's selection.

- A string of lights adds interest.
- Plastic letters are effective.

—*But*—

- Plain cardboard will do.

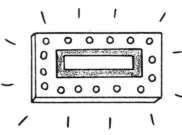

If table or shelf space is available, display books, record jackets, reproductions and realia that pertain to the day's selection.

MEMO

Investigate General Electric's Radio-Phono-Viewer

SHOW 'N TELL units

(6 transistor AM radio, viewing screen for film strips and 4-speed phono turntable).

Even very small children can easily manage these units. Over 100 picturesound programs are available in 18 categories (i.e., Fairy Tales, Children's Classics, Tales from Shakespeare, History, Science, Adventure, Biography, etc.).

Each program consists of an unbreakable, vinyl record (7", 33⅓ rpm) and a 15-picture mounted film strip housed in a hard cover jacket.

2. Keep a Record

Have each student keep a special notebook of the Culture Corner selections. Use the information for games, quizzes and reports.

Base part of the art, music and literature report card grades on Culture Corner activities. Prepare puzzles, stage contests, encourage projects and post manipulative charts that require the use of the information in the notebooks.

3. Choosing the Selections

Encourage your students to locate and bring in material suitable for the Culture Corner.

Assign committees to prepare an interest center, marquee and bulletin boards pertaining to the Culture Corner.

Make your selections from art, music and literature:

Listen to	. . . . the *Overture to Carmen*
Study	. . . . Watt's *Sir Galahad*
Enjoy	. . . . selections from Emerson
Hear	. . . . the recording of *The Midnight Ride of Paul Revere*
Discuss	. . . . . . an article from TIME's art section

4. "Story Hour"

If your schedule includes a daily story hour, read the classics to your students. For younger students select the abridged versions of the original work—those which eliminate many of the involved descriptive passages which are better appreciated in later years.

. . . I want them to learn to distinguish between what is written in haste to meet a demand for easy amusement and what is written with perception about people and conditions, what is written to appeal to the senses and what is written to appeal to the mind.
*—Georgena Goff **

* Quoted from "Culture for the Savages," by Georgena Goff from April, 1965 issue of *Redbook* magazine, © McCall Corporation 1965.

5. Listen to Literature

Hundreds and hundreds of selections are available on tape and on record. Seek them out! Robert Frost and Carl Sandburg have been recorded reading their own poetry; *Evangeline, Leaves of Grass, An Anthology of Negro Poets,* excerpts from Dante's *Inferno,* the Shakespearean Plays, *Poems and Letters of Robert Burns*—check with your school library, audio-visual library and public library. Write to Folkways Records, 117 West 46th Street, New York, New York for their catalog.

Literature is eavesdropping.
—Emerson

6. Dramatize Literature

Skits, choral readings, several-act plays, musicals and role playing all offer you and your students a chance to bring literature to life in the classroom.

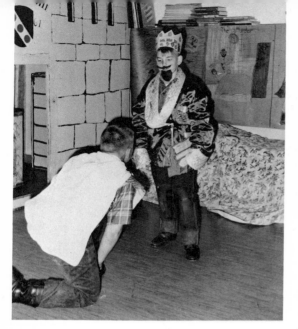

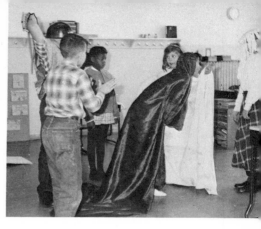

It will be objected that no one requires a justification for the study of great literature. That may be true of adults. But the young need to have such things proved to them. They are not even sure that literature is worth studying, they cannot tell whether the Homeric poems are great literature until after reading them, and they have only a vague intuitive grasp of the meaning of greatness in literature. It is not necessary to glorify a good subject; but you must explain it, allow its merits to display themselves, fill in a suitable background.

—Gilbert Highet

That, I said, is true of every great book: it either makes us want to do things, to go fishing, or fight harder or endure more patiently—or it takes us out of ourselves and beguiles us for a time with the friendship of completer lives than our own.

—David Grayson

7. Work With Literature

Find ways to work with the themes and passages which your students are studying. Assign special maps, murals, models, puppets, dioramas, drawings, essays, reports, exhibits and displays.

By Donald
Colson

The Tempest
February 24th 1966
by
William Shakespeare

I Like the story of "The Tempest"
because it has so many good characters in it.
The one I like the best is Caliban.
He was an old man and he smelled like a fish
when you caught it.
Prospero had learned magic from a book that
was old and he and a fairy studied from them.
A ship came to the Island and there was a
prince on the ship and his name was Ferdinand; he
was the King's son.
prospero had a daughter who did not know
that there were people in the world; she
thought all the people in the world had
a beard and were old like her father.
There were three more men.
They were the King, the butler, and the
Jester.

Literature only exists to express and develop that imaginative world which is our life, the kingdom that is within us. It follows that the literary side of a technical education should consist in an effort to make the pupils enjoy literature. It does not matter what they know, but the enjoyment is vital.
—Alfred North Whitehead

MEMO

Read Gilbert Highet's essays,

"The Birth of a Book"

and

"The First Few Words"

to your class. Give them an insight into the labor involved in writing and publishing a book, and the talent revealed by the great writers in their first few words.

TALENTS AND GENIUSES
Gilbert Highet

Oxford University Press
1957

8. Look at Literature

Comb audio-visual catalogs for slides, filmstrips and films of literary works. For example, among the 16mm sound films available through Coronet Films alone are:

Midsummer Night's Dream: Introduction to the Play
Scotland: Background for Literature
Legend of the Pied Piper
American Literature—Revolutionary Times
King Midas and the Golden Touch

Make your own movies of literature! Chapter 16 covers this in detail. Four hundred feet of film will give you a full half-hour show. Sound effects and music can be taped. Narration can be taped or given by the students as the film is shown.

*Enthusiasm is at its highest pitch when
we work creatively—no matter how
little our technical knowledge of the
medium—when we discover things for
ourselves, set our own moods, make
our own interpretations.*

—*Jacob Deschin*

9. Concerts in the Classroom

Record racks are filled with selections designed specifically to introduce young people to the classics. Plan a concert for the classroom—20 or 30 minutes of recorded music, with an intermission and refreshments, if you like.

Ditto the program or print it in a special place on the chalkboard.

Discuss concert manners. Ask students to "dress up"—the girls might wear gloves during the concert and the boys a tie—anything to set these times apart as *special*.

*Every great composition can stand
practically unlimited repetition, following the well-known law of the survival
of the fittest.*

—*Sigmund Spaeth*

10. Early in the Morning

During the first few minutes of the morning—during homeroom or while materials are being assembled or fees collected—play a classical selection on record or tape. No comments, just write the name of the selection and the performer on the board and insist that this be a "listening time."

*There is a particular excitement in dis-
covering a piece of music that grows
more fascinating with each successive
hearing—particularly if each time the
listener finds new beauties that he had
not suspected before.*

—*Sigmund Spaeth*

11. Work With Music

Sponsor a songfest. Invite parents and friends. Give a rhythm band concert for parents and friends. Learn the stories of the great operas. Dramatize them. Produce an opera in the classroom!

Take the music from pop songs, folk tunes, operatic arias, Broadway shows, and write your own words. These songs were written by student committees for units on pioneer life:

THE FINEST TOWN

5th Grade   "O Susannah"

We traveled covered wagon style
Across the countryside
Over steep and rocky mountain roads
Through valleys deep and wide.
The mud was thick
The rains beat down
The trip caused us to screech
But we pushed on through thick and thin
Till Robertsville we reached.
   Oh, Oh, the Roberts, the Pecks and Lecys too—
   They built the finest town of all
   It grew and grew and grew.

PIONEER LIFE

4th Grade   Turkey in the Straw

Oh, we're living in the woods
With the bullfrogs and the bugs
And the ladies spend their evenings
Making patch work quilts and rugs.
Every morning bright and early
Finds the men out in the field
Plowing, planting and a-praying
For good harvest and good yield.
We have a good life, hard though it be
Making U. S. History—
Back in time one hundred years
You'll find the best three families of pioneers.

*There was a great golden glory lasting
a half hour each week when Mr. Morton came to Francie's room to teach
music . . . he set his own words to
the great classics and gave them simple
names like "Lullaby" and "Serenade"
and "Street Song" and "Song for a Sun-
shiny Day."*

—*A Tree Grows In Brooklyn*

Let your students illustrate the music which asks for visual
interpretation: *Grand Canyon Suite, Swan of Tuonella, Night on
Bare Mountain, Tyll Eulenspiegel, Fountains of Rome, Mississippi Suite,* and the like. Play the selection while they are
drawing, sketching or painting.

Prepare puzzles and worksheets, games and quizzes, manipulative charts and contests to help students work with and remember the music they are studying and enjoying.

*There are a number of great composers
whose names should be as familiar as
those of statesmen, warriors and authors. They have contributed as much
as these to the life of the nation and
their names should be recognized and
honored.*

—*W. W. Charters*

12. Take a Good Look at Art

*Copies of good pictures are so cheap
that no school should be excused from
having many of the best in albums and
on the walls . . . The atmosphere of
the schoolroom should be pervaded
with the charm which emanates from
beautiful prints and pictures.*

—*W. W. Charters*

Let your students take a good look at art through slides,
prints, films, and field trips to museums.

Panorama Slide Programs visits a world famous art gallery each month. A subscription to the program includes 32 slides narrated by a well known art critic, a book of the paintings and the gallery and a special projector to show the slide cards.

Since all 32 slides are mounted on two cards, the paintings must be shown in order unless all slides are remounted in half-frame 2 x 2 mounts or you mask out any paintings you do not wish to include in your study program. Panorama is associated with the Columbia Record Club at 111 Fifth Ave., New York, N. Y.

Reproductions can be purchased from *Perry Pictures* at a price of from 2¢ to 25¢ per print, depending on size and color. Order the catalog from Perry Pictures, Inc., Malden, Massachusetts for 35¢.

No. 48—The Jester   Rijks Museum
Frans Hals (1580-1666)   Dutch School
    Artext Junior   Art Extension Society   New York—Westport, Conn.

Mexican Child   Diego Rivera, 1886., Mexican
Artext Junior No. 324. Also published as an Artext Print. Photographed in color from the original painting in a Private Collection.
                    Artext Prints, Inc., Westport, Conn.

No. 125—The Fighting Temeraire   National Gallery, London
J. M. W. Turner (1775-1851)   English School
        Artext Junior   Art Extension Society   New York—Westport, Conn.

The University Prints catalog can be obtained for 50¢. It lists 5,900 fine arts subjects in black and white and 145 in color. All prints are 5½" x 8" and cost 2½¢ each for black and white or 5¢ each for color. Order the catalog from The University Prints, 15 Brattle Street, Cambridge 38, Mass.

Art appreciation folders are available through the F. A. Owen Publishing Company, Dansville, New York. There are 100 art masterpieces to choose from, 9¾" x 12¾", and mounted on heavy mat paper. Each print comes in a folder with the story of the picture, the artist and study questions. The prints are divided into eight age-level series. Prints may be ordered separately or in folders. Junior prints which match the larger pictures are available for the pupils at 2¢ each in color.

- *Magazine* and *calendar* reproductions are available every month.
- Mount and frame your prints. Dimestore frames are inexpensive and come in a wide variety of materials and sizes.
- Change your selections frequently.
- Start an art lending library. Let students sign out the framed reproductions for a few days enjoyment in their homes.

13. Take Part in Art

After studying a particular painter and analyzing his style, let students attempt to paint in the same manner—first, copying one of his subjects, then trying to apply the same techniques to a composition of their own. Try a painting or drawing in the style of El Greco, Rembrandt, Cezanne, Van Gogh, or Picasso.

The best place to learn standards, the richest source of knowledge of pictorial unity, is from the masters . . . Study, compare and train your eyes as a musician trains his ear . . . Choose your favorite masters. Study them with your eyes and let your hands study them too by copying their drawings. You will find yourself in very good company: Manet copied Titian; Matisse copied Courbet; Liebermann copied Franz Hals; Braque copied Raphael; and long before them, Rembrandt copied Dürer.

—Gollwitzer

Let your students attempt not only painting, but sculpture, woodcarving, ceramics, mosaics, crafts, flower arranging. There is no better way to gain appreciation of an artist's genius.

To appreciate the works of other artists is not so difficult once you have tried to do it yourself. Nobody, however intelligent, can really hope to penetrate into the heart of a picture unless he does it for himself. However bad his efforts, however clumsy they may seem, through his attempts he will understand better the same problems and successes of the great painters, past and present . . .

—Alfred Daniels

Ask students to prepare a catalog of art objects in their homes or in the school: paintings, reproductions, sculpture, ceramics, special interior decoration features, landscaping, and the like.

(Tom Sawyer)

1. <u>Painting.</u> Original watercolor painted by Jean Wiselogel and given to the family by the artist.
2. <u>Painting.</u> Original oil painted by Ada Powell for the family.
3. <u>Reproduction.</u> PAINTER AND HIS MODEL by Picasso (1963). Framed
4. <u>Sculpture.</u> Madonna and Child, 14 inches high by Constance Ortmayer, 1955.
5. <u>Woodcarving.</u> Madonna and Child, 16 inches high, by Reichlin Anton. Purchased in Lucerne, Switzerland, 1959.
6. <u>Book.</u> JAPAN: A HISTORY IN ART by Bradley Smith. Book-of-the-Month Club Edition.

(Heidi)

14. Culture Corner Classwork

Assign maps, murals, dioramas, displays and projects of all kinds to illustrate what is being studied in the Culture Corner. Prepare puzzles, worksheets, games, quizzes and contests for classroom activities. Encourage special reports on the artists, composers, actors, musicians, sculptors, authors and dancers who have enriched the Culture Corner. Prepare special Who's Who bulletin boards featuring Culture Corner contributors.

Play Art Charades: An individual or a team member makes a sketch on the chalkboard which relates to something studied in the Culture Corner. Classmates try to guess the selection. Additional clues may be added, if necessary. The winner becomes the next sketcher.

Play Culture Corner Golf: Prepare 9 or 18 questions depending upon the number of holes you wish to play.

(Swan of Tuonela)

(Moses)

(Moby Dick)

1. Who painted this?
2. Who painted *Sir Galahad?*
3. Is this a concerto or a symphony theme?
4. From what opera is this aria?
5. Who wrote *La Boheme?*

HOLE	TEAM A	TEAM B
1		
2		
3		
4		
5		

HOLE	TEAM A	TEAM B
6		
7		
8		
9		

6. Who composed this folk song?

7. What book begins with the sentence, "Call me Ishmael."?

8. Is this an oil painting or a water color?

9. Who is the conductor of the Philadelphia Orchestra?

Every answer, correct or incorrect, counts as one stroke. The lowest score wins.

Someone with eyes keener than ours saw form in what we have passed by a thousand times. Someone has made uncommon, and very special, the common.

—Beaumont Newhall

CHAPTER 19

Something
to Live By

The purpose of a nation depends primarily
upon the way its children are brought up a
generation earlier. The way to improve the
nation for tomorrow is to enlighten and
strengthen the lives of children today.

—Robert J. Havighurst

Public schools and the teachers in those
schools are charged with the responsibility of
developing certain attitudes. The British edu-
cators in the nineteenth century called it
building character.

—James Bryant Conant

Failure to help students develop a philosophy
of life or commitment to a set of values which
will guide their behavior is a major weakness
of many schools.

—Kimball Wiles

295

From the time we are quite small we develop a personal philosophy—something to live by. It is formed by what we find in the world about us, good or bad.

As classroom teachers we have a tremendous opportunity to shape philosophy, to commit our students to a set of values. Take advantage of it! Introduce your students to that which has inspired, influenced and ennobled man since the beginning of time.

1. What Can You Do?

A child's mind is like a bank—whatever you put in, you get back in 10 years, with interest.*
　　　—Dr. Frederic J. Wertham

Spend a few minutes every single day showing your students some way in which men have met life with courage, honor, strength and conviction.

When the pupils come to you, their minds are only half formed, full of blank spaces and vague notions and oversimplification. You do not merely insert a lot of facts, if you teach them properly. It is not like injecting 500 cc of serum, or administering a year's dose of vitamins. You take the living mind and mold it.
　　　—Gilbert Highet

a. Present a selection—a story, quotation, anecdote, article, poem, epigram, apothegm, maxim or proverb.
b. Discuss it.
c. Post it.
d. Reflect upon it—through essays, poems, art and projects.
e. Keep it—in scrapbooks, notebooks and anthologies.
f. Use it—through memorization, deeds and outlook.

* Quoted from "Alfred Hitchcock and Dr. Wertham," by Dr. Frederic Wertham, from April, 1963 issue of *Redbook* magazine, © McCall Corporation 1963.

Ask your students to be alert for material—a sentence, a phrase, verse, picture or entire selection. Begin a file of the contributions.

2. Where Can You Find Material?

Everywhere! On buildings, in motion picture themes, on television and radio, in newspapers, magazines and advertisements, in books, speeches and from the students themselves.

3. To Get You Started . . .

Here are a few selections taken from the world about us. They have been gratefully acknowledged by the children as something special to live by.

> The January 28, 1964 issue of LOOK carried the picture essay, "Steady Hand in Vietnam's Hell Ward" and spoke of the work of Iowa-born Dr. Robert Norton. Dr. Norton, his wife and their three children have been in the Mekong since 1962,

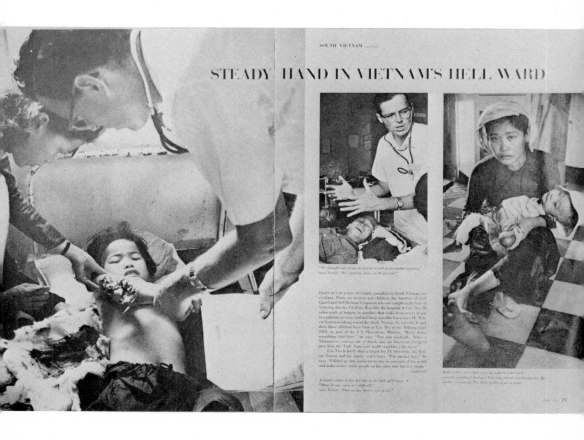

"Some people back in the states do nothing but rant about communism. In a way, we're lucky here. We can do something about it.

"I'm needed here. I didn't go into medicine to stay in one part of the world and make money while people on the other side bleed to death."

The difference between landscape and landscape is small but there is great difference in beholders.

—Emerson

There is not enough money in all America to relieve the misery of the under-developed world in a giant and endless soup kitchen. But there is enough know-how and enough knowledgeable people to help those nations help themselves.

—John F. Kennedy, Presidential Campaign Speech, November 2, 1960

We survive precisely as primitive man survived, that is by force and cunning. But we live by ideas and faiths.

—Clifton Fadiman

The September, 1963 issue of Reader's Digest carried the article, "New Food for Hungry Children" by Harland Manchester. A new cereal food mixture, Incaparina, has been developed to combat kwashiokor, the malnutrition disease that is a greedy child-killer in tropical and subtropical areas throughout the world.

Eight years of patient testing and research, first instigated by Dr. Robert S. Harris, Professor of Nutrition at MIT, resulted in this protein powder, Incaparina. The penny-a-glass life saver stands as an inspiring example of international team work, patience and dedication.

What are you giving room in your mind? Are you dumping just any old thing into it? If you use it as a garbage container, you will live a garbage-can existence.

—von Hesse

And when we come to think of it, goodness *is* uneventful. It does not flash, it glows. It is deep, quiet and very simple.

It passes not with oratory, it is commonly foreign to riches, nor does it often sit in the places of the mighty: but may be felt in the touch of a friendly hand or the look of a kindly eye.

—David Grayson
David Grayson's Omnibus

When I hear the people
Praising great ones,
Then I know that I too
Shall be esteemed,
I too when my time comes
Shall do mightily.
—*Chippewa Indian Song*

No matter what the mistakes are that you must make, do not be afraid of having made them or of making more of them. Trust your heart, which is a good one, to be right, and go ahead—don't stop. If you fall, tricked or tripped by others, or by yourself, even, get up and don't turn back.

—William Saroyan
The Human Comedy

Dr. Tom Dooley, founder of MEDICO, became acquainted with "the developing nations of the world" as a doctor in the United States Navy. After leaving the service, he went back to Southeast Asia in an effort to help the people help themselves:

"I'm going back to the jungle where my children don't have any clothes, nor any of the nice things you have. And you must never feel that what I do or anyone like me does was possible because I am an extraordinary person. I am not. I'm an ordinary man. This country was founded on the idea that the ordinary man can accomplish extraordinary things.

"Come to the developing nations of the world for a while. You will always know that you have given a fragment of your life for the good of many."

LOOK magazine carried an article by Chester Morrison, "A Study in Courage," telling of the infinite courage of Robert Bastion, a former fighter pilot, blinded and burned in a plane crash, who spent years in the hospital while doctors slowly rebuilt his

*face. He re-enrolled in the University of Southern
California under the GI Bill, graduated with honors
from law school, and is now Judge of the County
Court.*

From the advertising world—
portraits of our great patriots.

He led the chorus of the Union...

*Of the former Clementine Hozier, the present Lady
Churchill, Sir Winston once wrote, "What can be
more glorious than to be united in one's walk
through life with a being incapable of an ignoble
thought?"*

—AP news release from London

Three of the men who signed the Declaration of Independence were famous. They were truly extraordinary men: Thomas Jefferson, John Adams, and Benjamin Franklin. But what about the other fifty-three? For the most part they were, in all outward aspects, ordinary men. They came from various walks of life. Some were rich, others were poor. Some were scholars and educated persons, others were just barely literate. Some were immigrants, others were natives. Some were old, some young. They really had nothing much in common—nothing except a passionate love for their country. This was enough to bind them together for all eternity, enough to make their names a byword for patriotism and courage wherever liberty is understood and wherever freedom is enjoyed.

—Lifeline, January, 1963

We must aim above the mark to hit the mark.
—Ralph Waldo Emerson

Dr. Albert Schweitzer, author, teacher, philosopher, musician and medical doctor, turned his back on the rewards of European society and dedicated his life to the service of Man as a medical missionary in Africa.

"It struck me as incomprehensible that I should be allowed to lead such a happy life, while I saw so many people around me wrestling with care and suffering.

"It is unthinkable that we civilized peoples should keep for ourselves alone the wealth of means for fighting sickness, pain and death which science has given us. If there is any ethical thinking at all among us, how can we refuse to let these new discoveries benefit those who, in distant lands, are subject to even greater physical distress than we are?

"However much concerned I was at the problem of the misery in the world, I never let myself get lost in broodings over it; I always held firmly to the thought that each one of us can do a little to bring some portion of it to an end."

There is nothing weak and unmanly about clean hands and faces. A man who is strong and tough never needs to show it in his dress. Toughness is a quality of mind, like bravery or honesty or ambition. In a year or so some of you will be thinking about girl friends; believe me, they will think you much more attractive with clean teeth, hands and faces.

—E. R. Brathwaite
TO SIR, WITH LOVE

All life is an experiment. The more experiments you make, the better. What if they are a little coarse . . . what if you do fail and get fairly rolled in the dirt once or twice? Up again, you shall never be so afraid of a tumble.

—Ralph Waldo Emerson

When I get my report card I don't feel a bit ashamed because I know if I done work through the semester it just wasn't good enough and then the next semester, I'll try harder and if that isn't good enough I'll try with all my might. There's an old saying you get what you pay for, that's true and so is this "you get what you work for" so if I know that I tried there's nothing to be ashamed of. Some kids don't even work and try but they get low grades too but if you really try you'll get lots more out of it not on your report card but in you.

—Jerry Neuland, 7th Grader,
Essay

The S. S. Hope (former naval vessel Consolation), a 15,200 ton, 520 foot hospital ship, is manned by a permanent staff of handpicked nurses and technicians, and a rotating staff of doctors who serve for two month periods without pay.

The second voyage of the Hope was to Peru. The staff gave medical and surgical care to the Peruvians and taught local medical personnel directly and by example. The care given to these people by the United

States through the S. S. Hope made a tremendous impact. As North Americans worked side by side with Peruvians, they reported the experience to be one of the greatest of their lives.

"Project Concern: Somebody Has To Care" was the title of an article on the work of Jim and Martha Turpin, a young couple who took their children and their lives from a comfortable medical practice in Southern California to Kowloon, the slums of Hong Kong.

PROJECT CONCERN
Somebody has to care

Who could see a child with arms like chicken bones and the wounds of five rounds of chain around his leg without wanting to help? The trick that most of us manage is not to see him—not even in the mind's eye.

The world abounds in pitiful children. To look at them—really look at them; long enough to know that hunger multiplied by millions is still one small, desperate, private hunger—is a soul-shaking thing. An increasing number of Americans, blessed themselves with food, warmth, comfort and cleanliness, are opening their imaginations to the countless personal tragedies of privation around the world—and are committing their lives to help.

Two of them are Jim and Martha Turpin, who conceived a project so idealistic that not even a church or established relief organization could help. Both were born in the South, Jim in Kentucky, Martha in Alabama. Who knows where idealism starts? On the record, both were active in church work in their teens; Jim particularly admired his grandfather, John Wesley Duke, a state health-department physician who served and was loved throughout an entire rural county. By the time he was 12, Jim knew he wanted to be a medical missionary to China.

Jim and Martha were married on the day of their graduation from college. Six years later, Jim was both an M.D. and an ordained Methodist minister. Until last year, he practiced medicine in a Southern California town, and used to give one day a week to a clinic across the border in Tijuana. Martha used to accompany him. There they had their first jolting, exhilarating taste of what it is like to bring help and hope to the utterly lost—to those whose historic role it has always been to go unnoticed. "I found in Tijuana that I needed these people even more than they needed me."

Last year Dr. Jim Turpin and his wife were 34 years old, lived with their four children in a ranch house in prosperous Coronado, and led useful lives. But

Tijuana was not enough. Jim wanted to go to the greatest slum in the world, the very pit of urban civilization: Hong Kong. The more he investigated, the greater he found the need. Refugees from Red China are the British crown colony's teeming problem. Over a million of them, stripped of every possession, have poured onto the barren, waterless strip of mainland known as the New Territories or onto the jam-packed junks and sampans of Hong Kong harbor. On the mainland is the autonomous walled city of Kowloon, lawless, squalid almost beyond American conception. Its walls are ancient buildings encompassing an area 10 blocks square. Its passages are so narrow that every morsel of food and stick of fuel must go in on human backs. In its streets and warrens live a quarter of a million people—until last year without any medical care within the city walls whatsoever. On the pitiful harbor boats live another 200,000 people—until this year without any medical care in the harbor whatsoever.

Jim paid one visit to Hong Kong in 1961 and saw what he went to see. In August of 1962 he and Martha and the children, Keith, eleven, Payton, nine, Scott, four, and Jan, three, moved to Hong Kong.

The work they went to do had been conceived by Jim out of whole cloth. No organization had been before him. He was unwilling to bring doctrine to a people whose needs were so overwhelmingly physical, and he decided not to seek the support of a church. But all the people who knew and liked the personable young physician and his wife—home-town friends, college professors, Coronado friends—gathered together to create Jim's own organization, Project Concern. An old Navy friend, Paul Fleener, left his job at Kansas State University, and he and his wife came along to help. By the time the two families sailed, a relatively small handful of people had raised enough money to open the first clinic in Kowloon.

The clinic is in operation now, with the addition of two young Chinese refugee doctors, a biochemist and some British volunteers. Above it is

an opium den, next door a pig pen. The staff works seven days a week; when they arrive in the mornings, hundreds of children are lined up, and cry "Hal la!" in greeting. Every child is given a vitamin pill, some milk and two nutrient crackers. As one observer described it, "A British lady eagerly stuffs a pill into every open mouth in sight."

It was here Jim found the starved boy whose legs had been manacled because he had tried to run away. Here he treats some 50 cases of illness a day, most of them caused by malnutrition.

A second clinic is about to open as this is being written. This one will be in Hong Kong harbor, on a specially built junk with clinic area on deck and living quarters for the Turpins and Fleeners below. The junk is expected to be christened in late March with a bottle of water from the river in the Congo where Dr. Albert Schweitzer has his hospital.

Building the junk has swallowed $14,000. With donated drugs and volunteer help in both the United States and Hong Kong, Jim hopes to keep the running costs of the two clinics to $2,000 a month.

The Turpins' attitude is not sacrificial. "People who speak of sacrifice don't understand why we're doing this," begins Martha. More practically, until the junk is ready they are living in a decent bungalow that looks, to their shanty neighbors, like lordly wealth.

Their three bright and handsome sons are going to good British schools. Daughter Jan has a hundred playmates. "I doubt if I give pause for our children as often as a mother in America," Martha continues. "They are learning many things about life that children at home, protected by all their toys and comforts, never know. For example, the other day we found Scott, now five, handing out our precious rations of bubble gum to Cantonese children through the gate. Giving was his pleasure."

Somebody has to care. If you do, send your tax-deductible contribution to Project Concern, Inc., c/o Postmaster, San Diego, California.

Dr. Jim Turpin opened Hong Kong clinic on a shoestring, was soon flooded by undernourished children.

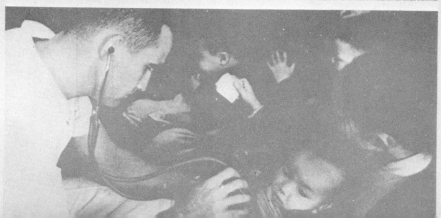

"An increasing number of Americans, blessed themselves with food, warmth, comfort and cleanliness, are opening their imaginations to the countless personal tragedies of privation around the world—and are committing their lives to help."

—*Ladies' Home Journal*

In 1966 McGraw-Hill published "Vietnam Doctor—the story of Project Concern," Dr. Turpin's account of the increasing world-wide interest and participation in this work.

Thousands of babies in the United States could have been born pitifully deformed, had it not been for the courage and conviction of Dr. Frances Oldham Kelsey, a U. S. Food and Drug Administration medical officer. She refused to be hurried into approving an application for marketing the drug thalidomide.

Be concerned about the future. The rest of your life will be spent there.

—*Charles Francis Kettering*

O God,
Give us serenity
    to accept what cannot be changed
Courage to change what should be changed
And wisdom to distinguish
    the one from the other.

—Reinhold Niebuhr

"The Enchanted Child" was only with her family three years. The way in which that family faced her death was as fine and as beautiful as the short years she spent on earth.

"There were so many things about Ceci that I look back on now as being somehow unusually enchanting, almost as if she were meant to live a lifetime in three years.

"I cannot help feeling that we should not be bitter that Ceci went so soon. Rather we should be grateful with all our hearts that it was our privilege to

be given her in the first place. It is a blessing beyond any we shall ever have again."

Ceci's mother enriched the life of every person who read her small article. What a beautiful experience it was for every teacher who shared it with her students.

"The Enchanted Child"
Shirley G. Goodrich
Ladies Home Journal

One should not hide visible emotion when it is genuine, for this can be just as unkind a wrong as holding back from a man what is due him. Your friend, your beloved, your child, or whoever is the object of your love, has a claim upon its expression also in words when it really moves you inwardly. The emotion is not your possession but the other's. The expression of it is his due, since in the emotion you belong to him who moves you and makes you conscious of belonging to him. When the heart is full you should not grudgingly and loftily short-change another, injure him by pressing your lips together in silence; you should let the mouth speak out of the abundance of the heart; you should not be ashamed of your feelings and still less of honestly giving to each one his due.

—Soren Kierkegaard
Works of Love

Reprints of Reader's Digest Articles such as "Let's Dare to Be Square" are available for all readers. This Charles H. Brower article examined the word "square," once one of the finest words in the language, but currently equated with "the man who never learned to get away with it. A Joe who volunteers when he doesn't have to. A guy who gets his kicks from trying to do something better than anyone else can." Mr. Brower points out that "this country was discovered, put together, fought for and saved by squares."

"Today, our country still has a choice. I believe it has already begun to make that choice. I believe it is going back to its old beliefs in such things as ideas, pride, patriotism, loyalty, devotion and even hard work."

—Let's Dare to Be Square
Charles H. Brower
The Reader's Digest, April, 1963

Each month the non-sectarian magazine, GUIDEPOSTS, offers a wealth of material for the teacher who is helping his students find something to live by. A practical guide to successful living, this little magazine exists to point the way to deeper faith and more creative living. A subscription costs $2.00 a year. Order yours from

Guideposts
Carmel
New York

People feel that genius and inner potential must come forth through personal expression, not through outside influence. But how can you help being influenced? How can you avoid seeing things created by others? . . . . It is what you choose to let take root in you and influence you that matters.
—Gollwitzer

CHAPTER 20

Sources and Resources

To read books passively does not feed a mind.
It makes blotting paper out of it.
>   —Mortimer J. Adler

Get your knowledge quickly, and then use it.
If you can use it, you will retain it.
>   —Alfred North Whitehead

PLANNING AHEAD

Armstrong, Frank Alexander. *Idea-Tracking*. New York: Criterion
    Books, 1960.
Ashton-Warner, Sylvia. *Teacher*. New York: Simon & Schuster, 1963.
Charters, W. W. *Teaching the Common Branches*. Boston: Houghton
    Mifflin Co., 1924.
Chase, Stuart. *The Tyranny of Words*. New York: Harcourt, Brace
    & Co., 1938.

307

Clark, Harold F., Harold S. Sloan. *Classrooms in the Military*. New York: Bureau of Publications, Teachers College, Columbia University, 1964.

Conant, James B. *The Education of American Teachers*. New York: McGraw-Hill Book Co., Inc., 1963.

Department of the Army, *Techniques of Military Instruction*. FM 21-6. Washington: Department of the Army, May, 1954.

Deschin, Jacob. *Say It With Your Camera*. New York: Ziff-Davis Publishing Company, 1960.

Dufay, Frank R. *Ungrading the Elementary School*. Parker Publishing Co., West Nyack, N.Y., 1966.

Eble, Kenneth E., *A Perfect Education*. New York: The Macmillan Co., 1966.

Flesch, Rudolf. *The Art of Plain Talk*. New York: Harper & Bros., 1946.

Highet, Gilbert. *The Art of Teaching*. New York: Vintage Books, 1956.

Hodges, Luther H. *"Are Our Children Half-Educated?"* LOOK: January 28, 1964, pp. 85.

Holt, John. *How Children Fail*. New York: Pitman Publishing Corp., 1964.

Keyes, Kenneth I., Jr. *How To Develop Your Thinking Ability*. New York: McGraw-Hill Book Co., Inc., 1950.

Lewis, Gertrude M. *Educating the More Able Children In Grades Four, Five and Six*. (U. S. Department of Health, Education and Welfare, Bulletin #1) Washington: Government Printing Office, 1961.

Mackintosh, Helen K., Wilhelmina Hill. *How Children Learn To Think*. (U. S. Department of Health, Education and Welfare, Bulletin #2) Washington: U. S. Government Printing Office, 1953.

Montessori, Maria. *The Absorbent Mind*. Adyar, Madras, India: The Theosophical Publishing House, 1963.

————. *The Secret of Childhood*. Bombay: Orient Longmans, 1963.

————. *Reconstruction in Education*. Adyar, Madras, India: The Theosophical Publishing House, 1961.

————. *Spontaneous Activity in Education*. New York: Schocken Books, 1965.

————. *Dr. Montessori's Own Handbook*. New York: Schocken Books, 1965.

McMurry, Charles A. (ed.) *Public School Methods, Vol. IV*. New York: School Methods Company, 1913.

————. *Public School Methods, Vol. V*. New York: School Methods Company, 1913.

Osborn, Alex. *Wake Up Your Mind*. New York: Charles Scribner's Sons, 1952.

Owen Publishing Company. (ed.) *347 Tips For Upper-Grade Teachers*. Dansville: F. A. Owen Publishing Company, 1955.

Phillips, Margaret M., Marjorie Carr Smith. *Try These Answers*. New York: Row, Peterson & Co., 1956.

Rambusch, Nancy McCormick. *Learning How To Learn*. Baltimore: Helicon Press, 1962.

Ryan, Nellie. *What Every Teacher Should Know*. Chicago: Lyons & Carnahan, 1961.

Sheppard, Lila. *Dancing on the Desk Tops*. Evanston: Row, Peterson & Co., 1960.

Simon, Henry W. *What Is A Teacher*. New York: Collier Books, 1964.

Standing, E. M. *The Montessori Method: A Revolution in Education*. Fresno: The Academy Library Guild, 1962.

Tiedt, Sidney W. and Iris M. Tiedt. *Elementary Teacher's Complete Ideas Handbook*. W. Nyack: Parker Publishing Co., Inc., 1965.

Wiles, Kimball. *The Changing Curriculum of the American School*. Englewood Cliffs: Prentice-Hall, 1963.

————. *Teaching For Better Schools*. New York: Prentice-Hall, Inc., 1953.

————. *Supervision For Better Schools*. New York: Prentice-Hall, Inc., 1950.

Whitehead, Alfred North. *The Aims of Education*. New York: The New American Library, 1957.

Wilkes, L. *Teach Yourself to Teach*. London: The English Universities Press, Ltd., 1959.

CLASSROOMS AS WORKSHOPS

Black, Gretchen Z. *"Creating A Stimulating Learning Environment For Third Graders."* Unpublished Masters Problem in Elementary Education, The Graduate School of Cornell University, 1957.

Carmel, James H. *Exhibition Techniques: Traveling and Temporary*. New York: Reinhold Publishing Corp., 1962.

Gilbreth, Lillian M., Orpha Mae Thomas, Eleanor Clymer. *Management In The Home*. New York: Dodd, Mead & Co., Inc., 1954.

TIME SAVERS: RECORDS, FILES AND FORMS

Collison, Robert L. *Modern Business Filing and Archives*. New York: John de Graff, Inc., 1963.

Gore, Michael. *How To Organize Your Time*. Garden City: Nelson Doubleday, Inc., 1959.

Weeks, Bertha M. *How To File and Index*. New York: Ronald Press Company, 1956.

FIRST DAY FEVERS

Abraham, Willard. *A Handbook For The New Teacher*. New York: Rinehart & Co., Inc., 1960.

Tarbell, Harlan. *Chalk Talk Manual*. Minneapolis: T. S. Denison & Co., Inc., 1962.

SETTING STANDARDS

Fine, Benjamin. *The Modern Family Guide to Education*. Garden City: Doubleday & Co., Inc., 1962.

———. *Stretching Their Minds*. New York: E. P. Dutton & Co., Inc., 1964.

Lewis, Gertrude M. *Educating the More Able Children In Grades Four, Five and Six*. (U. S. Department of Health, Education and Welfare, Bulletin #1) Washington: Government Printing Office, 1961.

Rambusch, Nancy McCormick. *Learning How To Learn*. Baltimore: Helicon Press, 1962.

CLASSROOM TESTING AND EVALUATION

Ebel, Robert L. *Measuring Educational Achievement*. Englewood Cliffs: Prentice-Hall, Inc., 1965.

Huff, Darrell. *Score: The Strategy of Taking Tests*. New York: Appleton-Century-Crofts, Inc., 1961.

Odell, C. W. *How To Improve Classroom Testing*. Dubuque: W. C. Brown, 1953.

Schneider, Elsa. *Games and Self-Testing Activities for the Classroom*. (U. S. Department of Health, Education and Welfare) Washington: Government Printing Office, 1961.

Thorndike, Robert L. and Elizabeth Hagen. *Measurement and Evaluation in Psychology and Education*. New York: John Wiley & Sons, Inc., 1955.

TEACHING THEM TO STUDY

Anderson, Paul S. *Language Skills in Elementary Education*. New York: The Macmillan Co., 1964.

Cevasco, George A. *Grammar Self-Taught*. New York: Frederick Fell, Inc., 1963.

Coon, Horace. *Speak Better—Write Better English*. New York: New American Library, 1954.

Cooper, Gosvenor W. *Learning To Listen*. Chicago: Phoenix Books, The University of Chicago Press, 1957.

Fader, Daniel N. and Morton H. Shaevity. *Hooked On Books*. New York: Berkley Publishing Corp., 1966.

Funk, Wilfred. *Words of Power*. New York: Pocket Books, Inc., Cardinal Edition, 1955.

————, Norman Lewis. *30 Days To A More Powerful Vocabulary*. New York: Washington Square Press, 1960.

Furness, Edna L. *Spelling for the Millions*. New York: Appleton-Century, 1964.

Hansen, Carl F. and Dorothy I. Johnson, LaVerne C. Walker, Octavia E. Webb. *A Handbook for Young Writers*. Englewood Cliffs: Prentice-Hall, Inc., 1965.

Hegarty, Edward J. *How To Write A Speech*. New York: McGraw-Hill Book Co., Inc., 1951.

Hodges, John C. *Harbrace Handbook of English*. New York: Harcourt, Brace and World, Inc., 1959.

Hook, J. N. *Writing Creatively*. Boston: D. C. Heath & Co., 1963.

Kahn, Gilbert, Donald J. D. Mulkerne. *The Term Paper—Step By Step*. Garden City: Doubleday & Co., Inc., 1964.

Lewis, Norman. *Word Power Made Easy*. New York: Permabook, 1961.

Linn, James W. *The Essentials of English Composition*. New York: Charles Scribner's Sons, 1912.

Morris, William. *It's Easy To Increase Your Vocabulary*. New York: Harper & Bros., 1957.

Nichols, Ralph G. *Listening*. Ft. Belvoir: U. S. Army Management School, 1965.

O'Donnell, James J., Raymond L. Taylor, Paul J. McElaney. *Help Your Child Succeed in School*. New York: Dell Publishing Co., Inc., 1962.

Pankey, George E., J. J. Sachs. *Five Thousand Useful Words*. Nashville: Southwestern Co., 1937.

Powers, David Guy. *How To Say A Few Words Effectively*. Garden City: Nelson Doubleday, Inc., 1958.

Rapp, Stanley. *How To Get Information—Fast!* Garden City: Nelson Doubleday, Inc., 1959.

Sandwick, Richard L., Anna Tilden Bacon. *The High School Word Book*. Boston: D. C. Heath & Co., 1908.

U. S. Army Ordnance School. *Staff Writing Handbook*. Aberdeen: U. S. Army Ordnance School, 1957.

Wallace, Sarah Leslie. *So You Want To Be A Librarian*. New York: Harper & Row, 1963.

Warriner, John E. *English Grammar and Composition*. New York: Harcourt, Brace & Co., 1957.

COMPETITION, RECOGNITION AND REWARDS

Gellerman, Saul W. *Motivation and Productivity*. New York: American Management Association, Inc., 1963.

Highet, Gilbert. *The Art of Teaching*. New York: Vintage Books, 1956.

Whitehead, Alfred North. *The Aims of Education*. New York: The New American Library, 1957.

CLASSROOM PUBLICITY AND PUBLIC RELATIONS

Griswold, Glenn and Denny (ed.). *Your Public Relations—The Standard Public Relations Handbook*. New York: Funk & Wagnalls Co., Inc., 1948.

Holder, Robert. *A Complete Guide to School Publications*. Englewood Cliffs: Prentice-Hall, 1964.

Kindred, Leslie W. *How To Tell The School Story*. Englewood Cliffs: Prentice-Hall, 1960.

DRILLING WITHOUT DRUDGERY

Adler, Mortimer J. *How To Read A Book*. New York: Simon & Schuster, 1940.

Anderson, Paul S. *Language Skills in Elementary Education*. New York: The Macmillan Co., 1964.

Armstrong, Leila and Rowena Hargrave. *Building Reading Skills: Teacher's Guidebook*. Wichita: The McCormick–Mathers Publishing Co., 1951.

Basch, Lester D., Milton Finkelstein. *Spelling Self-Taught*. New York: Sterling Publishing Co., 1962.

Black, Gretchen Z. *"Creating A Stimulating Learning Environment For Third Graders."* Unpublished Masters Problem in Elementary Education, The Graduate School of Cornell University, 1957.

Brown, Myra B. *"Science Activities of the Eight Year Old in Duval County, Florida."* Unpublished Masters Problem in Elementary Education, The Graduate School of Cornell University, 1957.

Cox, Claire. *Rainy Day Fun For Kids*. New York: Association Press, 1962.

Crescimbeni, Joseph. *Arithmetic Enrichment Activities for Elementary School Children*. West Nyack: Parker Publishing Co., Inc., 1965.

————. *Teaching the New Mathematics*. West Nyack: Parker Publishing Co., Inc., 1966.

Cuisenaire, George, Caleb Gattegno. *Numbers In Colour*. Third Edition. London: Heinemann Ed. Books Ltd., 1957.

Depew, Arthur M. *The Cokesbury Game Book*. Nashville: Cokesbury Press, 1939.

Doman, Glenn. *How To Teach Your Baby To Read*. New York: Random House, 1964.

Eisenberg, Helen and Larry. *The Pleasure Chest*. Nashville: Parthenon Press, 1949.

Flowerdew, Phyllis, Ronald Ridout. *Reading to Some Purpose, Books 1-8*. Edinburgh: Oliver & Boyd, Ltd., 1952.

Forbush, William Byron, Harry R. Allen. *The Book of Games for Home, School and Playground*. Philadelphia: John C. Winston Co., 1954.

Fraser, Phyllis, Edith Young. *A Treasury of Games, Quizzes, and Puzzles*. New York: Grosset & Dunlap, Inc., 1947.

Gans, Roma. *Common Sense in Teaching Reading*. Indianapolis: The Bobbs-Merrill Co., Inc., 1963.

Gattegno, Caleb. *Modern Mathematics With Numbers in Color*. Reading: Educational Explorers Ltd., 1960, 1961.

————. *Book A, Mathematics With Numbers in Color*. Mt. Vernon: Cuisenaire Company of America, Inc., 1958, 1961.

————. *Arithmetic: A Teacher's Introduction to the Cuisenaire-Gattegna Methods of Teaching Arithmetic*. Mt. Vernon: Cuisenaire Company of America, Inc., 1960.

Gowland, Peter. *How To Take Better Home Movies*. New York: Arco Publishing Company, 1960.

Hay, Julie, Charles E. Wingo. *Teachers Manual for Reading With Phonics*. Philadelphia: J. B. Lippincott Co., 1954.

Hook, J. N. *Writing Creatively*. Boston: D. C. Heath & Co., 1963.

Hunt, W. Benjamin. *Indian and Camp Handicraft*. Milwaukee: The Bruce Publishing Co., 1945.

Jackson, Lora Z. *Around the Clock*. New York: Grosset & Dunlap, 1937.

Johnson, Donovan A. *Paper Folding for the Mathematics Class*. Washington: National Council of Teachers of Mathematics, NEA, 1957.

Kittle, Ruth. *Kittle's Penmanship*. New York: American Book Company, 1961.

Leeming, Joseph. *Money-Making Hobbies*. New York: J. B. Lippincott Co., 1948.

Matill, Edward L. *Meaning in Crafts*. Englewood Cliffs: Prentice-Hall, 1965.

Morton, Robert Lee. *Teaching Children Arithmetic*. New York: Silver Burdett Co., 1953.

Mueller, Francis J. *Arithmetic—Its Structure and Concepts*. Englewood Cliffs: Prentice-Hall, Inc., 1964.

McKee, Paul. *The Teaching of Reading*. Boston: Houghton Mifflin Co., 1948.

Norinsky, Sid. *The Amateur's 8mm Movie Guide*. New York: Universal Photo Books, 1957.

Orlick, Emanuel and Jean Mosley. *Teacher's Illustrated Handbook of Stunts.* West Nyack: Parker Publishing Co., Inc., 1963.

Parker, Don H. *SRA Reading Laboratories Manual.* Chicago: Science Research Associates, Inc., 1960.

Perceptual Development Laboratories (ed.). *Reading Improvement Course.* St. Louis: Perceptual Development Laboratories, 1963.

Rosenhaus, Max. *Penmanship Step By Step.* Columbus: The Zaner-Bloser Company, 1954.

Schneider, Elsa. *Games and Self-Testing Activities for the Classroom.* (U. S. Department of Health, Education and Welfare) Washington: Government Printing Office, 1961.

Spalding, Romalda Bishop with Walter T. Spalding. *The Writing Road to Reading.* New York: William Morrow & Co., 1957.

Swain, Henry. *How To Study Mathematics.* Washington: National Council of Teachers of Mathematics, NEA, 1955.

Trivett, John V. *Mathematical Awareness.* New York: Cuisenaire Company of America, Inc., 1962.

PROJECTS, DISPLAYS AND EXHIBITION TECHNIQUES

Blough, Glenn O., Marjorie Campbell. *Making and Using Classroom Science Materials in the Elementary School.* New York: Dryden Press, Inc., 1954.

Carmel, James H. *Exhibition Techniques: Traveling and Temporary.* New York: Reinhold Publishing Corp., 1962.

Coplan, Kate. *Poster Ideas and Bulletin Board Techniques: For Libraries and Schools.* Dobbs Ferry: Oceana Publications Inc., 1962.

De Kieffer, Robert and Lee W. Cochran. *Manual of Audio-Visual Techniques.* Englewood Cliffs: Prentice-Hall, 1962.

De Lemos, John. *Planning and Producing Posters.* Worcester: The Davis Press, Inc., 1950.

Huff, Darrel. *How To Lie With Statistics.* New York: W. W. Norton & Co., 1954.

Johnson, Donovan A. and Clarence E. Olander. *How To Use Your Bulletin Board.* Washington: National Council of Teachers of Mathematics, NEA, 1955.

Kinder, James S. *Audio-Visual Materials and Techniques.* New York: American Book Company, 1959.

Liechti, Alice O., Jack R. Chappell. *Making and Using Charts.* San Francisco: Fearon Publishers, Inc.

Long, Paul E. *Teaching With The Flannel Board.* Philadelphia: Instructo Products Co., 1960.

Modley, Rudolf and Dyno Lowenstein. *Pictographs and Graphs:*

How To Make and Use Them. New York: Harper & Bros., 1952.

Power, Gertrude Lenore. *Making Posters, Flashcards and Charts for Extension Teaching.* (Federal Government Extension Service Miscellaneous Publication #796) Washington: Government Printing Office, October, 1956.

TEACHING THEM TO DRAW AND TO LETTER

Daniels, Alfred. *Painting and Drawing.* New York: Arc Books, Inc., 1962.

Famous Artists Course. Westport: Institute of Commercial Art, Inc., 1950.

Freedman, Edward H. *Conversational Drawing.* New York: Farrar, Straus & Co., 1949.

————. *How To Draw.* New York: Bantam Books, Inc., 1965.

Freer, Howard. *You Can Paint With A Pencil.* New York: The Studio Publications Inc., 1951.

Gollwitzer, Gerhard. *Express Yourself in Drawing.* New York: Sterling Publishing Co., Inc., 1962.

Ham, Jack. *Drawing the Head and Figure.* New York: Grosset & Dunlap, Inc., 1963.

Holmes, Carl. *ABC of Lettering.* Laguna Beach: Walter T. Foster Art Service.

Holub, Rand. *Lettering Simplified.* New York: Watson-Guptill Publications, Inc., 1957.

Laker, Russell. *Anatomy of Lettering.* New York: The Studio Publications, 1959.

Longyear, William. *Type and Lettering.* New York: Watson-Guptill Publications, Inc., 1950.

Loomis, Andrew. *Creative Illustration.* New York: The Viking Press, 1947.

Peck, Ruth L. and Robert S. Aniello. *What Can I Do For An Art Lesson?* West Nyack: Parker Publishing Co., Inc., 1966.

Tarbell, Harlan. *Chalk Talk Manual.* Minneapolis: T. S. Denison & Co., Inc., 1962.

White, Peter. *The Second Easy Drawing Book.* New York: Sterling Publishing Co., Inc., 1955.

FAR-REACHING FIELD TRIPS

Johnson, Donovan A. and Dirk Ten Brinke, Lauren G. Woodby. *How To Use Field Trips in Mathematics.* Washington: National Council of Teachers of Mathematics, NEA, 1956.

Michaelis, John U. *Social Studies for Children in a Democracy.* Englewood Cliffs: Prentice-Hall, Inc., 1956.

TEACHING THROUGH "MAKE BELIEVE" TRIPS
THE ACTIVITY DAY
TEN UNITS TO TRY

American Home Economic Association. *The World's Favorite Recipes from the United Nations*. New York: Harper & Bros., 1951.

Bryson, Lyman. *An Outline of Man's Knowledge of the Modern World*. New York: McGraw-Hill Book Co., Inc., 1960.

Cleveland, Harlan and Gerard J. Mangone, John Clarke Adams. *The Overseas Americans*. New York: McGraw-Hill Book Co., Inc., 1960.

Committee for the Study of the Social Studies. *Teaching the Social Studies in Caddo Parish Schools,* Bulletin #19. Shreveport: Caddo Parish, 1963.

Coon, Horace. *150 Budget Vacations*. New York: David McKay Co., Inc., 1955.

Crane, Burton. *The Practical Economist*. New York: Simon & Schuster, 1960.

Evlin, Enid. *So You're Going Abroad*. New York: Comet Press Books, 1958.

Fodor, Eugene. *Jet Age Guide to Europe 1960*. New York: David McKay Co., Inc., 1960.

Hill, Wilhelmina. *Social Studies in the Elementary School Program*. (U. S. Department of Health, Education and Welfare, Bulletin #5) Washington: Government Printing Office, 1963.

Hunt, Sarah and Ethel Cain. *Games The World Around*. New York: A. S. Barnes & Co., 1941.

Junior League of Tampa. *The Gasparilla Cookbook*. Tampa: The Junior League of Tampa, Florida, 1961.

Keene, Frances W. *Fun Around the World*. Pelham: Seahorse Press, 1955.

Liebman, Rebekah R., and Gertrude A. Young. *The Growth of America*. Englewood Cliffs: Prentice-Hall, Inc., 1959.

Macfarlan, Allan and Paulette. *Fun With Brand-New Games*. New York: Association Press, 1961.

Michaelis, John U. *Social Studies for Children in a Democracy*. Englewood Cliffs: Prentice-Hall, Inc., 1956.

Millen, Nina. *Children's Games From Many Lands*. New York: Friendship Press, 1963.

O'Donnell, Mabel. *Guidebook for Singing Wheels*. New York: Row, Peterson & Co., 1940.

Pan American World Airways (ed.). *New Horizons World Guide*. New York: Pan American World Airways, 1960-61.

President's Council on Youth Fitness. *Youth Physical Fitness.* (U. S. Department of Health, Education and Welfare.) Washington: Government Printing Office, July, 1961.

Reader's Digest Assoc. (ed.). *Our Human Body, Its Wonders and Its Care.* Pleasantville: Reader's Digest Assoc., 1962.

Robinson, Marshall A., Herbert C. Morton, James D. Calderwood. *An Introduction to Economic Reasoning.* Washington: The Brookings Institution, 1959.

Strong, William M., and A. Milton Runyon. *Travel Abroad at Low Cost.* Garden City: Doubleday & Co., Inc., 1960-61 edition.

Tooze, Ruth Anderson and Beatrice Perham Krone. *Literature and Music as Resources for Social Studies.* Englewood Cliffs: Prentice-Hall, Inc., 1955.

Tunis, Edwin. *Frontier Living.* Cleveland: The World Publishing Company, 1961.

Von Baumann, Cyril and Beulah Phelps Harris. *The Four Winds Cookbook.* New York: Thomas Y. Crowell, Co., 1954.

Ward, Barbara. *The Rich Nations and The Poor Nations.* New York: W. W. Norton & Co., Inc., 1962.

Wilson, Mitchell. *The Human Body: What It Is and How It Works.* New York: Golden Press, 1959.

PUTTING ON A PROGRAM

Bacon, W. Stevenson (ed.). *Ideas for Science Fair Projects.* New York: Arco Publishing Co., Inc., 1963.

Barton, Fred B. *Music As A Hobby.* New York: Harper & Bros., 1941.

Berg, Ester L., and Florence B. Freedman (ed.). *The Recording As A Teaching Tool.* New York: Folkways Records, 1955.

Bernstein, Leonard. *The Joy of Music.* New York: Simon & Schuster, 1959.

Blough, Glenn O., and Paul E. Blackwood. *Teaching Elementary Science.* (U. S. Dept. of Health, Education and Welfare, Bulletin #4) Washington: Government Printing Office, 1960.

————, and Marjorie Campbell. *Making and Using Classroom Science Materials in the Elementary School.* New York: Dryden Press, Inc., 1954.

Brown, Myra B. *"Science Activities of the Eight Year Old in Duval County, Florida."* Unpublished Masters Problem in Elementary Education, The Graduate School of Cornell University, 1957.

Burnett, Will. *Teaching Science in the Elementary School.* New York: Rinehart & Co., Inc., 1953.

Ewen, David. *Complete Book of the American Musical Theatre.* New York: Henry Holt & Co., 1958.

Gowland, Peter. *How To Take Better Home Movies.* New York: Arco Publishing Co., 1960.

Miller, Kurt R. *"A Little Creativity in Children's Music."* Munich: Dependents Education Group, 1961.

Norinsky, Sid. *The Amateur's 8mm Movie Guide.* New York: Universal Photo Books, 1957.

Obourn, Ellsworth S. *Science As A Way of Life.* (U. S. Department of Health, Education and Welfare) Washington: Government Printing Office, 1961.

Plummer, Gail. *The Business of Show Business.* New York: Harper & Brothers, 1961.

Scholastic Magazines & Book Services. *How To Hold A Successful Scholastic Paperback Book Fair.* Englewood Cliffs: Scholastic Magazines & Book Services.

Shapley, Harlow (ed.). *A Treasury of Science.* New York: Harper and Brothers, 1958.

Spaeth, Sigmund. *Music For Fun.* Garden City: Blue Ribbon Books, 1942.

Thompson, Nellie Zetta. *High Times.* New York: E. P. Dutton & Co., Inc., 1950.

UNESCO. *Source Book for Science Teaching.* France: UNESCO, 1962.

CULTURE CORNER

Barton, Fred B. *Music As A Hobby.* New York: Harper & Bros., 1941.

Bernstein, Leonard. *The Joy of Music.* New York: Simon & Schuster, 1959.

Burnett, Will. *Teaching Science in the Elementary School.* New York: Rinehart & Co., Inc., 1953.

Fadiman, Clifton. *The Lifetime Reading Plan.* Cleveland: The World Publishing Co., 1960.

Faverty, Frederic E. *Your Literary Heritage.* Philadelphia: J. B. Lippincott Co., 1959.

Hennessy, David E. *Elementary Teacher's Classroom Science Demonstrations and Activities.* West Nyack: Parker Publishing Co., Inc., 1964.

Highet, Gilbert. *Talents and Geniuses.* Fair Lawn: Oxford University Press, Inc., 1957.

Hook, J. N. *Writing Creatively.* Boston: D. C. Heath & Co., 1963.

Mason, Jerry (ed.). *Creative America.* New York: The Ridge Press, 1962.

Miller, Kurt R. *"A Little Creativity in Children's Music."* Munich: Dependents Education Group, 1961.

Nye, Robert E. and Vernice T. Nye. *Music In the Elementary School: An Activities Approach to Music Methods and Materials.* Englewood Cliffs: Prentice-Hall, Inc., 1964.

Smith, Betty. *A Tree Grows In Brooklyn.* New York: Harper & Brothers, 1947.

Stefferud, Alfred (ed.). *The Wonderful World of Books.* Boston: Houghton Mifflin, 1952.

Time-Life Editors. *Life History of the United States, Volumes 1-12.* New York: Time Inc. Book Division, 1964.

SOMETHING TO LIVE BY

Dooley, Thomas A. *Deliver Us From Evil.* New York: Farrar, Straus & Co., Inc., 1956.

———. *Edge of Tomorrow.* New York: Farrar, Straus & Co., Inc., 1958.

———. *The Night They Burned the Mountain.* New York: Farrar, Straus & Co., Inc., 1960.

Emerson, Ralph Waldo. *Basic Selections From Emerson.* New York: The New American Library, 1954.

Grayson, David. *David Grayson Omnibus.* Garden City: Garden City Publishing Co., 1946.

Kopplin, Dorothy. *Something To Live By.* New York: Permabooks, 1948.

Madow, Pauline (ed.). *The Peace Corps.* New York: H. W. Wilson Company, 1964.

Nichols, William (ed.). *Words To Live By.* New York: Simon & Schuster, 1962.

Schweitzer, Albert. *Out of My Life and Thought.* New York: Mentor Books, 1957.

Von Hesse, Elisabeth Ferguson. *So To Speak.* Philadelphia: J. B. Lippincott Co., 1959.

Ward, Barbara. *The Rich Nations and The Poor Nations.* New York: W. W. Norton & Co., Inc., 1962.

Any materials or techniques which make learning more dynamic and more realistic will undoubtedly foster better learning.

—James S. Kinder

BE A CATALOG COLLECTOR!

HELPFUL CATALOGS

American Medical Association
535 N. Dearborn Street
Chicago, Illinois 60610
. . . The AMA Health Education Materials catalog lists posters and pamphlets which promote better health.

Barth's Colonial Garden
Valley Stream, New York
. . . catalog of foods, gifts and accessories: American regional and foreign.

Bridger Displays
305 East 1st St.
Jacksonville, Florida
. . . all materials to make up displays, projects, scenery.

Creative Playthings
Princeton, New Jersey
. . . equipment, materials, games.

Cuisenaire Co. of America, Inc.
9 Elm Avenue
Mt. Vernon, New York
. . . catalog of Cuisenaire math kits, texts, worksheets and supplementary aids.

Edmund Scientific Company
Barrington, New Jersey
. . . science, math, teaching aids, science fair projects.

John Hancock Mutual Life Insurance Company
200 Berkeley Street
Boston, Mass. 02117
. . . *Great Americans* portraits and word sketches, and historical booklets.

Ideal School Supply Co.
83220 Birkhoff Avenue
Chicago 20, Illinois
. . . materials, teaching aids.

Instructo Products Co.
1635 N. 55th Street
Philadelphia 31, Penn.
. . . materials, teaching aids.

Instructor Teaching Aids
F. A. Owen Publishing Co.
Dansville, N. Y.
   . . . materials, teaching aids.

Lifeline
620 Eleventh St. NW
Washington 1, D. C.
   . . . patriotic records, books, maps, freedom
documents, and radio transcripts.

NASCO
Ft. Atkinson, Wisc. 53538
   . . . extensive listing of scientific and mathematic
materials.

Newton School Equipment Co.
2221 Pearl Street
Jacksonville, Florida
   . . . equipment, supplies, aids, materials.

Perry Pictures
Malden, Mass. 02148
   . . . 35¢ . . . prints of art and historical subjects

Pioneer Historical Society
Harriman, Tennessee 37748
   . . . exact reproductions of posters, handbills,
playbills, prints, advertisements and books from
American history (recommended by Henry Steele
Commager in THE NATURE AND STUDY OF
HISTORY).

School Teaching Aids and Supplies
Models of Industry, Inc.
2100 Fifth Street
Berkeley, California 94710
   . . . this exciting and unusual catalog is itself a
valuable teaching resource. It has a center section
science guide and a cross reference index of
equipment in the catalog. Books, aids, models,
equipment, kits (Playground Geography, Model
Oil Refinery, Story of Paint, etc.)

University Prints Catalog
15 Brattle Street
Cambridge 38, Mass.
   . . . 50¢ . . . prints of art and historical subjects.

INEXPENSIVE PUBLICATIONS

NEA Publications Catalog
1201 Sixteenth Street, NW
Washington, D. C. 20036

Price List of Government
Publications

Ask for *Price List 31-Education*
Superintendent of Documents
Government Printing Office
Washington 25, D. C.

NEED TO BE INSPIRED?

Get a copy of:

► The Art of Teaching
Gilbert Highet
Vintage Books
1956

► Creativity in Teaching
Alice Miel (ed.)
Wadsworth Publishing Co., Inc.
1961

► Teacher
Sylvia Ashton-Warner
Simon & Schuster
1963

► What Is A Teacher?
Henry W. Simon
Collier Books
1964

► A Perfect Education
Kenneth E. Eble
The Macmillan Co.
1966

► How Children Fail
John Holt
Pitman Publishing Corp.
1964

Have you thought about the power of
the spoken word?

► Tyranny of Words
Stuart Chase
Harcourt, Brace & Co.
1938

"I wish from my heart that you could somehow induce every politician, teacher, preacher, and all who listen to them, to read it."
—Julia Peterkin

PROFESSIONAL HELP FROM THE MAGAZINE RACK

Classroom-tested suggestions, aids, plans, devices and practices! Practical classroom help prepared by educational experts!

Take a look at what's going on outside of the elementary classroom. What new and exciting projects are being tried at the secondary level? Can they be adapted for your students?

To which of these magazines do you or your school subscribe?

Administrators Swap Shop
1201 Sixteenth St., NW
Washington, D. C. 20036
$2 for 4 issues
Newsletter

Arts and Activities
Skokie, Illinois
$6 for 10 issues

Art Education
National Art Education Assoc.
1201 Sixteenth Street, NW
Washington, D. C. 20036
$5 per year

Arithmetic Teacher
National Council of Teachers of Math
1201 Sixteenth Street., NW
Washington, D. C. 20036
$5 per year

Classroom Clipper
Educational Services
Pan American Airways
Pan Am Building
New York 17, New York
Bi-monthly
Free!

Education Digest
416 Longshore Drive
Ann Arbor, Michigan

Educational Summary
100 Garfield Avenue
New London, Conn.

Elementary English
National Council of Teachers of English
508 South 6th Street
Champaign, Illinois
        $5 per year

Elementary School Journal
University of Chicago Press
5750 Ellis Ave.
Chicago 37, Illinois

Grade Teacher
Darien, Connecticut
        $5 for 10 issues

Highlights for Children
2300 W. Fifth Avenue
Columbus, Ohio 43216

The Instructor
F. A. Owen Publishing Co.
Dansville, N. Y.
        $6 for 10 issues

It Starts in the Classroom
National School Public Relations Association
1201 Sixteenth Street, NW
Washington, D. C. 20036
        $3 per year
        Monthly newsletter

National Geographic School Bulletin
National Geographic Society
Washington, D. C.
        $2 for 30 issues

NEA Journal
1201 Sixteenth Street, NW

Washington, D. C. 20036
    NEA membership

Pack-o-Fun, The Scrap Craft Magazine
Clapper Publishing Co., Inc.
14 Main Street
Park Ridge, Illinois
    $3 per year

Plays
Plays, Inc.
8 Arlington Street
Boston, Mass.
    $6 per year

School Arts
State College, Pa.
    $6 for 10 issues

School Life
U. S. Dept. of Education
Washington 25, D. C.

School Management
School Management Magazine, Inc.
22 W. Putnam Ave.
Greenwich, Conn.

Science and Children
National Science Teachers Assoc.
1201 Sixteenth Street, NW
Washington, D. C. 20036
    $4 per year

Science Newsletter
Science Service, Inc.
1719 N Street, NW
Washington, D. C. 20036
    $5.50 per year

Scholastic Magazine Publications
902 Sylvan Avenue
Englewood Cliffs, N. J.
    Grades 1-4: 50¢ per year
    Grades 5-6: 80¢ per year

THEY HANDLE FILMS

- Association Films, Inc.
  347 Madison Avenue
  New York 37, New York

- Blackhawk Films
  Davenport, Iowa

- Coronet Films
  Coronet Building
  Chicago 1, Illinois

- Encyclopedia Brittanica Films, Inc.
  1150 Wilmette Avenue
  Wilmette, Illinois

- Eye Gate House Inc.
  146-03 Archer Ave.
  Jamaica, New York 11435
    (Catalog of more than 2000 filmstrips and visual teaching aids)

- National Children's Council, Inc.
  175 Fifth Avenue
  New York, New York 10010

- Teaching Film Custodian, Inc.
  25 West 43rd Street
  New York, New York

- Telephone Company
    (Contact the Business Office of your local telephone company. Most Bell Telephone Companies offer a lecture series, instructional sound films, and telephone teaching equipment.)

- United World Films
  1445 Park Avenue
  New York 29, New York

- Walt Disney Productions
  2400 W. Alameda Avenue
  Burbank, California

Monthly Bulletin of
Travel Slides
8mm Films
16mm Films
Projectors
Photographic
Equipment

—

Blackhawk Films
Davenport
Iowa

So You Want To Start A Picture File—50¢

Sources of Free and Inexpensive Teaching Aids—50¢

> *Bruce Miller*
> *Box 369*
> *Riverside, Calif.*

Free History Teaching Aids—$1.95
Pioneer Press
Harriman, Tenn. 37748

THEY MAKE SLIDES:

PROJECTION SLIDES, INC.

B. J. Anderson   P. O. Box 26072   Indianapolis, Ind. 46226

All Slides 35mm Double Frame Size Only

BLACK & WHITE SLIDES

1 - 2 x 2 B&W Slide from Any Size B&W Negative......20¢
1 - 2 x 2 B&W Slide from Any Size Photo.............35¢

Time Varies from 10 to 20 Days

No Minimum Order - - No Discounts
No Slides from Color Negatives - B&W or Color
All Slides Mounted in Good Cardboard Mounts
Original Material Size from 35mm Double Frame Up to 10 x 12
In Indiana Add Sales Tax
Please Include Return Postage With Payment

They Handle Records:

> *Audio Education*
> *American Book Co.*
> *55 Fifth Avenue*
> *New York 3, N. Y.*

> *Children's Reading Service*
> *106 Beekman Street*
> *New York 38, N.Y.*

> *Decca Distributing Corp.*
> *511 E. Clybourn Street*
> *Milwaukee, Wisc.*

MEMO

Motivation Records *publishes a series of albums designed to "delight the mind while they enchant the heart:"*

SINGING SCIENCE RECORDS

Weather, Space, Energy & Motion, Experiment & Activity, Nature, and More Nature Songs.

$3.95 each

All six are 12", 33⅓ rpm records with printed lyrics available. Hearing is believing how fine these records are.

Order through:
NASCO
Ft. Atkinson, Wisc. 53538

Educational Record Sales
157 Chambers Street
New York, N.Y. 10007

Enrichment Materials Inc.
246 Fifth Avenue
New York, New York

Folkways Records, Inc.
117 West 46th Street
New York 36, N.Y.

Henry Holt & Co.
383 Madison Avenue
New York 17, N.Y.

NASCO
Ft. Atkinson, Wisc. 53538

Simon & Schuster, Inc.
Golden Book Records
650 Fifth Avenue
New York, New York

HELPFUL ADDRESSES

The American Library Association
50 East Huron Street
Chicago 11, Illinois

American Youth Hostel Association
East Northfield
Massachusetts

National Council of Teachers of English
508 South 6th Street
Champaign, Illinois

National Council of Teachers of Mathematics
1201 Sixteenth Street, NW
Washington, D. C. 20036

International Reading Association
5835 Kimbark Avenue
Chicago 37, Illinois

The Children's Book Council, Inc.
175 Fifth Avenue
New York, N.Y. 10010

National Science Teachers Association
1201 Sixteenth Street, NW
Washington, D. C. 20036

National Council for the Social Studies
1201 Sixteenth Street, NW
Washington, D. C. 20036

National Council for Geographic Education
450–454 Ahncup Street
Menasha, Wisconsin

NEED INFORMATION on Foreign Countries and
Geographic Areas?

Write to these folks:

Africa
East Africa Tourist Travel Assoc.
750 3rd Avenue
New York 17, N. Y.

South African Tourist Corp.
610 5th Avenue
New York 20, New York

Alaska
State of Alaska
Division of Tourist and Economic Dev.
Klein Bldg.
Juneau, Alaska

Arab States
Arab States Tourist Office
120 East 56th St.
New York 22, N. Y.

Australia
Australian National Travel Assoc.
636 5th Avenue
New York 20, New York

Austria
Austrian State Tourist Dept.
444 Madison Ave.
New York 22, N. Y.

Belgium
Official Belgian Tourist Bureau
589 5th Avenue
New York 17, N. Y.

Brazil
Brazilian Government Trade Bureau
551 5th Avenue
New York 17, N. Y.

Britain

The British Travel Association
680 5th Avenue
New York 19, N. Y.

Canada

Canadian Government Travel Bureau
680 Fifth Avenue
New York 19, N. Y.

Caribbean

Caribbean Tourist Association
20 East 46th St.
New York 17, N. Y.

Columbia

Columbia National Tourist Board
608 5th Avenue
New York 20, New York

Denmark

Danish National Travel Office
588 5th Avenue
New York 36, N. Y.

Ecuador

Ecuadorean-American Chamber of Commerce, Inc.
15 Whitehall Street
New York 4, N. Y.

Finland

Finnish National Travel Office
10 East 40th Street
New York 16, N. Y.

France

French Government Tourist Office
610 Fifth Avenue
New York 20, New York

Germany

German Tourist Information Office
500 5th Avenue
New York 36, N. Y.

Greece

National Tourist Organization of Greece
601 5th Avenue
New York 17, N. Y.

Guatemala

Guatemala Tourist Office
331 Madison Ave.
New York, New York

Haiti
Haiti Government Tourist Bureau
30 Rockefeller Plaza
New York, New York

Hawaii
Hawaii Visitors Bureau
2051 Kalakaua Avenue
Honolulu 15, Hawaii

Hong Kong
Hong Kong Travel Association
501 Madison Avenue
New York 22, New York

Iceland
Icelandic Consulate General
551 5th Avenue
New York 17, N. Y.

India
Government of India Tourist Office
19 East 49th Street
New York 17, New York

Ireland
Irish Tourist Office
33 E. 50th Street
New York 22, N. Y.

Israel
Israel Government Tourist Office
574 5th Avenue
New York 36, N. Y.

Italy
Italian State Tourist Office
626 5th Avenue
New York 20, N. Y.

Japan
Japan Natl. Tourist Association
45 Rockefeller Plaza
New York 20, N. Y.

Luxembourg
Luxembourg Consulate General
200 East 42nd Street
New York, New York

Mexico
Mexican Govt. Tourist Department
630 5th Avenue
New York 20, N. Y.

Monaco
Monaco Information Center
610 5th Avenue
New York 20, N. Y.

Netherlands
Netherlands National Tourist Office
605 5th Ave.
New York 18, N. Y.

New Zealand
New Zealand Travel Commissioner
630 5th Avenue
New York 20, N. Y.

Norway
Norwegian National Travel Office
290 Madison Avenue
New York 17, New York

Nova Scotia
Nova Scotia Information Office
30 West 54th Street
New York, New York

Pacific Area
(Burma, Korea, Malaya, Thailand, and others)
Pacific Area Travel Association
153 Kearney Street
San Francisco 8, Calif.

Philippines
Philippines Travel Office
535 5th Avenue
New York, New York 10017

Poland
Polish-American Information Bureau
55 W. 42nd Street
New York 36, N. Y.

Portugal
Casa de Portugal
447 Madison Avenue
New York 22, N. Y.

Spain
Spanish National Tourist Office
589 5th Avenue
New York 17, N. Y.

Sweden
Swedish National Travel Office
630 5th Avenue
New York 20, N. Y.

Switzerland
Swiss National Travel Office
10 W. 49th St.
New York 20, N. Y.

Turkey
Turkish Information Office
500 5th Avenue
New York 17, N. Y.

Venezuela
Venezuelan Chamber of Commerce of the U.S., Inc.
233 Broadway
New York 7, N. Y.

Yugoslavia
Yugoslav State Tourist Office
509 Madison Avenue
New York 22, N. Y.

TRAVEL POSTERS

- *Girls in Native Costumes*
    28" x 42"—$1.00 per set
  - Europe (Spain, France, Italy)
  - Pacific (Japan, Hawaii, Philippines)

- *Twelve Scenic Views*
    21" x 16"—$1.00 per set
  - 1963 Reprints (West Indies, Hawaii, Mexico, England, France, Italy, Spain, Germany, USA, Japan, Brazil, Argentina)
  - 1964 Reprints (USA, Hawaii, Italy, Thailand, Great Britain, France, Germany, Yugoslavia, Japan, Hong Kong, Peru, Brazil, Trinidad)
  - 1965 Reprints (USA, Hawaii, Austria, Tahiti, Thailand, Italy, Belgium, Alaska, Brazil, Hong Kong, Jordan, Argentina, Curacao)

- *WORLD ROUTE MAPS*
    18" x 32"—50¢
    3' x 5'—$2.00
    5' x 10'—5.00

Order from: Pan American Airways
P. O. Box PAA
Jamaica, N.Y.

PARTING THOUGHTS . . .

It is the individual's own interest, efforts, experiments, errors, adjustments, study of his pupils and his material that will lead him to success in teaching.

—L. Wilkes

. . . a book cannot tell you how to be creative. It may cause you to see something differently, or to do something you have not done before, or to understand better what you have been doing all along. At best, a book can only start you off on a way of your own and be a resource to you as you go ahead. It can do little, compared to what you yourself must do.

—Evelyn Wenzel

Bibliography

The authors are indebted to the following authors, publishers, and agents for permission to use the material indicated:

Academy Guild Press for excerpts from MARIA MONTESSORI: HER LIFE AND WORK and an excerpt from THE MONTESSORI METHOD—A REVOLUTION IN EDUCATION both published by the American Library Guild, Inc., Fresno, California, 1962.

American Book Co. for excerpts from AUDIO-VISUAL MATERIALS AND TECHNIQUES, 1959, by James S. Kinder.

American Management Association, Inc. for excerpts from MOTIVATION AND PRODUCTIVITY by Saul W. Gellerman © American Management Association 1963.

Appleton-Century-Crofts, Inc. for excerpts from SCORE: THE STRATEGY OF TAKING TESTS, copyright 1961 by Darrell Huff.

Arc Books, Inc. for an excerpt from PAINTING AND DRAWING by Alfred Daniels, published by Arc Books, Inc. 1962.

Association Press for an excerpt from FUN WITH BRAND-NEW GAMES, by Allan and Paulette Macfarlan published by Association Press.

A. S. Barnes & Co., Inc. for excerpts from SAY IT WITH YOUR CAMERA by Jacob Deschin.

Mr. Peter Berger for photographs taken in the Hohenfels American School, Western Germany.

The Book of the Month Club for an excerpt from their brochure READING SKILLS by Dr. Calvin E. Gross.

The Boy Scout World Bureau for an excerpt from SCOUTING FOR BOYS by Lord Baden-Powell.

Mrs. Clifford Chang for an excerpt from her spelling worksheet.

Mr. Carlton Chorley, Photographer, for photographs taken at Liverpool Elementary School.

Dr. James Bryant Conant for an excerpt from THE EDUCATION OF AMERICAN TEACHERS published by McGraw-Hill Book Co., Inc. and to Mr. John Hollister for permission granted as Project Administrator, Conant Studies.

Conde Nast Publications, Inc. for an excerpt from "Maine Beach Party" by Helen Brown, July, 1961 edition of HOUSE AND GARDEN.

Collier Books for excerpts from WHAT IS A TEACHER, 1964, by Henry W. Simon.

F. E. Compton & Co., for an excerpt from HELPING CHILDREN STUDY A STATE, a teaching guide, © F. E. Compton & Co.

Thomas Y. Crowell Co. for excerpts from THE FOUR WINDS COOKBOOK, by Cyril von Baumann and Beulah Phelps Harris. Copyright 1954 by Elizabeth von Baumann and Beulah Phelps Harris. Thomas Y. Crowell Company, New York, publishers.

The Cuisenaire Company of America, Inc., for an excerpt from a newspaper article by Caleb Gattegno.

The Curtis Publishing Company for the following material from LADIES' HOME JOURNAL:

excerpts from "Project Concern: Somebody Has to Care," April 1963 © 1963 by LADIES' HOME JOURNAL.

excerpts from "Hearty British Food," by Miss Ward-Hanna, January-February, 1964 © 1964 by LADIES' HOME JOURNAL.

The Davis Publishing Company for an excerpt from PLANNING AND PRODUCING POSTERS by John de Lemos, published by The Davis Press, Inc., 1950.

The Daytona Beach Morning Journal for excerpts from an article in the April 30, 1963 edition, "Youngsters See Famed Collection."

Dell Publishing Company for excerpts reprinted from HELP YOUR CHILD SUCCEED IN SCHOOL by James J. O'Donnell, Raymond J. Taylor and Paul J. McElaney. Copyright © 1962 by James J. O'Donnell, Raymond J. Taylor and Paul McElaney, and used with permission of the publisher, Dell Publishing Co., Inc.

T. S. Dennison & Co., Inc. for an excerpt from CHALK TALK MANUAL by Harlan Tarbell.

The Department of the Army for excerpts from Field Manual 21-6, TECHNIQUES OF MILITARY INSTRUCTION.

Dodd Mead & Company for an excerpt from MANAGEMENT IN THE HOME, 1954, by Lillian M. Gilbreth, Orpha Mae Thomas and Eleanor Clymer.

Doubleday & Company, Inc. for excerpts from DAVID GRAYSON OMNIBUS, by David Grayson. Copyright 1925 by Doubleday & Company, Inc. Reprinted by permission of the publisher; for excerpts from HOW TO SAY A FEW WORDS, by David Guy Powers. Copyright 1953 by David Guy Powers. Reprinted by permission of Doubleday & Company, Inc.; and from TRAVEL ABROAD AT LOW COST, by William A. Strong and A. Milton Runyon. Copyright © 1937, 1939, 1959, 1960, by Doubleday & Company, Inc. Reprinted by permission of the publisher.

E. P. Dutton & Co., Inc. for an excerpt from STRETCHING THEIR MINDS by Benjamin Fine.

William B. Eerdmans Publishing Co., for an excerpt from WHAT SHALL WE PLAY? by Kathleen Tiemersma © William E. Eerdmans Publishing Co., Grand Rapids, Michigan, 1952. Used by permission.

The English Universities Press Ltd., for excerpts from TEACH YOURSELF TO TEACH by L. Wilkes, published by English Universities Press, Ltd.

Farrar, Straus & Giroux, Inc. for excerpts from DELIVER US FROM EVIL by Thomas A. Dooley, copyright 1956, for excerpts from EDGE OF TOMORROW by Thomas A. Dooley, copyright 1958, and for excerpts from THE NIGHT THEY BURNED THE MOUNTAIN by Thomas A. Dooley, copyright 1960, all published by Farrar, Straus & Giroux, Inc.

The *Florida Times-Union* for reprinting articles on the activities of classes from Stockton School, Jacksonville, Florida.

Mr. Edward H. Freedman for an excerpt from his book CONVERSATIONAL DRAWING.

Gemini Industries for use of sample stamps.

Mr. Harry Golden for excerpts from ONLY IN AMERICA by Harry Golden, published by World Publishing Co., 1958.

The John Hancock Life Insurance Co., for use of one of their advertisements.

Harcourt, Brace and World for an excerpt from THE HUMAN COMEDY by William Saroyan, © Harcourt, Brace and World, also for an excerpt from a review by Julia Peterkin of TYRANNY OF WORDS.

Harper and Row Publishers, Inc. for excerpts from THE BUSINESS OF SHOW BUSINESS, by Gail Plummer, published by Harper and Brothers, 1961; for an excerpt from DANCING ON DESKTOPS, by Lila Sheppard, published by Harper and Row, 1960; for an excerpt from A TREE GROWS IN BROOKLYN, by Betty Smith, published by Harper and Brothers, 1947; and for an excerpt from WORKS OF LOVE, by Soren Kierkegaard, copyright © 1962 by Howard Hong, published by Harper and Row Publishers.

Dr. Robert J. Havighurst for an excerpt from CADDO PARISH BULLETIN #19, TEACHING THE SOCIAL STUDIES IN CADDO PARISH SCHOOLS.

Helicon Press for excerpts from LEARNING HOW TO LEARN by Nancy McCormick Rambusch, Helicon Press, Inc., Baltimore, Maryland.

Dr. Wayne L. Herman for material reprinted from "How to Construct This Covered Wagon."

Holt, Rinehart and Winston, Inc. for excerpts from OUT OF MY LIFE AND THOUGHT by Albert Schweitzer, published by Holt, Rinehart and Winston.

Houghton Mifflin Company for excerpts from EMERSON'S WORKS published by Houghton Mifflin Co., and for excerpts from TEACHING THE COMMON BRANCHES by W. W. Charters, published by Houghton Mifflin Co., 1924.

The Junior League of Tampa for material from THE GASPARILLA COOKBOOK.

David Kahn, Inc., and their advertising agents S. R. Leon Co., for material from the Wearever Handwriting Kit.

Life Line for excerpts from their radio transcript.

J. B. Lippincott Co. for an excerpt from SO TO SPEAK by Elizabeth von Hesse. Copyright © 1959 by Elizabeth Ferguson von Hesse. Published by J. B. Lippincott Company.

LOOK magazine for material reprinted from "What Johnson Faces in South Vietnam" by Sam Castan, LOOK Magazine, January 28, 1964, Copyright © 1964 by LOOK Magazine and for an excerpt from "Teacher of the Year" by Daniel Chapman, LOOK Magazine, April 19, 1966.

Lyons and Carnahan for excerpts from WHAT EVERY TEACHER SHOULD KNOW by N. F. Ryan.

Macmillan Company for excerpts reprinted with permission of the Macmillan Company from THE AIMS OF EDUCATION by Alfred North Whitehead. Copyright 1929 The Macmillan Company, renewed 1957 by Evelyn Whitehead, and for an excerpt from LANGUAGE SKILLS IN ELEMENTARY EDUCATION by Paul S. Anderson, published by the Macmillan Company, 1964.

McCall Corporation for an excerpt from "Culture for the Savages" by Georgena Goff, from the April 1965 issue of REDBOOK magazine, © McCall Corporation, 1965; for an excerpt from "Alfred Hitchcock and Dr. Wertham" by Dr. Frederic Wertham, from the April 1963 issue of REDBOOK magazine, © McCall Corporation, 1963; and for an excerpt from "Festive Food from An Early American Kitchen" from the December 1963 issue of REDBOOK magazine, © McCall Corporation, 1963.

McGraw-Hill Book Company for their permission to use excerpts from *Music For Fun* by Sigmund Spaeth, Copyright 1939 by Sigmund Spaeth.

McGraw-Hill, Inc. for reprinting ECONOMICS WITH ABC'S from BUSINESS WEEK magazine, © 1964 McGraw-Hill, Inc. and for an excerpt from THE OVERSEAS AMERICANS by Cleveland, Magone, and Adams. Copyright © 1960 McGraw-Hill, Inc. Used by permission of McGraw-Hill Book Co.

David McKay Co., Inc. for an excerpt from THE MAKING OF A PUBLIC RELATIONS MAN by John W. Hill.

Mrs. Cornelia L. Meigs for reprinting HASTY PUDDING, from CHILD LIFE Magazine, Copyright 1936, 1964 by Rand McNally & Co.

Dr. Kurt Miller for excerpts from his directives to teachers.

William Morrow and Co., Inc. for an excerpt from THE WRITING ROAD TO READING, by Romalda Bishop Spalding, published by William Morrow and Co., 1957.

The Murine Company for permission to reproduce art work in one of their advertisements.

Mr. Beaumont Newhall for an excerpt from SAY IT WITH YOUR CAMERA by Jacob Deschin.

Mr. Arnold Newman for an excerpt from SAY IT WITH YOUR CAMERA by Jacob Deschin.

Newsweek, Inc. for permission to reprint "Minnesota's Vikings" from NEWSWEEK Magazine, March 29, 1948, copyright NEWSWEEK, Inc., March 1948.

W. W. Norton and Co., Inc., for an excerpt from HOW TO LIE WITH STATISTICS by Darrell Huff, Pictures by Irving Geis. Copyright 1954 by Darrell Huff and Irving Geis. W. W. Norton and Co., Inc., New York, New York.

The Parker Pen Company for material concerning their International Penfriend Program.

Perry Pictures for materials regarding their prints and advertisements.

Pictograph Corp. for the use of their prepared charts.

Prentice-Hall, Inc. for excerpts from THE CHANGING CLASSROOM, 1963, by Dr. Kimball Wiles, for an excerpt from SOCIAL STUDIES FOR CHILDREN IN A DEMOCRACY, 1956, by John U. Michaelis, and for an excerpt from TO SIR, WITH LOVE, 1960, by E. R. Brathwaite, published by Prentice-Hall.

Public Relations News for quotations by Joseph W. Hicks, John M. Shaw, and James W. Irwin from YOUR PUBLIC RELATIONS, THE STANDARD PUB-

LIC RELATIONS HANDBOOK, 1948, edited by Glenn and Denny Griswold.

Random House, Inc. for excerpts from THE ART OF TEACHING, 1957, by Gilbert Highet and HOW TO TEACH YOUR BABY TO READ, 1964, Glenn Doman, both published by Random House.

Reader's Digest for excerpts from "Let's Dare to Be Square" by Charles H. Brower.

Reinhold Publishing Corp. for an excerpt from EXHIBITION TECHNIQUES: TRAVELING AND TEMPORARY, 1962, by James Carmel, published by Reinhold Publishing Corp.

Norman Rockwell for use of one of his drawings.

The *Saint Augustine Record* for articles about Ponte Vedra-Palm Valley School.

San Diego City Schools for the use of MY READING BOOKCASE.

Science Research Associates for material on the Elkhart experiment and OUR WORKING WORLD.

Charles Scribner's Sons for an excerpt from THE ESSENTIALS OF ENGLISH COMPOSITION, 1912, by James W. Linn and for an excerpt from SHAKESPEARE, TWENTY-THREE PLAYS AND SONNETS, Thomas Marc Parrott; New York, Charles Scribner's Sons, 1953.

Simon and Schuster, Inc. for excerpts from TEACHER by Sylvia Ashton-Warner, 1963; for excerpts from HOW TO READ A BOOK by Mortimer Adler, 1940; and for an excerpt from WORDS TO LIVE BY, 1962, edited by William Nichols. Published by Simon and Schuster.

State University of Iowa for permission to reproduce the Leonard P. Ayres Handwriting Scale.

Mr. Edward Steichen for an excerpt from SAY IT WITH YOUR CAMERA by Jacob Deschin.

Sterling Publishing Co. for excerpts from EXPRESS YOURSELF IN DRAWING by Gerhard Gollwitzer © 1962 by Sterling Publishing Co., Inc., New York, New York.

The John N. C. Stockton School for the use of their permission slip and photographs taken at their school.

Studio Vista Limited for an excerpt from ANATOMY OF LETTERING, 1959, by Russell Laker, published by the Studio Publications.

Summit Industries for use of advertising material concerning their illustrated grading and marking stamps.

Time-Life Books for permission to reproduce one of their record jackets.

The UNESCO Publications Center for excerpts from THE UN COOKBOOK.

The U. S. Army Photographic Laboratory for pictures from Giessen, Western Germany.

The U. S. Department of Health, Education, and Welfare; Office of Education for an excerpt from SCIENCE AS A WAY OF LIFE, #OE-29023, 1961, by Ellsworth S. Obourn.

Viking Press, Inc. for excerpts from CREATIVE ILLUSTRATION, 1947, by Andrew Loomis, published by the Viking Press.

The Wadsworth Publishing Company, Inc., Belmont, California for an excerpt from "Finding Meaning in Teaching" by Evelyn Wenzel which appears in CREATIVITY IN TEACHING, ed. Alice Miel, 1961.

Watson-Guptill Publications for an excerpt from TYPE AND LETTERING, 1966, by William Longyear.

Wm. Wrigley Jr. Co. for use of their advertisements regarding construction of a covered wagon.

World Publishing Co. for an excerpt from FRONTIER LIVING, 1961, by Edwin Tunis and for excerpts by Clifton Fadiman from THE LIFETIME READING PLAN, The World Publishing Company.

Zaner-Bloser Company for the use of an advertising brochure on the Freeman Handwriting Evaluation Scales.

The authors have made diligent efforts to trace the ownership of all copyrighted material in this work. It is believed that all necessary permissions have been secured. If an error has been made inadvertently, proper corrections will be made in future editions.

Index

A Handbook for Young Writers, 67
A Tree Grows in Brooklyn, 289
Accentuating positive, 75
Acetate cover sheets for projects, 128
Activities, follow-up, for field trip, 181
Activity day, 203-216
Adapting play from article, 223-224
Adapting play from classics, 222-223
Adapting play from story, 221
Adler, Mortimer, 9, 55
Adventures in Appreciation, 68
AERO Products, 109
Alphabet charts, 108
American Medical Association, 276
Anderson, Paul S., 12
Animals of the Sea and Seashore, 153
Animals, teaching familiar, 168
Anthologies by students as gifts, 97-98
Appearance, setting standards of, 40
Arithmetic Enrichment Activities for Elementary School Children, 107
Armstrong, Leila, 119
"Art gallery," 243-244
Art, working with in culture corner, 289-293
Ashton-Warner, Sylvia, 12, 13, 37, 128
Assignment, attacking, 57-72
   building vocabulary, 60-63
   locating and gathering information, 58-59
   memorization, 70
   oral reports, 66-67
   outlining, 64-65
   preparing speech, 65-66
   reading improvement, 59-60
   reviewing, 70-71
   summarizing material, 65
   survey, 57-58
   taking notes, 63-64
   taking tests, art of, 71-72
   thinking on their feet, 66
   written composition and reports, 67-70
Assignment sheets, student, 3
Assignments, challenging, 4-7
Assignments, specific, for students on field trip, 178-179
Atlantic Advertising, Inc., 20
Attitude, evaluating, 52
Audio Visual Materials and Techniques, 176
Awards, classroom, 96
Awards, special, 85
Ayres Handwriting Scale, 51, 123

Baden-Powell, Lord, 74
Banners, 85
Barth's Colonial Garden, 195
Barton, Bruce, 51, 66
Bathroom facilities for field trip, 178
Beecher, Henry Ward, 31
Beginning day, 31-36
Behavior, evaluating, 52
Behavior standards, establishing, 37-40
   of appearance, 40
   on field trip, 178
Bernstein, Leonard, 231
Book fair, 241-242
Bostwick, Prudence, 18
Brathwaite, E. R., 302
Brightness in classroom, 32
Brower, Charles H., 305
Brown, Helen Evans, 197
"Buddy system," 13, 177
Building Reading Skills, 119
Bulletin boards, 128-137
Bulletin, classroom, 90

Calendars by students as gifts, 99
California Test Bureau, 47
Camelot, 227
Cards, greeting, 93
Carmel, James H., 142
Carousel, 227
Cartooning, 169-170
Cat in the Hat Beginner Book Dictionary, 108
Certificates of achievement, 84
"Chalk talk," 33-34
Chaperones on field trips, 177-178
Chappell, Jack, 71, 136
Charters, W. W., 12, 159, 193, 280, 289
Charts, 137-138
Charts, manipulative, 71, 105-106
Check list for field trips, 179-180
Child Life, 221
Children's Plea for Peace, 124
Churchill, Clementine, 301
Clarke, Irwin & Co., Ltd., 15
Class list, 27
"Classroom Bowl," 84
Classroom, importance of on first day, 31-32
Classrooms as workshops, 17-23
   display space, creating, 21
   interest center, 21-22
   sketching on paper, 18

Classrooms as workshops (*cont.*)
    storage space, creating, 19-20
    work stations, creating, 18-19
Columbia Records, 194, 290
Columbia University, 46
Community, bringing into classroom, 96-97
Competition, recognition and rewards, 73-86
    accentuate positive, 75
    banners, pennants, flags, 85
    certificate of achievement, 84
    emblems, letters, 85
    gimmicks, 84
    honor roll, 75-76
    learning from each other, 79
    news, 80
    papers, posting, 76
    plaques, 84
    progress, picturing and charting, 77
    reading, 78
    ribbons, 85
    special awards, 85
    "telling tales," 79
    tournaments and contests, 80-81
    trophies, 84
Composition, teaching, 170
Compositions, written, 67-70
Conant, James Bryant, 295
Concert and community sing, 230
Concerts in classroom, 287
Conference, 52-53
Contests and tournaments, 80-81
Conversation, punctuating, 123
Coronet Films, 286
Correspondence, classroom, 90-93
Cost of field trips, 177
Costume creating, 244-245
Creative writing corner, 109-110
Crescimbeni, Joseph, 107
Cuisenaire Company of America, 16, 124
Culture corner, 121, 280-294
    art, 289-293
    choosing selections, 282
    classroom, 293-294
    concerts in classroom, 287
    keep record, 281-282
    literature, working with, 283-287
    music, working with, 288-289
    "story hour," 282
"Culture for the Savages," 282
Cylindrical objects, perspective of, 164-165

Daniels, Alfred, 292
David Kahn, Inc., 123
Dayton, Mona, 73
de Lemos, John, 10
Deschin, Jacob, 287
Dewey, John, 3, 56, 58
Diaries about "make believe" trips, 201

Dioramas, 138
Display of projects, 96
Displays, 21, 125-158
    (*see also* "Projects, displays, exhibition techniques")
Doman, Glenn, 12
Dooley, Dr. Tom, 299
Drawing and lettering, teaching, 159-174
    basic strokes, 161-162
    cartooning, 169-170
    composition, 170
    expression, 168
    familiar animals, 168
    form, 162-164
    hand and foot, 168
    head and face, 166-167
    human figure, 166
    lettering, 172-174
    shape, 162
    simple perspective, 164-166
    sketch sessions, 170-172
    standard symbols, 169
    tools, 161
Dress, standards of, for field trips, 179
Drilling without drudgery, 102-124
    alphabet charts, 108
    arithmetic with Cuisenaire Rods, 124
    "beat the clock" drill, 107
    Bingo, Lotto, Quizmo, 112
    creative writing corner, 109-110
    culture corner, 121
    egg carton contests, 107
    flashcards, 103-105
    gold star papers, 108
    grammar kit, 122-123
    hand puppets, 119-120
    "Interesting Things to Do" sheets, 119
    listening corner, 116
    magic slates, 109
    manipulative charts, 105-106
    movies, making, 114
    penmanship, 123-124
    postage stamps, work with, 115
    punctuating conversation, 123
    puzzles and worksheets, 108
    reading skill-builders, 119
    role playing, 113
    slide shows, 114-115, 116
    "speeches," extemporaneous, 111
    sports, using student interest in, 110-111
    supplementary reading material, 116-118
    textbook relay, 112
    twenty questions, 113
    Viewmaster corner, 116
Dwellings, 138

Eastman, P. D., 108
Edison, Thomas A., 48, 55

Egg carton contests, 107
Emblems, 85
Emerson, Ralph Waldo, 1, 2, 41, 55, 283, 298, 301, 302
English Grammar and Composition, 68
Essay vs. objective tests, 45-46
Evaluation in classroom, 42-53
  (*see also* "Testing and evaluation in classroom")
Evlin, Enid, 189, 191, 202
Exhibition techniques, 125-158
  (*see also* "Projects, displays, exhibition techniques")
Exhibition Techniques—Traveling and Temporary, 142
Express Yourself in Drawing, 160
Expression, teaching, 168

F. A. Owen Publishing Company, 84, 291
Fadiman, Clifton, 280, 298
Field trips, 175-183
  advance preparations, 177
  all-day excursions, 177
  bathroom facilities, 178
  behavior standards, 178
  check list, 179-180
  cost, 177
  follow-up activities, 181
  how many?, 177
  ingredients of successful trip, 181
  meals, 178
  publicity, 181-183
  safety factors, 178
  specific assignments for students, 178-179
  standards of dress, 179
  supervision, 177-178
  transportation, 177
  where should you go?, 176
File for each student, 26
Financial records, 27
Financing "make believe" trip, 190-192
Fine, Dr. Benjamin, 42, 53
Flags, 85
Flannel boards, 143
Flashcards, 71, 103-105
Florida Times-Union, 175, 207, 266
Flowerdew, Phyllis, 15
Fodor, Eugene, 192
Folkway Records, Inc., 186-187, 199, 283
Food on trip, 195-197
Form, teaching, 162-164
Forms as time savers, 24-30
Four Winds Cookbook, 195
Freedman, Edward H., 160, 162
Freedoms Foundation, 81
Freeman Scientific Evaluation Scales, 51, 123
Frost, Robert, 283
"Fun tests," 47-50

Games of other lands, 199-200
Gasparilla Cookbook, 197
Gattegno, Caleb, 9
Gellerman, Saul W., 73, 75
Gemini Industries, 52
Getting to work on first day, 34-36
Gilbreth, Lillian M., 28
Gimmicks to motivate and interest, 84
Goff, Georgena, 282
Gold star papers, 108
Golden, Harry, 54
Gollwitzer, Gerhard, 160, 162, 164, 292, 306
Grammar kit, 122-123
Graphs, 143-146
Grayson, David, 284, 299
Greeting cards, 93
Gross, Dr. Calvin E., 59
Gross, Ruth, 98, 175
Guideposts, 306

Hagen, Elizabeth, 47
Hand and foot, teaching, 168
Hansel and Gretel, 225, 227
Hargrave, Rowena, 119
Harris, Beulah Phelps, 195, 196, 197
Havighurst, Robert J., 295
Head and face, teaching, 166-167
Helping Children Study a State, a Teaching Guide, 248
Hicks, Joseph W., 87
Highet, Gilbert, 10, 74, 275, 284, 286, 296
Hill, John W., 101
Holub, Rand, 173
Honor roll, 75-76
Hook, J. N., 97
Houghton-Mifflin Company, 47
How to Draw, 160
How to Improve Classroom Testing, 47
How to Lie with Statistics, 144
How to Read Better and Faster, 60
Huff, Darrell, 44, 71, 144
Human figure, teaching, 166

Information, locating and gathering, 58-59
Interest center, 21-22
Introducing yourself on first day, 32-34
Irwin, James W., 94
It Starts in the Classroom, 101
Itinerary for "make believe" trip, 189

Jet Age Travel Guides, 192
John Gunther's High Road, 265-266
Johnson Smith and Company, 85
Joseph Dixon Crucible Company, 123

Kahn, Gilbert, 69
Kelsey, Dr. Frances Oldham, 304
Kennedy, John F., 298

Kettering, Charles Francis, 304
Kierkegaard, Soren, 305
Kinder, James S., 116, 176, 203, 217
Kiss Me Kate, 227
Kit, project, 158

Labelling, 25
Ladies' Home Journal, 303-304, 305
Laker, Russell, 172
Language, 197-199
League of Friendship, 124
"Learn From Each Other" worksheets, 14, 79
Leedy, Paul D., 60
Leonard P. Ayres Scale, 51, 123
Lessons, successful, record of, 27
Lettering Simplified, 173
Lettering, teaching, 159-174
    (*see also* "Drawing and lettering, teaching")
Letters, 85
Letters home from "make believe" trips, 201
Lewis, Norman, 60, 61
Liechti, Alice, 71, 136
Lifeline, 301
Li'l Abner, 227
Linn, James W., 67
Listening to music, 116
Literature, working with in culture corner, 283-287
Longyear, William, 174
LOOK, 297, 299
Loomis, Andrew, 9, 87

Macbeth, 222, 273
Macfarlan, Allan and Paulette, 199
Magic slates, 109
Magnetic charts and boards, 146
"Make believe" trips, 184-202
Making and Using Charts, 71, 136
Manchester, Harland, 298
Manipulative charts, 71, 105-106
Maps by students as gifts, 100
Marking made easy, 51-52
McAllister, Anne, 278
Meals on field trips, 178
Measurement and Evaluation in Psychology and Education, 47
Meigs, Cornelia, 221
Memorization, 70
Michaelis, John U., 42, 138, 148, 176
Miller, Dr. Kurt R., 199-200, 224
Models of Industry, Inc., 127
Montessori, Maria, 9, 11, 102, 159
Morrison, Chester, 299
Motivation, teaching, 55-56
Movies, making, 114, 233
Mulkerne, Donald, 69
Murals, 149-156

Music, working with, 288-289
Musical in classroom, planning and producing, 225-227
My Fair Lady, 215, 227

National Audubon Society, 236
National Children's Book Council, Inc., 242
National Council of Teachers of Mathematics, 134
National Defense Education Act, 124
National School Public Relations Association, 101
Newhall, Beaumont, 294
Newman, Arnold, 125
News, 80
Newspapers, 88
Newsweek, 223
Newton School Equipment Company, 84
Niebuhr, Reinhold, 304
Norinsky, Sid, 114, 233
Norton, Dr. Robert, 297
Note taking, 63-64
Notebooks, 200
Nutcracker of Nuremberg, 227

Objective vs. essay tests, 45-46
Obourn, Ellsworth S., 11
Odell, C. W., 47
Oklahoma, 227
Omnibus, 231
Open house, 235
Oral tests, 50-51, 66-67
Organizing students' work, 41
Our Singing World, 225
Outlining, 64-65

Packing for "make believe" trip, 192
Paintings by students as gifts, 99
Pan-American Airways, 185
Papers, posting, 76
Parker Pen Company, 92-93, 124
Passport for "make believe" trip, 188
"Password," 84
Pen pals, 92-93
Penmanship program, 123-124
Pennants, 85
Perry Pictures, 121, 194, 290
Perspective, teaching simple, 164-166
Pictograph Corporation, 145
Pictographs, 143-146
Plaques, 84
Plan book, weekly, 2-3
Planning activity day, 204-205
Planning ahead, 1-16
    challenging assignments, 4-7
    day by day, 3
    for yourself, 8
    guidelines, 8-16

Planning ahead (*cont.*)
  projecting for year, 1-2
  student assignment sheets, 3
  weekly plan book, 2-3
Plans for "make-believe" trip, 185-187
Plummer, Gail, 24, 27, 245
Poetry assembly, 231
Postage stamps, work with, 115
Posters, 156-157
Pot plants by students as gifts, 99
Preparations, advance, for field trip, 177
Program, putting on, 217-247
  adapting play from article, 223-224
  adapting play from classics, 222-223
  adapting play from story, 221
  "art gallery," 243-244
  book fair, 241-242
  classroom musical, 225-227
  concert and community sing, 230
  costume creating, 244-245
  movie, 233
  open house, 235
  planning, 217-218
  poetry assembly, 231
  scenery and props, 245-247
  science fair, 235-240
  sound effects and slides, 234-235
  writing original play, 219-220
  your own "telecast," 231
Programs, classroom, 94
Progress, picturing and charting, 77
Projection Slides, Inc., 115, 235
Projects, displays, exhibition techniques, 125-158
  acetate cover sheets, 128
  bulletin boards, 128-137
  charts, 137-138
  dioramas, 138
  dwellings, 138
  exhibits and displays, 140-142
  flannel boards, 143
  graphs and pictographs, 143-146
  magnetic charts and boards, 146
  maps, 146-148
  murals, 149-156
  posters, 156-157
  project kits, 158
  sandtable displays, 157
  setting up period, 127-128
  type, 126-127
Projects for "make believe" trips, 201-202
Props, 245-247
Psychological Corporation, 47
Publicity for field trip, 181-183
Publicity and public relations, classroom, 87-101
  awards, 96
  bulletin, 90

Publicity and public relations (*cont.*)
  community, bringing into classroom, 96-97
  correspondence, 90-93
  gifts reflecting school skills, 97-101
  greeting cards, 93
  newspapers, 88
  project display, 96
  programs, 94
Punctuating conversation, 123
Puppets, hand, 119-120
Puzzles, 108

Ralston Purina Company, 265
Rambusch, Nancy McCormick, 9, 11, 74, 102, 120, 161
Reader's Digest, 298, 305
Reading improvement, 59-60
Reading Improvement for Adults, 60
Reading, incentive for, 78
Reading to Some Purpose, 41
Reason for tests, 44
Recipe books by students as gifts, 100-101
Records as time savers, 24-30
Rectangular objects, perspective of, 165-166
Redbook, 197, 282, 296
Reference files, 28-29
Reports, written, 67-70
Ribbons, 85
Ridout, Ronald, 15
Role playing, 113
Runyon, A. Milton, 191
Ryan, N. F., 223, 229

S.S. Hope, 302-303
Safety factors on field trip, 178
Sandburg, Carl, 283
Sands Point Country Day School, 53
Sandtable displays, 157
Saroyan, William, 299
Scenery, 245-247
Scholastic Book Services, 16, 117
Schweitzer, Dr. Albert, 184, 301-302
Science fair, 235-240
Science Research Associates, Inc., 15, 47, 278, 279
Score: The Strategy of Taking Tests, 72
Scrapbooks, 200
Sears, Roebuck and Company, 20
Selections, choosing, for culture corner, 282
Self, planning for, 8
Senesh, Professor Lawrence, 278, 279
Setting up project period, 127-128
Shape, teaching, 162
Shaw, John M., 10
Sheppard, Lila, 10
Shot records for "make believe" trips, 188-189
Sightseeing, 192-194

Silver Burdett Company, 230, 251, 255, 259
Simon, Henry W., 11, 12, 32, 38
Sketching room arrangement, 18
Sketching sessions, 170-172
Skill-builders, reading, 119
Slide shows, 114-115, 116
So You're Going Abroad, 191
Social Studies for Children in a Democracy, 138, 148, 176
Songbooks by students as gifts, 99
Sound effects and slides, 234-235
Sound of Music, 227
Spaeth, Sigmund, 231, 287
Spalding, Romalda Bishop and Walter T., 9, 273
Special awards, 85
Specialist, visiting, file for, 29-30
Speech, preparing, 65-66
"Speeches," extemporaneous, 111
Sports, using student interest in, 110-111
Standards, setting, 37-41
    establishing, 37-40
    on first day, 36
    organizing work, 41
    scholastic, 41
Standing, E. M., 119
Stationery, personalized, by students as gifts, 100
Storage space, creating, 19-20
"Story hour," 282
Strokes, basic, of drawing, 161-162
Strong, William A., 191
Student committees for "make believe" trips, 187
Study plan, 56-57
Study, teaching how to, 54-72
    attacking assignment, 57-72
    guidelines, 56
    plan, 56-57
    teaching motivation, 55-56
Substitute, folder for, 29
Summarizing material, 65
Summit Industries, 52
Supervision on field trips, 177-178
Supplementary reading material, 116-118
Surveying assignment, 57-58
Symbols, teaching standard, 169

Talents and Geniuses, 286
Tarbell, Harlan, 170
Techniques of Military Instruction, 50
"Telecast," 231
"Telling tales," 79
Test taking, art of, 71-72
Testing and evaluation in classroom, 42-53
    conference, 52-53
    essay vs. objective, 45-46
    evaluating behavior and attitude, 52

Testing and evaluation in classroom (*cont.*)
    evaluating tests, 46-47
    "fun tests," 47-50
    marking made easy, 51-52
    oral tests, 50-51
    reason for tests, 44
    test construction, 44-45
    what is evaluated, 43
Textbook relay, 112
The Amateur's 8MM Movie Guide, 114, 233
The Human Comedy, 299
The Overseas Americans, 192
The Term Paper, Step by Step, 69
The Whales Go By, 153
The Wonderful Human Machine, 276
The Writing Road to Reading, 273
Think on their feet, teaching students to, 66
Thorndike, Robert L., 47
Ticket counter in classroom for "make believe" trips, 192
Tiemersma, Kathleen, 203
TIME, 81
Time-Life Books, 230
Time savers, 24-30
    class list, 27
    on desk top, 30
    "Executive's Diary," 25
    file for each student, 26
    financial records, 27
    inventory, 25
    label, 25
    reference files, 28-29
    substitute, folder for, 29
    successful lessons, record of, 27
    visiting specialist, file for, 29-30
Times-Union of Jacksonville, 175, 207, 266
Tools, proper, for drawing, 161
Tournaments and contests, 80-81
Transportation for field trips, 177
Transportation, planning, for "make believe" trips, 189-190
Travel Abroad at Low Cost, 191
Trophies, 84
Tunis, Edwin, 197
Tuttle, Stella, 152
Twenty questions, 113

UN Cookbook, 195
Units, ten, to try, 248-279
University of Iowa, 46, 51, 123
University of Minnesota, 124
University Prints, 121, 194

Viewmaster, use of, 116
Vital Statistics Sheet, 34-35
Vocabulary building, 60-63
von Baumann, Cyril, 195

Ward-Hanna, Elaine, 197
Warriner, John E., 69
Wearever Handwriting Kit, 123
Wenzel, Evelyn, 334
Wertham, Dr. Frederic J., 296
Whitehead, Alfred North, 11, 74, 125, 286
Wiles, Kimball, 11, 12, 17, 23, 35, 40, 42, 74, 200, 217, 295
Wilkes, L., 56, 70, 102, 184, 334
Work stations, creating, 18-19
Works of Love, 305

Worksheets, 108
Workshops, classrooms as, 17-23
    (see also "Classrooms as workshops")
World Book Company, 47
Writing Creatively, 97
Writing original play, 219-220
Written compositions and reports, 67-70

Yearly plan, 1-2

Zaner-Bloser Company, 51, 123, 173